6140162712

Making Site-Specific Theatre an

D1758006

Phil Smith

Making Site-Specific Theatre and Performance

A Handbook

 macmillan
international
HIGHER EDUCATION

 RED GLOBE
PRESS

First published 2019 by
RED GLOBE PRESS

Red Globe Press in the UK is an imprint of Springer Publishers Limited, registered in England, company number 785998, of 4 Crinan Street, London, N1 9XW.

Red Globe Press® is a registered trademark in the United States, the United Kingdom, Europe and other countries.

ISBN 978–1–352–00323–9 hardback
ISBN 978–1–352–00317–8 paperback

This book is printed on paper suitable for recycling and made from fully managed and sustained forest sources. Logging, pulping and manufacturing processes are expected to conform to the environmental regulations of the country of origin.

A catalogue record for this book is available from the British Library.

A catalog record for this book is available from the Library of Congress.

Contents

List of Illustrations

Acknowledgments

I would like to acknowledge the inspiration and education that I have received from countless colleagues, visiting artists and students while working on site-specific performance modules at the Universities of Plymouth and Exeter and at the much-missed Dartington College of Arts. I would like to thank Professor Roberta Mock for asking me, some 15 years ago, to create a site-specific performance module for the University of Plymouth (and as I write this I am preparing for the first lesson of a new one tomorrow) and my colleagues in Wrights & Sites for first setting me off down this path. Finally I would like to thank my partner, Nikki Sved, and our children Rachel and Daniel, for their love and support over the years and their putting up with my occasional disappearances 'into the field'.

Arriving: A Fluid Sort of Prologue

One evening in 2001, I cadged a lift on a coach. It was full of performers on their way to Buckland Abbey, a medieval religious house in Devon (UK) that had been converted to a private residence early in the sixteenth century during the Dissolution of the Monasteries. Once we had arrived, I wandered around this heritage site, now owned and managed by the National Trust, chancing upon various scenes from the performance of *The Tempest* being staged in different parts of the house and grounds. This was a very early production by Punchdrunk, a company that was shortly to become central to a rise in international popularity for site-specific theatre.

Although built as a Cistercian monastery, Buckland Abbey is now known almost exclusively, to the frustration of its managers, as the home of Sir Francis Drake, who bought it from fellow privateer and slaver Sir Richard Grenville. These maritime connections sat well with a play that opens with an apparent shipwreck. Some of my fellow audience members, meetings with whom feature as strongly in my memories as those of the scenes themselves, were, however, somewhat at sea. They were ill at ease with the ambulatory roles they had been given. I met some spectators who were desperately rushing from space to space in the hope of 'collecting' the scenes from the play 'in the correct order' and fearing incompleteness, while there were others who had become becalmed in a Sargasso Sea of uncertainty, waiting on a staircase in the hope that the performance would eventually come to them.

I had rather enjoyed the confused swirl of audience and actors around the old building and its gardens. A sense of theatrical maelstrom was created, and I was happy to surrender my grasp on the linearity of plot in order to be swept along in the accidents of the event. My wandering about the abbey eventually brought me to its enormous medieval barn – almost 90 metres long and 10 metres to its rooftop. It was the medieval equivalent of a giant industrial steel mill or a vast retail distribution centre; the commerce there would have deeply affected the lives of those who lived tens of miles around it. Kept almost entirely empty now, I felt its vastness and hollowness.

As I tentatively entered the almost pitch darkness of this barn, I could hear something. I thought at first that it was the sound of water dripping; then maybe of a clock softly ticking. I stood stockstill. Perhaps it was breathing, and I was interrupting a theatrical action? In the deep gloom I thought I detected a very gentle, rhythmic movement. I stared hard into the shadows. The giant roof beams and the grey lines of the cavernous space of the barn gradually emerged from the murk. After that, I sensed nothing additional to these initial impressions. The clock continued to drip and the spectral, almost abstract movement in the shades of darkness, possibly an effect inside my eyes rather than anything in the barn, continued to shift. I left after 20 minutes, still unsure whether I had experienced some very subtle theatrical scene or accidentally trespassed alone into an off-limits part of the heritage complex. Whichever it was, I exited the barn with an impression that has never left me: that with or without human performers a site will always have an agency of its own that can hold a spectator rapt by its performance.

Because this book is as much a handbook for making performance as a description of certain kinds of performance making, each section of the book, even this one, will contain guidance towards some principles or ideas that I hope will be useful to you in forming your own thoughts about site and performance; a few exercises for you to try; and sometimes a pointer towards a reading or two that may challenge you to widen or deepen your thinking about what 'site' is and how 'site-specific theatre' can be made. But, then, because this book is also a site and a performance, it may all change between the moment of your choosing to enter and the moment of your disappearance from it.

Idea

Think about the different *kinds* of spaces there are: spaces that take you to somewhere else, places of arrival, ritual and holy spaces, retail spaces of commercial exchange (trading, buying and selling), transport hubs, 'peace and quiet' spaces, institutional spaces, mines and quarries, Wendy houses and model villages, secret spaces and gigantic spaces, sub-atomic spaces and quantum fields, snow globes and train sets, airport runways and athletic tracks, auditoria and stages, legislative spaces, democratic spaces, rubbish tips, and rooms where judgements are handed down. How would you list these? Under what headings would you group different collections of them?

Is it possible to draw up a meaningful list of 'kinds' or 'qualities' of site? Would actual places sit happily under your headings, or would they defy categorisation? If one of the qualities was 'enclosed space' and you listed 'prison', 'tunnel' and 'bunker' under that title, could 'chapel' or 'classroom' also go under that heading? Consider how you think about, define and identify places. Consider how and why you give value to one kind of place and not to another; reflect on your spatial values and whether you need to acquire some new ones.

Exercise

Plunge in. Create a micro-performance (no more than one minute in duration) for a micro-space. This could be any kind of space with clear limits: doorway, cupboard, pavement slab, beanbag, photo booth, confessional, cardboard box. Take no more than five minutes to choose the space, and no more than ten to devise your performance. Other than yourself, do not bring any extra resources into the space, but work with the resources it gives you; say, the swinging of a door, the instability of a beanbag, or the muffled acoustics of a cupboard (Illustration 0.1). Whatever you perform, try to 'get it' from that small space. If the idea of using such a micro-site strikes you as a little too abstract and formalistic, consider how such a performance can become politically controversial. Think how your choice of micro-site might become contentious. Consider how you might respond to the invitation to choose 'a location as site for generating material: one square foot of planet earth' (Hulton, 2008, p. 96). A performance called *the still small voice of the people* (Cyprus, 2003–2006) responded to this offer by choosing two sites: the work, a collaboration between Echo-Arts Living Arts Center in Cyprus and Theatre Alibi (UK), had two performers. One was dancer Arianna Economou (a co-director of the project) from one side of the military border that divides Cyprus and the second was musician Ilker Kaptanoglu from the other. Working with co-director Dorinda Hulton, they created a performance for one 'square foot' on each side of the border, in the capital Nicosia. On the predominantly Greek Cypriot side, accompanied by an armed soldier, they were able to choose a micro-site very close to the border. On the mostly Turkish side this was not possible. Prohibitions and restrictions are often revealing, and sometimes productive: on this occasion the nearest site to the border on the Turkish side that the company could use turned out, suggestively, to be an apiary. Among a number of actions made for the two square feet were two performances that each began with a walk to their site and were peppered with small actions and stories along the way; both moved along the same piece of railway line now cut off at the border. The walk on the predominantly Greek Cypriot side 'ended with a "marking" of the square foot – with a mirror, chalk, water, and some blossoms similar to those used in the wayside shrines within the Greek Orthodox tradition'. On the Turkish Cypriot side the performers marked the 'chosen square foot in the apiary with two halves of a honeycomb... a promise of reconnection as well as communication' (Hulton, 2008, p. 96).

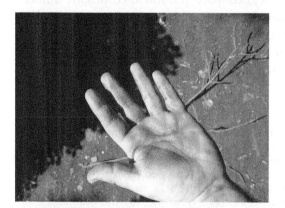

Illustration 0.1   Rather than create your own micro-space, find an existing one and use that.

Photo: Phil Smith.

Exercise

Try again, but with a transferable dimension: lie down on a rock, a table or a pavement and chalk around your body, then create a performance while staying within the chalk line. Again, use the resources within the line; but this time decide if you want to refer to what you can see and hear beyond the line. Work with the contents and qualities of your space, without the benefit of any research about its history or particular qualities; maybe there is something in the texture and materials of the surface that can help you. Use what you immediately find and create a micro-performance that the space seems to be inviting. Once you have drawn or defined your micro-site, take no more than ten minutes to devise a performance of a minute or less in duration; then, do it. Maybe perform it to the space itself first, and then show it to a friend.

Exercise

Find a place that evokes a particular scene from a movie. Stage a low-budget spontaneous re-enactment.

Exercise

Lay down an A4 piece of paper, draw a line around it, then make a performance for that space; then draw a shape the size of a small motor car around the A4 shape and make a performance for that; then 'draw' a shape the size of a football field around the two smaller shapes. Make a performance for the football field shape. In each of the three spaces include in your performance a lie and a belief that is important to you. Then create a performance that uses all three performances, switching from one to the other as they pass repeatedly across the boundaries that separate/define them.

(In these exercises, worry less about how to change or manipulate the space to make it theatrically effective and impactful, and more about how the space can direct you – how it can give you what you need for a performance of it.)

Readings

Take a look at the 'Two Prefaces' that begin Steve Mentz's *book Shipwreck Modernity: Ecologies of Globalisation, 1550–1719*. In them Mentz, a New York literature professor, proposes two spatial dynamics for the sea-based colonialism that shaped and continues to shape much of the terrain you are likely to be searching through for your performance sites. The first is 'theft' and is characterised by land grabs, ruptures, cutting things into bits and parcelling them up; the second is 'composure' and is defined by oceanic fluidity, decay, exchanges and transformations. Rooting these broad spatial dynamics in harsh historic events, Metz makes them useful to the site-artist: they are sharpening and dissolving lenses through which you can read some general features in any space coloured by colonialism (that's just about everywhere) and its relation to the oceans (same applies; those limestone pavement slabs you are walking on began as sediment at the bottom of warm, shallow seas). Metz's idea of 'shipwreck modernity' addresses all our recent human encounters with planetary space, particularly those characterised by ecological disaster. Any performance that is rigorously specific to its site is in some way an ecological one (attentive to how everything connects to everything else); it is bound to address how a performance adds to or subtracts from its site's prospects.

Ask of a space: What features here have been copied from an elsewhere, a faraway elsewhere? What was made there and brought here? What has been imposed here from there? What was fragmented or excavated before it was transported? Is there something missing? How have warmth, decay or fusion changed the things here?

Readings

Complementarily, particularly to Mentz's broad brush, is the concluding chapter of Tasmanian biologist Lisa-ann Gershwin's *Stung!: On Jellyfish Blooms and the Future of the Ocean*. In a few pages her chapter 'The Rise of Slime' summarises the human-made challenges facing the world's oceans – overfishing, climate change, acidification and plague species – and then speculates on what these waters might look like if the present momentum continues: larger fish and marine mammals exterminated, worms and clams suffocated, shellfish and corals disintegrated. Not a new state of evolution in any accepted sense, but a perverse reducing down to the remnants of an older and more homogeneous ecology: 'No spectacular coral reefs. No vast filtering mussel beds. No sharks slicing through the water as menhaden multitudes flee. Just jellyfish... lots of jellyfish' (Gershwin, 2013, p. 344).

So, what has that got to do with your site? Jellyfish, oceans, really?

Well, the rock beneath you and many of the buildings around you are probably the remains of ancient oceans. The pavement slabs and stone gutters may once have been around in the form of billions of tiny sea creature corpses, sinking to the bottom of warm seas, where they became compressed into limestone; those were seas from which our distant ancestors would crawl, and to which we may soon be accommodating or returning, as sea levels rise as a result of climate change. Making performance that is specific to its site is not just about the specificity of its immediate past or present, but of its deep past and far future too. If the seas change, everywhere changes.

What can you see in your site that anticipates what may be coming? Trivial or world changing? What choices do you have and what consequences may there be? What better materials for performance could you ask for than these life-or-death questions? Where is the coast in your space, where are the depths, where are the currents, where is the tsunami, where is the reef, where is the dead sea, where are the lagoon and the harbour, where is the school and where is the shoal?

Part I

Finding a Site

1

Why Make Site-Specific Performance?

There is good cause to challenge any use of the word 'site'. The word implies far more than, say, 'space' or 'place'. It suggests that a human choice has already defined its boundaries, meaning and identity. A site is always the site *of* something; with the implication that it is a kind of container for what is really important, for the valuable property that is in it but is different from the space itself. It says that space accrues its meaning through its use by humans; which, in an overwhelmingly unhuman cosmos, is an odd way of describing things. ...

A section headed 'Finding a site', particularly in a handbook, might be expected to begin with some inventive tactics for exploring cities and natural expanses. Instead, it is important to begin by getting at what the 'whys' of site-specific theatre are; if only to dispel the idea that sites are neutral, natural places, blank pages on which you can write with impunity. Site-specific theatre is often characterised in terms of an impulsive and instinctual break from the dead weight of intellectual, building-based arts traditions, an escape to the freshness of the outdoors, to the randomness of the everyday world, even to the shock of the wild; but it is also a choice with its own traditions and legacies.

Where did site-specific performance come from? Why did it appear at all? What were, and what remain of, the original impulses, motives and motivations for making theatre and performance that consciously refuses designated sites and heads off in pursuit of a something 'more real' than staged illusions? Why turn to the churning of everyday life? And what new drives, if any, are emerging now to sustain this momentum?

Una Chaudhuri is just one of any number of academic critics and historians who identify the origins of these impulses with 'an experimentation that began with Dadaism' and that climaxes with 'finally, site-specific theater' (1995, p. 22). The extraordinary 'moment' of Dada in 1916, with its products and performances made and shared by exiled anti-war artists gathered together in neutral Zurich, meeting regularly to create the Cabaret Voltaire in a small bar, was goaded by a transnationalist bloodbath and reinforced in its escalating radicalism by the influence of the artists, thrown together by total war, on each other.

Dada has become a touchstone for artworks that seek to break from existing conventions of staging, presentation and representation. Dada's paintings escaped from their frames. The episodic structure of its cabarets was used to parody to death live presence and representational performance. Through blasphemous pseudo-rituals, trances, contrived outrages and confrontations, and grotesquely masked buffoonery, the Dadaists generated an assault on nationalistic common sense and 'rationality'. They disrupted artistic individualism, incorporated everyday things into privileged aesthetic discourses and macerated the literal and metaphorical meaningfulness of words.

Dada's precedence for site-specific performance is manifest in the 'Dadaist excursions', inspired by Baudelaire's rhetorical query 'does there exist anything more charming, more fertile and more positively *exciting* than the commonplace?' These 'excursions' were anti-touristic visits to places that had struck their organisers as lacking any reason for existing; most famously a 1921 foray to the repeatedly adapted and repurposed Church of Saint-Julien-le-Pauvre in Paris where the Dadaists yelled gnomic slogan-poems at passers-by.

The 'moment' of Dada has become something of an event horizon for radical art, a phenomenon from before which little information is allowed to radiate. Dada's principles of rupture, rootlessness, fragmentation, nihilistic repetition, anti-art, irony and parody have often prevailed both in subsequent cultural practice and in critical theory, and they continue to inform an important seam of site-specific performance which is often closer to live art than theatre. These principles, however, are not the whole story of site-specificity's roots. There are other less iconoclastic, though perhaps equally radical, strands.

Some of the later influences on site-specific performance have come from art forms that seem far from performance. Sculpture, painting and drawing, particularly through the fusions of land art as practised by the likes of Kazuo Shiraga and the Gutai group, Robert Smithson or Ana Mendieta, have all informed site-specific performance. These artists, given their prioritising of sensitivity to and enthusiasm for materials – Gutai is Japanese for 'concreteness'; Smithson used heavy machinery to make his installations; Mendieta sank her body into mud and snow – and their preference for immersion in and communion with terrains, over rupture and separation from them, showed that site-specific works could be just as critical and political as those based on modernist fragmentation and disruption.

Other strands of influence spring directly from building-based theatre. Most crudely this can consist of existing plays, often with naturalistic dialogue, linear narratives and psychological characterisations that are almost directly 'lifted out' of theatre buildings and restaged in spaces not usually designated for theatre. While theatre scholar Bertie Ferdman suggests that this is far from a recent phenomenon and that 'Theater has a rich history of taking place outside the traditional theatre build- ing … Long before modernism' (2013, p. 16), her citing of individual productions (e.g., a 1934 staging of *The Merchant of Venice* in a Venetian street and a play about the anarcho-syndicalist Buenaventura Durruti performed in a French factory in 1964) suggests an impulse repeatedly re-found and practice re-invented rather than a coherent ongoing tradition incrementally built upon.

In such productions, there are varying degrees of adaptation of the play to their new 'grounds', and varying degrees of adaptation of the spaces themselves. Today, there are numerous examples of companies making such work: Changeling Theatre in Kent (UK), the Castle Tours of the American Drama Group Europe/TNT throughout Europe, the plays staged on the plaza of the Art Tower Mito in Japan by the Mito Yagai-Geki and those of the many affiliates of the Institute of Outdoor Theatre in the USA. While it is possible to question quite what it is about many of these performances that is 'specific' to their sites, a significant proportion of what is described as site-specific theatre, particularly by journalists, looks much like this.

More profoundly, however, though far less obviously, there is another building-based theatrical influence on site-specific performance. Long before Dada, there was a break from the burgeoning dominance of the binary of extravagant melodrama on the one hand and realist or natural-istic appearance on the other over nineteenth-century theatre; one that resonates in continuing attempts to represent things beyond and above appearance. This was Symbolist Theatre. Spectral and idealist, mostly now derided or ignored as reactionary or effete, its proponents set out to dissolve and transcend the same conventions and frames that Dada would smash, disrupt and escape. Their performances 'ow[ed] much to the interdisciplinary fusions ... arguably evolved from Richard Wagner's *Gesamtkunstwerk* ... and early Romantic arguments for the inherent unity of all the arts' (Machon, 2013, p. 29); an explosive concoction that all the time threatens to burst the limits of the theatre building. So, when Sara, a renegade Gnostic nun in Villiers De L'Isle-Adam's *Axël* (1890), plunges a dagger into a heraldic sign and 'the entire mass of the wall section [of the castle] cleaves into a wide, vaulted opening, glides and sinks gradually underground' (De L'Isle-Adam, 1986, p. 149), or when the avalanche at the end of Henrik Ibsen's *Brand* (1867) swallows everything in ice, or when in his *The Master Builder* (1893) the steeple is built right up through the ceiling of the theatre, these are not just visual effects. They are ques-tionings of the physical frame of appearance and representation itself. They point theatre out beyond the container of the theatre building – just as much as a work like Max Ernst's *Culture Mechanism: The Robing of the Bride* (1924) is encouraging painting to escape from its frame, literally and prefiguratively – while retaining a deep commitment to the theatrical as a heightened form of life that is distinct from the everyday.

An example of the continuing resonance of this Symbolist theatre for site-specific theatre is evident in an immersive performance created by the American director Robert Wilson (much of whose stage work is suffused by Symbolist aesthetics) working with two young Dutch artists and theatre makers, Boukje Schweigman and Theun Mosk, for the Oreol Festival on the island of Terschelling. *Walking* (2008) required its audience/participants to walk for around three hours at half 'normal' pace, one by one, at intervals, along a designated path through dunes and bushes, encountering various portals, installations and soundscapes, both natural and artificial. While the attentive supervision of the participants by usher-guides, called 'angels', was suggestive to some participants of preparations for a trip through an 'underworld' or 'otherworld', Wilson and his collaborators were careful to leave literal space and symbolic ambiguity through which their ambulatory audience could explore their own associations with the augmented landscape by way of an altered moving and seeing.

These theatrical strands of influence share some things in common with older lineages of performance that were, or are, sited outside of designated or conventional performance spaces. As Anna Wilson observes, although groups like Punchdrunk have often been contextualised in academic writing as inheritors of a tradition from high modernist groups of the 1960s like The Performance Group led by Richard Schechner, in fact their 'ancestry has more in common with … [an] aesthetic reframing of populist everyday forms such as that of the game or theme park' (2016, p. 173).

In discussions about site-specific art, the influence of these older (and sometimes imagined) traditions has been dampened by critical discourses that privilege 'modernism' and by the event horizon of Dada. Nevertheless, these much older traditions are demonstrably inspirational to site-based performances, from one-off productions like the Krampus play or 'Nikolausspiel' performed in the Church of the Angels at Pasadena (USA, 2016) to significant and long-standing practices like that of Red Earth (UK, founded 1989 and ongoing) who draw on or appropriate iconography and rituals from other cultures and from other times to inform spectacular landscape events and processions and even the speculative imagining of 'lost' prehistoric performances: 'Butoh dancer Atsushi Takenouchi … his flowing movement balancing the stillness of the landscape and the restless energy of the sheep. The enclosure is opened, and the sheep run down the valley, weaving around him' (Prior, 2011, p. 26). The range of these influential traditional performances – often informed to some degree by re-creation, the finessing of repertoire, creative excavation of archives, reforms and speculative imaging – include plough plays, carnival parades, the devotional dancing of the Mevlevis, eighteenth-century freemasonic rituals performed on a chalked ground plan, the two 'horses' (with their teasers and supporters) of Padstow's *'Obby 'Oss*, and the processing of sacred Christian statues around cities and villages during Easter.

In the mid-1990s I attended a processing of church statues around the Andalusian town of Aracena (Spain). I was struck by the many modes of performance that were deployed that night; a multiplicity at odds with the narrow formal rigours that characterise much representational building-based theatre or even modern-day Catholic church services. Here was a rich resource of performance forms and discourses that a theatre, freed of its buildings, could draw upon or indulge itself in. There was the shattering physical labour of those lifting and carrying the *pasos* (floats), the hypnotic repetitions of simple creaky marching music, the thrill of the shaking ornaments each time the unsteady *pasos* were raised up, the randomness of a halt for one of the statues to be serenaded (with a secular aria) by a professional singer from the upstairs window of her home, and the high theatricality of the *nazarenos* (penitential robes) with their distinctive *capirotes* (pointed hoods) not quite fully explained by the requirement of anonymity.

Here, procedure stood in for dramatic plot; rather than the events unfolding in novelty, the mystery was excavated predictably and always 'once again', high emotion erupted without preparation or crescendo as if there was always something hot and molten beneath the surface that the ritual could directly tap into. I was struck by the ways that rich symbolism and ordinariness were woven very closely; how beneath the ornately decorated *paso* the men lifting and carrying were only partially concealed, their fluorescent trainers shining and their heavily muscled and hairy legs straining beneath the frills.

Cathy Turner, in her book *Dramaturgy and Architecture* (2015), has described how performance, having burst out from the theatre building in the early twentieth century (in ways prefigured by Ibsen and others), did not then abandon architecture in the flurry of idealism and abstraction. Instead, performance often redirected its straining against the limitations of the stage onto new material 'grounds'. Through various arts and esoteric groups, there were stagings of masques, pageants and processions that tied varieties of collectivist politics and (often theosophy-based) idealism to the new architectural forms of innovative institutions and communities. Mass choreographed movement played a part in this; human beings performing as parts of a eurhythmic social machine. Turner shows how, alongside the Symbolist Theatre's drive towards a realistic representation of the unreal (ambience, death, mystery) and a Gnostic aspiration to be realised in its own negation, something else was advanced that was far more material, at times even steely and scaffolded, informed by the Constructivist and Bauhaus movements' exposures of the mechanics, forms and philosophies of design as agencies in themselves.

This particular influence has been represented, more recently, in the work of those small professional groups that were characteristic of post-1960s experimental performance. So, for example, in Brith Gof's *Gododdin* (1988), a seventh-century Celtic 'last stand' against Anglo-Saxon invaders was staged in the engine room of a disused car factory, directly engaging with and protesting the London-controlled neo-liberal dismantling of the architecture of heavy industry in Wales through the material revenant of its fading history. Even more explicitly in tune with the architectural performances of the 1920s are the interventions of the Office of Subversive Architecture (1995 and ongoing), mostly in Germany and Austria. These range from performative installations to the erection of 'permanent' structures as parts of a continuum of production along which the company can disperse narratives, objects, ideas and activism. They call this entanglement of their physical and intellectual products the 'fictionalisation' of their sites.

Developments in technical, artistic and productive practices and a renewed attention to terrains have all been crucial to repeated 'turns' to site-specificity; but theoretical ideas have also been influential. Such ideas have included the idealisation of fluidity and the privileging of rhizomic dispersal over and against fixed, vertical rooting in the work of critical theorists such as Gilles Deleuze and Felix Guattari, the popularisation of neo-vitalism, the 'lure of the local' and the dematerialisation of the art object (as both theorised by Lucy Lippard), the ideas of the vibrant energy of non-human things in the work of Jane Bennett and the Object-Oriented Ontologists, the study of the performance of everyday life developed from pioneering work by Erving Goffman, the 'spatial turn' in geography, the 'mobilities paradigm' championed by John Urry and the increasing seriousness with which disciplines outside the arts, like human geography and anthropology, have come to regard performance as a tool of research.

The 'why' of site-specific performance, then, has arisen in numerous and various guises: in cultural-political subversion, in strains within theatre and theatre architecture which have then reached out to a more general architecture, in a nostalgia for older (or the invention of something *like* older) performance forms, in the uncontainable qualities of the numinous, and in shifts within critical theory that move across categories.

A cautionary note, however, is necessary here. Where these performances are driven by bright new ideas (or respect for and excavation of old ones) and take the form of transgressions of accepted or conformist practices, there is a temptation to assume that a common idealism, generous politics and thoughtful ethics inform all these works. Not always so. It is important to note that some artists have been accused of an indifference to the impact and sustainability of their interventions in the terrain involved in making spectacular land art. Localism can turn into petty nationalism and chauvinism. Critics have identified an opportunistic commercialism and neo-liberal individualism at work in some of the more immersive examples of site-specific theatre. The popularity of labour-intensive site-based theatre events like those of Secret Cinema and Punchdrunk have generated some unease, both around issues of unpaid or low-paid work of associate artists, the 'hidden "scripting" – in terms of what is forbidden' and policed at Punchdrunk performances by the company's 'black-masked crew' (Wilson, 2016, pp. 168–169) – and the subservience of content to the imperative of sensorial impact. The initially enthusiastic critic Alice Saville (2016) explained how, now, for her, 'immersive theatre feels like a capitalist playground, inviting the audience to play "freely" in an environment that is full of invisible restrictions, and costs'.

There is nothing easy here. Today, practitioners have to navigate their own ways between aesthetic drives and the tempting opportunities for 'added value' offered by occupying and capitalising upon unfamiliar and spectacular spaces; at the same time as finding a way through compromising practicalities and 'an admixture of desire and necessity, the implementation of sets of both programmatic and pragmatic addresses to the possibilities and problems of a location' (Pearson, 2012, p. 69). Performances, like young artists' studios before them, play a recognised role in the redevelopment, gentrification and monetisation of 'run-down' neighbourhoods; indeed, Michael McKinnie redefines site-specificity as 'monopolistic performance' generating 'value by appropriating and trading self-consciously on the non-replicable qualities of places'; he identifies this specificity as part of a raw material with its own value, while the 'experiential benefits of the theatre event' are what makes it exchangeable and tradable (2012, p. 23). Rather than a radical escape from property, site-specific performance, in this analysis, is a 'rent-seeking' (p. 24) process; and this is not simply due to the accidental fallout of using, for example, derelict (and subsequently developed) space. According to McKinnie, this proprietorial quality is integral to the nature of site-specific performances, taking 'temporary "ownership" over a distinct and non-replicable time, place and experience' comparable to other forms of private property and encouraging an audience experience that 'allows spectators to imagine themselves as productive economic subjects of a particular kind – the property owning bourgeoisie' (p. 29). All of this, according to Anna Wilson, is 'underpinned by an individualist drive where participants compete against each other to receive the "optimum" experience' (Wilson, 2016, p. 172).

While McKinnie's thesis is reductive, it is no more than a theoretical version of complaints that have been made by spectators and critics about the latest (late 2000s to mid-2010s) trends in immersive theatre experiences. The ecology of a site is rarely so limited that performance makers have only aesthetics to consider; and McKinnie's argument is a corrective to instances of such a blinkered view. Instead, site-specific performance making is an eclectic, conflicted and ambivalent business; and requires a matching set of inspirations, motivations and justifications.

Whatever your own 'why' or 'whys' for studying or making site-specific performance, they will find their place in some relation to this ragtag and contradictory range of issues and to others that I have omitted.

Exercise

In site-specific performance you need to pay the closest attention to exactly what is in your site; what is specific to it. But there is another kind of specificity. What is missing? What is evidently and explicitly absent? Say, a swimming pool with no water in it. What happens when you perform as if the missing thing were still present, although you have not replaced it?

Your 'why?'

Write you own reasons for making site-specific performance in the space below.

Your 'whys' may be heartfelt, immediate, strong and clear. They may be ambiguous, vague, negative or obliged; just the same, write them. Creativity can begin with resistance. Your reasons may be conjectural – 'if I *were* to make site-specific performance, why would I be doing it?' – and that is just as valid. Leave room for future crossings out and rewriting.

If you need a model:

Because our cities are increasingly policed, militarised and made banal. Because there is a conspiracy of boredom against cities. Because the Great God Pan is long dead and we still don't have the new myths we were promised. Because the city is chopped and parcelled up like a rack of meat, streamlined for ignorance and meaninglessness. Because hidden inside the functionality of the city are the secrets of texture and the funny ghosts of pattern. Because the purloined symbols of the city are all still available for us to steal back. Because the self-possession of the non-rich has always been a work of imagination, and it needs to be practiced to be retained. Because of the erosion of public space. Because there are accidental playgrounds and launch pads and caves. Because of violence, property, loss and neglect. Because we are mobile and we want a fine time. For the sake of remnants and traces. To be prepared and spontaneous and happy whenever we need to be. And because we are prepared to be spontaneous. Right now...

(Crabman & Signpost, 2012, p. 5)*

*Reprinted with permission from *A Sardine Street Box of Tricks*, Phil Smith & Simon Persighetti, Triarchy Press, 2012, HYPERLINK "http://www.triarchypress.net/sardine" www.triarchypress.net/sardine

The broad range of motivations for, and influences upon, the making of site-specific performance does go some way to explaining why site-specific practices are quite as variegated, and sometimes as conflicted and contradictory, as they are. However, there is another significant part of that explanation lying within the very idea of specificity to site: if it truly is the sites that primarily determine the nature of the performances then there is nothing particular to the techniques or stylistics used in one site that would necessarily recommend them for use in any other.

The sheer breadth of the ranging across scales, across spectacle and intimacy, across image-theatre and autobiography, across mass choreography and one-to-one performance would suggest that there is little point in seeking *anything* in common among the narratives, interventions, concepts, personae and performance styles deployed in site-specific performances. Nevertheless, to give a sense both of the extreme disparities involved and how despite these there *are* significant affinities woven within these differences, I will point to two very different, but relatable performances from the early 1970s: firstly, the performance by the International Centre for Theatre Research of the Ted Hughes-scripted *Orghast* (1971) in the ruins at Persepolis as part of the prestigious Shiraz Festival and, then, Ana Mendieta's *Rape Scene* (1973) for which the artist created a private performance for fellow University of Iowa students in her own apartment.

Orghast was directed by Peter Brook, who had by 1971 combined considerable critical and popular success with classic plays in major theatre institutions with adventurous smaller-scale experimentally devised works, shifting productively between a literary tradition of theatre making and the serious social engagement, monkish corporeality and spiritual-theatricality of experimentalists such as Joan Littlewood, Jerzy Grotowski and Vsevolod Meyerhold. Brook is the author of the classic anti-specificity text: 'I can take any empty space and call it a bare stage. A man walks across this empty space whilst someone else is watching him, and this is all that is needed for an act of theatre' (1968, p. 7– a statement of universality that has been challenged on multiple accounts: Why specifically a man? In what sense is any space empty, free of its past and the events that took place there? And who is the 'I' that 'can take'? Another 'man'? These questions continued to be at work in *Orghast*, with its starting point in the myth of Prometheus, with Hughes's invention of a language – 'the language of man' (Smith, 1972, p. 108) – that would be less symbolic and 'more audial/visceral/muscular' (1972, p. 45), and with Brook's choosing the austere tomb of Artaxerxes II for one of the two spaces for *Orghast*'s performance at Persepolis, rather than a large terrace of ruins which he rejected as being 'too fussy as an image' on which to stage his production (Brook, 1968, p. 103).

Despite all that, there *was* an attention to the narrative of place; taking themes of fire, light and darkness from the seventh-century BCE Zoroastrianism that predates the building of the complex at Persepolis by a century and Hughes's aspiration to 'mak[e] the place itself the main character of the work' (Brook, 1968, p. 141). Although Brook had arrived with the idea of building an acoustic cube 'suggested by the shape of a glass-walled garden in the centre of Tehran airport' (p. 61) in the ruins, he decided not to augment the site, except with ladders (which had previously been features of the site), and chose natural light and fire over electrical illumination and effects. Once in rehearsal, elements of the site began to perform with the cast: '[T]he actress playing the Vulture found her voice being doubled by a jackdaw' (p. 182).

In stark contrast to the high-profile nature of the *Orghast* event and its 'world heritage' setting, both the location and the initial social exposure for Ana Mendieta's performance were intimate. *Rape Scene* was her response to the rape and murder of Sarah Ann Ottens, a nursing student in a student hall of residence at the University of Iowa. On arrival at Mendieta's apartment, a handful of invited student colleagues found the front door ajar and Mendieta inside, motionless, and slumped across a table, arms tied and her face hidden, her buttocks exposed and covered in fake blood. A pool of this fake blood had collected at her feet. All this was lit from a low source that threw long shadows onto the walls. Mendieta remained motionless for the hour's duration of the performance; the audience remained, then sat down, shocked by what they had found, and talked about the work and what they felt. The performance was documented in a series of photographs, later supplemented by others taken with Mendieta in a similar pose in outdoor locations on the perimeter of the university campus.

Rape Scene was not a staging like that of *Orghast*, searching for some kind of universal cultural field, but rather it referenced recent and specific events, in a space like those where there was a fear those events would be repeated, and performed the very sharpest of power imbalances and disjunctions. Social structures, behaviours and assumptions bore directly down on and marked a single female body. Where *Rape Scene* was literally self-effacing, *Orghast* was a global festive gesture, covered by international media. Nevertheless, and despite so many unlike qualities, within the opposites and contrasts of *Rape Scene* and *Orghast*, there are certain common features that arise from their attention to location in each piece.

(Resist any temptation to draw a conclusion that the common elements shared between a 'signature' intercultural high-art production for a celebration organised by a dictatorship and a female student-artist's self-financed action against rape on her campus indicate a comforting demonstration of a broad liberal and progressive quality inherent in site-specific performance. It is just as likely to signify that site-specific practices can be put to work, equally, for radical, collective, exploitative, indifferent and authoritarian purposes.)

The performers' bodies in both cases were put 'at the mercy' of the site. The actors at Persepolis were threatened by soldiers, struggled in the intense heat, and were joined in rehearsal and performance by snakes and scorpions, while Mendieta's audience were relieved to arrive at her home before anyone uninvited arrived, fearing that they might have taken advantage of her. In both events there is an oblique reference to ritual; while Brook acknowledged 'the ceremonial aspects of the work in Persepolis ... made by a cultural conspiracy of all those who meet to partake in it' (Smith, 1972, p. 253), Mendieta's copious use of blood (at odds with the forensic descriptions of the actual crime scene) was inspired by Santería rituals from her native Cuba; its excess was perhaps an attempt to go beyond reproducing the appearance of victimisation. Invitation and targeted selection (one based on conviviality and colleagueship, the other on cultural and political status and media access) played a role in who was able to access each of the two performances; mediation and documentation – visual and textual – have since their performances distributed both works to far broader audiences than the few that experienced them live. Both involved places of death: one a tomb, the other 'recreations' of a murder scene.

The last of these connections, the nature of their sites (although the other connections also resonate, variably, with other examples of site-specific performance), is particularly relevant here. Following the logic of specificity, where there are commonalities, repetitions and connections these often seem to arise where certain 'kinds' of sites are favoured by performance makers. This was one of the findings of Fiona Wilkie (2002) in her pioneering paper 'Mapping the Terrain: A Survey of Site-Specific Performance in Britain', written on the wave of a sudden growth in site-specific performance in the UK in the late 1990s and around the millennium. Wilkie noted, then, the popularity of certain kinds of places over others, with makers particularly favouring parks, disused or 'out-of-hours' workplaces, churches, beaches, museums and tunnels. She speculated on how various qualities of playfulness, inhabitability, self-reflexivity, affordance for heightened emotion and reusable symbolic codes might have drawn the artists to these particular kinds of sites.

As well as the common qualities in the sites chosen, site-specific performance makers may also have been influenced by each other. One maker, or group of makers, may have been initially alerted or attracted to site-specific arts by the works of another; a certain influence may have been sustained when others heard of or attended performances. Equally, information about practices and sites was dispersed indirectly through publications, blogs, university courses and 'industry chatter', in shared anecdotes and tactics taught in workshops, and in discussions of notions of ethics and traditions (to be observed or transgressed). These varied, if ephemeral, discourses have engendered certain consistencies across what is otherwise an uneven field. So, for example, an impetus towards 'immersiveness' seems to have accelerated in the first decade after the millennium as the work of existing groups like Royal de Luxe, Blast Theory or De La Guarda began to reach greater numbers of people, spreading from their countries of origin to international festivals and high-profile events, and this impetus was repeatedly added to by the emergence of new groups like Ontroerend Goed, Punchdrunk or Coney. In various combinations, and under different categories, these works were then narrated by journalists, researchers, audiences and theorists as if they were parts of a shared practice; at times a tradition was unified for reasons of intimate collaboration and skill-sharing, at others for no better purpose than the requirements of a journalistic narrative or an academic convenience.

Part of what all this means is that any site you choose is no more empty of enticing scripts and scores than it is of cosmological and geological materials or of a history of human engagement. Feedback loops develop, in mainstream and social media as well as academic discourses, so that certain kinds of effects and experiences are privileged, and the kinds of sites that favour the production of those effects and experiences also become privileged in turn. Thus, it may be important to see that what is valued across the range of site-specific performances – from the 'why' of motivations to any commonly perceived affordant qualities ascribed to certain kinds of sites – are not empty categories, clean tools or discrete spatial entities to be taken up without obligation or significance in themselves. Rather, they should all be regarded with some suspicion; all are likely to carry with them influences, histories and values that arrive from across the range of site-specific practices and practitioners as well as from elsewhere.

So, here is a paradox to give any maker of site-specific performance pause: because site-specific performance is now communicated as a 'thing', a discipline (enough to trigger this publication and others similar to it), a recognisable and significant cultural activity, each specificity that a performance maker now approaches, whether that be a new site or a performance idea, is likely to be interpreted by others – critics, colleagues, audiences – through conventions shared with others engaged with making or discussing site-specific performances. This means that site-based performances – whether they be ceremonies, processions, solo dance pieces, activist interventions, walks, augmented reality games, museum interpretation, plays or fire spectacles, and whether their sites be epic ruins or night-time suburban streets, sports stadia or intimate domestic settings – are always in danger of succumbing to a site-specific homogenisation. By acknowledging these conventions, however, it may become possible to do more than discuss the problem as a recognisable one, and either skirt the conventions or transform them.

Thus, in order to realise a genuine and rigorous specificity to your site not only will it be necessary to surrender some of your accustomed power and autonomy – as The Olimpias say of their 'Salamander' project (2013), 'the water is the director, the choreographer' – it will also help (or be necessary) to know what the tics, habits and etiquettes of similar work might be, in order, if appropriate, to strip them away and get to what is special about your site. On the other hand, it may be more true to the dynamics of your site, to knowingly commandeer existing conventions in order to create work that plays between what you bring to the site and what you find there.

One of the conventions, probably best avoided, is an assumption that an essential identity for a site can be discovered in the documentation of its past; that the everyday and living transformations of the contemporary site are but an ephemeral distraction from the essence that can be established by historical (or some other absolute) veracity. This need not apply only to antiquarian performances, but to any that seek to find and express the fixed essence of a site. Indeed, there is always some danger in any rigorous insistence on the specificity of performance to its site; particularly when such faithfulness to the specifics through performance reproduces them in a rigid, doctrinal and monocular account. In Victoria Hunter's schematic model of 'influence' in site-specific performance 'detailing the relationship between the site and the creative process', a quite different rigour (which Hunter, boldly, claims as 'perhaps the "true" and desired outcome of site-specific performance') is described in which the emphasis is not on what can be fixed by definition, but on an 'interaction between the spatial and the performative [that] is ephemeral in nature, existing only in the moment'. Hunter uses a diagram to demonstrate the variety of interactions; what then drops down from, or out of, the model's linear trajectory from 'site' to 'product' is 'New space created' (2015, pp. 36–38).

There is something in common here with one of the outcomes of a partnership between performance maker Mike Pearson and archaeologist Michael Shanks, to find a mutual illumination of their own disciplines in the workings of that of the other. Indeed, they also found traces of each other's disciplines in their own, and this interwoven-ness is pertinent to Hunter's formula. When Shanks writes of archaeology as 'a practice of cultural production ... within which the archaeologist is implicated as an active agent of interpretation' there is a clear echo of the work of the performance maker, of making something new rather than simply recording and finessing documentation in another form. Furthermore, Shanks describes an archaeologist 'work[ing] with material traces, with evidence, in order to create something – a meaning, a narrative, an image – which stands for the past in the present'. All this could just about be sustained within a making rigid, an essentialising of the multiplicity of those traces in a dogmatic telling of the site, except that what Shanks then concludes about archaeology is that 'Rather than being a reconstruction ... this is a recontextualisation' (Pearson & Shanks, 2001, p. 11).

Together, Hunter's model and Shanks's description constitute a general 'why?' for site-specificity that is not about its veracity to a fixed idea of the site, either to its past history or to its present-day norms, or even about fixing the meaning of the site in the moment, but – by acknowledging a performance's implication in the production of the space in materials and meanings; a process that is never completed, even in the fluidity of performance – it takes responsibility for the next iteration of the place, for its part in its production as new space and the transformation of its contexts from one set of frames to a whole new other.

So, depending on where you mark the origins in site-specific performance, after at least half a century of practice, this break from conventional cultural spaces not only has accrued its own conventions, but – through criticism and experiment – has also questioned an imperative at least partially driving that break; that new spaces would revivify art and performance. Hunter, Pearson and Shanks (and many practitioners who not only attend carefully to their sites, but reflect unflinchingly on their work) emphasise the reciprocity that was not always acknowledged: that the 'why?' of site-specificity is equally, maybe primarily, about how its attention revives the site. Is this why so many of the sites chosen are ones of abjection (abandoned or in ruins), of trauma (empty hospitals and institutions), of colonial heritage (and un-restituted appropriation) and so on? Is the primary emerging 'why?' of site specificity the making of new sites?

Idea

'Asymmetric action' is a term with two core meanings; firstly, it describes a general imbalance (e.g., where the limbs on one side of a body are better coordinated than those on the other), and secondly – and this is where the idea is probably more helpful to you – it describes where a weak force generates disproportionate effects by recruiting (and sometimes transforming) circumstances to its own ends and as its own allies. This second sense is often exemplified in terms of warfare. A famous instance of asymmetric warfare is at the Battle of Thermopylae (480 BCE), recently popularised by the *300* graphic novel and movie: a small force raised by an alliance of Greek city states took advantage of a feature in the local terrain, a very narrow defile, to limit the effectiveness of a much larger Persian enemy.

The 9/11 attacks on the World Trade Center in New York were asymmetrical; both immediately and in the longer term. Not only were a handful of individuals, armed only with small blades and rudimentary flying skills, able to capture commercial airliners and turn them into flying bombs, but the subsequent media coverage of the destruction and killing and then the political-military responses to them triggered regional and global events which are far from resolved at the time of writing. Compared to the fairly simple advantage-taking of one small feature of the landscape at Thermopylae, the 9/11 attackers and those organising them were able to exploit and redirect the resources and tendencies of a variety of powerful and complex systems.

A far more creative example of asymmetric action might be the way that the makers of some prehistoric structures, including the third millennium (BCE) Stonehenge, and the more recent planners and builders of the Midsummer Boulevard in modern Milton Keynes (a new town built in the UK beginning in the 1960s) have aligned their architecture so as to recruit the predictable rise of the sun on Midsummer's Day morning. Not only does this enhance the impact of their structures by annual illumination, but it culturally implants the idea that they (and their stewards) are, or were, connected, imaginatively if not spiritually, with the rhythms of the cosmos.

If a theatre maker approaches their site with the assumption that they are not entering a fixed state or exploiting a backdrop, but addressing themselves to living systems, then, by understanding what those systems are and how they work, those makers can amplify, prolong and entangle their interventions. Spending sustained periods of time in a site can reveal all sorts of unexpected dynamics; for example, a modern workplace being used 'after hours' might begin to perform its own sound score as central heating closes down overnight and the materials in the building contract at different rates. This could become the incidental and predictable music for your performance. A suburban garden might receive brief but regular visits from bats feeding on the wing, becoming reliable performers in a twilight piece. The question, then, for the observant and site-engaged performance maker is how to 'recruit' these reliable rhythmic systems; dancing to the creaks of the building may be all it takes. But how would you recruit the bats?

The above examples are of living, material and biological circumstances; but more elusive and ephemeral systems can also be engaged. So, in 1997, in a piece called *The Rumor*, Francis Alÿs – an artist who has paid very careful attention to the sites of his art making – visited a small Mexican town and was able to initiate gossip about a guest at a local hotel who had, he suggested, disappeared without explanation. The circulation, retelling, development and embroidering of this story (and various emerging subplots) reached sufficient levels of distribution and complexity for the local police to have an artist's impression of the 'missing person' drawn up and circulated on posters. This is fecund, powerful and perilous practice, not far from 'fake news' in its effects if dissimilar in intention; when not explained, it can produce attractive simulacra which others then colour with their assumptions.

So, if you were to create a similar project to Francis Alÿs's, how could you connect your own intervention to powerful assumptions and, rather than simply amplifying them (as is the dynamic with 'fake news'), transform and recruit them to your own dynamic? How would you use rumour to change assumptions?

The 'why' of performance shifts the grounds – and is the bridge – from a moment when you are most interested in how a site affects you, to one where you are more interested in finding out how – by using its own resources – you can affect it. This is the moment when neither the site's agency nor yours need be dominant; when site-specificity becomes a kind of reciprocity.

Exercise

The resources for Claire Blundell Jones's *Tumbleweed* (Loughborough and Cardiff [UK], Kuopio [Finland], 2007–2009) were simple, if partly exotic: a tumbleweed purchased online and a leaf blower. By deploying these, blowing the tumbleweed with the blower through city streets, Jones's action could transform the ambience of a busy shopping area or a financial district into that of a ghost town. The associations conjured by the sight of the tumbleweed blowing past a bank, a department store or along the pavement of a busy arterial road gave pause to the passers-by who witnessed it. The future dereliction of the bank, silence of the bankrupted retail centre, stillness of the road blocked by the rusting chassis of abandoned cars, all these were for a moment imaginable possibilities emerging out of the busy city. For some this was a momentary discordance, but the more that an observer looked the more the ordinariness was challenged, while Jones's focus on her task and lack of interaction with other trajectories (other than the wind) magnified the disjunction she caused. Follow Jones's example. Use a practically simple, but visually powerful associative intervention in an everyday space that you are familiar with. Maybe it will require a machinic assemblage like Jones's. Maybe a particular way of moving. Maybe the placing of a barely obstructive obstacle that begs a question, or the alteration of a sign. Consider what low-impact and gentle intervention you can make to generate a disproportionately profound effect on the imaginations of audiences/passers-by. Begin by studying the place; working out what its dynamics might be, and how you can recruit them for your intervention. Are there large windows in which to manipulate the reflections? Do the crowds flow in predictable, but subtly disruptable ways? Is there some ignored element that you could use to transform the space simply by illuminating, highlighting or signposting? Recruit the resources of the powerful space to your own meaning. What kinds of site do you discover by this performative visiting?

Exercise

Walk arm in arm with a blindfolded spectator (eyes shut may suffice), keeping them safe, telling them lies about what you see. Then swap roles. A variation: arm in arm, blindfold, but this time describe the terrain through the eyes of a character.

Exercise

The Russian movie director Ilya Khrzhanovsky, responsible for the highly regarded film *4* (2004), reputedly shot footage over more than two years (2008–2011) in a specially constructed set assembled near the city of Kharkiv in Ukraine. This film set, called 'The Institute', was the largest one ever made in Europe; 12,000 square metres in extent, a micro-world recreation of a 1950s Soviet-era institute in which the actors were resident throughout the filming period and barred from bringing modern devices onto the set. Journalists who visited were given 1950s costumes to wear and were expected to accept the fiction that this was no film project; but a science institute. The editing of the movie itself has as yet (2018) to be completed, but reportedly continues. Not all sites are real. Or not what they present themselves to be. Investigate simulations, recreations and simulacra as places to perform.

Reading

Environmental Theater by Richard Schechner (first published in 1973) is a book that both illuminates the dynamic history and developments of site-specific practices and contains numerous general ideas and technical models for making such performances. The earlier introductory sections and the chapter on 'Space' will be particularly useful to read prior to undertaking a first site-specific project; Schechner discusses principles but in a practical way and with plenty of concrete examples, many from his own work with The Performance Group (founded in New York in 1967 and evolving into the Wooster Group after Schechner's resignation as artistic director in 1980).

While mostly what are cited in this book are projects and performance makers that broke from theatre-designated building-based productions, Schechner articulates performance aesthetics that are committed to the particularities of the site of performance and yet describe principles, forms and techniques that can survive transfer from site to theatre or from rehearsal room to street. Emblematic of this (and in a move similar to the escape of the painting from its frame), in The Performance Group's production of *Dionysus in 69* (1968) the action erupted out of the theatre and the final scenes were played in the surrounding streets: the actors chanting 'no more rituals, we want the real thing!' (de Palma, Fiore & Rubin, 1970).

Schechner is not, however, unmindful of the problems and tensions that arise from a transfer between sites. Rehearsing *Makbeth* with the Performance Group in 'an open pasture bordering a stream and a small woods' (1978, p. xvii) in Boacic, near Dubrovnik (then Yugoslavia) and then returning to perform it on the street in New York in 1969, Schechner describes how their 'big mistake… was that we rehearsed it in Baocic… [because] the space-field of that outdoor meadow stayed with us' (1994, p. 27). The continuing impact of the original site did not fit well with the demands of urban streets; rather than simply transferring the performance, they had also transferred the imprint of the earlier site: 'I hope I've learned the lesson: *Text, action, and environment must develop together*' (p. 28, emphasis in original). The site for Schechner is not a container, nor a backdrop: 'environments ecological or theatrical can be imagined not only as spaces but as active players in complex systems of transformation. Neither… are passive' (p. x).

Schechner does not distinguish between high art and popular cultural forms when discussing space and performance; whether it is 'Peter Brook's "Tempest" and "Orghast"... or a pig kill and dance at Kurumugl in New Guinea... each example is of an event whose expression in space is a complete statement of what the event is' (p. 25); so the expression of the art is not what remains in a text or even in the experiences of all participants, but is realised in its spatial expression: the controlled site of the theatre building is not abolished, but it is expanded and its accoutrements (box office, lobby, bar, kiosk, fixed seating, boxes, flying gallery, stage door and dressing rooms) are absorbed into the organic site. There is no immutable separation of spectators from actors, all the space is available to both. Likewise everyday life and theatre are interwoven (see Schechner 1994, pp. 20–22); and Schechner describes a number of variations on this entanglement.

Finally, Schechner is aware (even in 1973) of the dangers and opportunities accompanying the incorporation of site-specificity. He describes a '"new mainstream" rang[ing] across the gamut of performance from the educational to the avant-garde, from crass commercialism to experimentation' and cites 'the Disney theme parks and their imitators; the hundreds of "restored villages" and "living museums" that entertain and educate millions' (1994, p. xv) as instances of incorporation of radical, environmental ideas. This appropriation is not always the work of giant corporations, however, but can be present in small-scale 'innocent' projects, such as Sandra Jiménez's *Se Traspasa* (2017), a show about objects, ornaments, costumes and romance performed in a small antiques and vintage clothing store in Madrid, where the proprietor seeks to 'combine both retail and theatre experiences' (Barrero, 2017). Flagging up the issues under discussion here, Schechner, almost generations ago, was alerting us to how they are active from the edges of a marginal artform to the very centre of the currents of the mainstream.

2

Drifting and Quest: In Search of Sites

Finding and choosing a site for a performance is more than an instrumental matter. Particularly now, when the performative qualities of ambulatory exploring are emerging as part of the continuum of site-specific performance itself. Just as the Symbolists first broke through the packaging of the theatre building, so walking artists, digital designers and other nomadic thinkers have been exploding the notional fixedness or any sense of the 'at rest' of the site of site-specific art. Exponentially increasing numbers of artists, performers, dancers, geographers and others are now using performative journeys as part of their production process, or as the product itself (which perhaps ought to be re-categorised as 'route-specific performance').

By 2017 the Walking Artists Network (WAN) had attracted over 600 members. 'Walking art' had once been the preserve of a few high-profile individuals, like Richard Long or Hamish Fulton, or consisted mostly of one-off, often spectacular actions – for example, Lonnie van Brummelen's epic dragging of a plaster sculpture of Hermes from her apartment in Amsterdam to the caves at Lascaux (documented in Siebren de Haan's film *Route Sedentaire* [2001]). Now, performative journeys, even when epic, are likely to have a convivial or social quality. *The Walking Library* (2012 and ongoing) created by Deirdre Heddon and Misha Myers, for example, gathers together groups of walkers who carry, and read from, a selected library that evolves along the way, and has journeyed in Scotland,

Belgium and the USA. Even where an epic quality remains, there is often a clearer social connection; so, for her *Plastic Crusader* walk (2012) from Amsterdam to Utrecht, Monique Besten collected every piece of waste plastic she found, adding them to a growing burden that grew such that she soon appeared like a snail carrying a giant shell on her back, eventually delivering and releasing her burden at the 'Metaal Kathedraal' (formerly a metal works, now an artists' workspace) where it was added to an installation responding to the so-called '8th continent' of plastic that has collected in the ocean at the North Pacific Gyre.

Uniting these different practices is the putting of the participants' bodies, in some sense or other, real or metaphorical, 'at the mercy' of the road; at times these adventures have the intensity of the transgressive missions of 'urban-explo' (see Ninjalicious, 2005; Garrett, 2013; and Solis, 2013). At its most extreme, there have been fatalities like that of the poet and activist Mark Baumer, killed when struck by a 'sports utility vehicle' on a bare-footed walk across the USA in 2017, and Richard Swanson whose walk, dribbling a football from Seattle to the World Cup in Brazil in 2014, ended in death beneath the wheels of a truck in Oregon. More positively, and more gently, are equally unplanned encounters such as those of Jess Allen's *tracktivism* (2012 and ongoing) in which she wanders rural footpaths, mostly in Wales, carrying 'prompts' to begin conversations around energy; or Walk and Squawk's collecting of stories as they instigated community explorations of desire paths in Detroit and KwaZulu-Natal (2003–2006); or Elspeth Owen's *Grandmother's Footsteps* (2009) in which, on becoming a grandmother, she crossed 15 UK counties delivering gifts to others who had also become grandparents for the first time, unsure what terrain the next gift would require her to cross.

Among other factors speeding this shift from 'sites' to 'routes' are the superior versatility of many human bodies over exploratory machines. The multi- and anti-located properties of Wi-Fi that allow a walker connections to elsewhere through area networks, the attractiveness of walking's sustainability, the rising popularity of (often now secularised) pilgrimage and the influence of relational aesthetics have also been factors. Given its minimum cost and lack of the need for mediation, a prepared, disrupted and improvisatory walking is often seen as an egalitarian and non-specialist performance without an audience. For just such a walking, some artists – exemplified by the 54 WAN members contributing their tactics and 'scripts' to Claire Hind and Clare Qualmann's *Ways to Wander* (2015) – have chosen to create toolkits and handbooks for such lay ambulatory performances additional to, or in place of, their own ambulations.

There is a strand within this walking, which is less about the journey and more about what is experienced; the atmospheres savoured and the data gathered. Along with some resilient reverberations from the first Romanticist movement, the most important impetus for this walking are the tactics of the 'drift' or '*dérive*' (destination-less meanders) of the International Lettrists/situationists; something known to, if not influ-ential upon, a majority of walking artists. Devised in the 1950s by a group of revolutionaries and iconoclasts based mostly in Paris, the '*dérive*' is a walk for gathering information – 'psychogeography' – to be used in creating 'situations'. These 'situations' are temporary manifestations, including performances, constructed against a manipulated life that has become mediated by images. Hyper-sensitivity to ambience on a '*dérive*' enables a radical walker to intuit and map anomalous areas that are resist-ant to the brutal homogenisation of planned cities and the image-soaking of space by the mass media and social media through handheld devices. These are places where it might be possible to live outside the dominant ideology, places where everyday life might be 'taken back', experienced fully and transformed. Although the International Lettrists/situationists realised their aspirations only in fragments (itself a contradiction of their struggle against the impetus to separation and pixilation), nevertheless, the attraction of a hyper-sensitised walking, alive to the 'feel' of place – and with precedents in the figures of the *flâneuse* and *flâneur* (see Elkin, 2016), of the early twentieth-century 'trampers', and of literary walkers from Thomas de Quincey to Virginia Woolf – continues to be felt and applied while 'psychogeography', particularly in the UK, morphed into a baroque, sometimes occult, literature of space and place and is now being rescued for activism by the annual Fourth World Congress of Psychogeography at Huddersfield (UK) (no matter how many times it is held it is always 'the Fourth').

The tactics and techniques of the *dérivistes, flâneuses*, occult psycho-geographers, space-activists, urban explorers and literary wanderers are a resource for a maker of site-specific theatre and performance, particularly at the start of their producing process; the emphasis on sensing the atmosphere of a place, and on how a place's shaping, symbols and texture might invite particular actions, or contain certain histories, are deployable in the search for sites for performance.

Tactics range from the simple 'zig-zag' walk of the tramper Stephen Graham – take the first left turn, then the next right, then the next left, and so on – to situationist 'catapults' such as taking a random bus and choosing which stop to get off by a throw of dice, or taking a taxi blindfolded and asking the driver to drop you somewhere remote and unsigned. These are tricks meant to shake you from the norms of everyday looking and get you beyond familiar places and routines, and maybe a little out of your comfort zone. Hyper-sensitising yourself during the explorations can include walking at an extreme slow pace, paying obsessive attention to textures, materials, fungi, eroded signs and other texts and litter; or walking with a 'theme' (colours, tensions, patterns) or a category of place in mind.

Exercise

Search for micro-worlds: limited places that are like a miniature cosmos, a small world in themselves; a microcosm. These can range from a furniture showroom to a garden shed to a pile of abandoned toys, and they can make powerful sites for performance.

Exercise

Sometimes an exploratory walk will begin to develop a narrative of its own; similar features appear repeatedly, what was evident at first becomes mysterious, a quest emerges, a stranger encountered along your way invites you to a restricted place or lays down a challenge. If such a narrative emerges on a walk, can you then follow it, making choices that develop the story of the walk or the walk as a story? You may want to record your thoughts and observations as you go. You can use a digital camera or the camera on your phone as a notebook. Or pause every now and again, lie down and write for 10 minutes. Or leave messages on an ansaphone. Map as you go, by GPS, sketch possible sites in a notepad. Or scratch your notes in the sand or riverbank, or chalk them on walls, and photograph them. On completing your journey, ask yourself: what place or moment was closest to performance?

Exercise

If you are working in a group, each individual member should choose one land artist and research their artwork. Then seek out a site that in some way reflects their work or the sites they chose for their work: pipes and Nancy Holt, concrete bunkers and Michael Heizer, lakes and Robert Smithson. Or if you already have a site, research the artist and then seek out an aspect of your site that reflects their work. In your site or the site you have found, each of you give a short (say, five minute) presentation about your chosen artist and a performance (of equal length) based on your understanding of their work. Various issues might inform your visit, presentation and performance. You might consider the criticism made of some land artists for their aggressive interventions in the landscape – Robert Smithson moved almost 7,000 tons of earth and rock by mechanical means for his 'Spiral Jetty' (Great Salt Lake, USA, 1970) – and make your interaction with the materials of a site (invasive or not) the basis of a performance. Many land art interventions work by their framing of a space, provoking and staging the performing of the place by itself. Changes of light will animate the naked-eye observatory, set within a huge volcanic cone in the Arizona desert, of James Turrell's 'Roden Crater' (Painted Desert, USA, construction ongoing). Turrell's project has lasted almost half a century and is still incomplete; how can you recruit a similarly epic landscape with a framing as light and intangible as Turrell's is large-scale and architectural? Grandness of scale or extremity of location are no guarantors of longevity; Michael Heizer's 'Rift 1', a long zig-zag trench dug into the exposed bed of Jean Dry Lake (USA) was wholly reabsorbed after a few years, while 'Spiral Jetty' has been inundated and has then re-emerged due to rising and falling water levels. Can you create a piece whose main agency is one of depredation: eroding, burning, shrivelling, draining, dissolving?

Idea

Ask a few friends to take a pen and paper and to draw the first image that pops into their head when you say 'the world'. Usually, a majority will draw some kind of globe or circle. As the anthropologist Tim Ingold has pointed out, without thinking about or choosing to, the person drawing such a shape has placed themselves far, far away from the thing they are trying to depict, adopting a view like that of a satellite or a spacecraft high above the Earth (pp. 31–32). Ingold proposes an alternative model for imagining 'the world', whereby knowledge of it comes not by remoteness, but by an ever deepening immersion in its detail and texture, as if you were descending through the layers of the Earth, the planet made of spheres nested within other spheres (1993, pp. 32–35). Hold that thought as you walk. Then hold another, at the same time. For the geographer Doreen Massey argued for exactly the satellite view that Ingold rejected, as a means to understand cities not by their boundaries, but by their movements. The satellite observes the 'power geometry' that is written into those mobilities and the varying access that different people have to the 'time-space compression' afforded by accelerating communications and transport (Massey, 1994, p. 154). As you walk, hold that thought too. Then deploy a binocular looking, attentive both to the unfolding textures close up and the trajectories that pass you by as they arrive and depart and churn (and of which your journey is now one).

Exercise

Referencing Vito Acconci's *Following Piece* (New York, 1969) and Sophie Calle's *Suite Vénitienne* (Paris and Venice, 1980), go to a busy public space and choose someone at random, then follow them at a considerable distance, being sure not to let them, or anyone else, know that you are following them. If you feel for a moment they may suspect, drop the exercise and move away. Make sure you always choose someone who is unlikely to already feel vulnerable; or to constitute a threat to you. The point of this exercise, a non-invasive following, is to do as Acconci attempted; to hand over power to an unknowing guide who 'leads' you into places you might not otherwise go. If this unknowing guide leaves public space, then move away and choose another guide to follow.

Exercise

Walk with the 'wrong' map. Walk in one city, but with another city's map; walk with a recipe, a diagram of an electrical circuit or a piece of carpet for your map.

Exercise

Walk a city's streets with a map of its buried wiring; or interpret as directions for your route those spray-painted instructions for maintenance workers on pavements/sidewalks (the ones some people imagine to be burglars' code).

Exercise

Use the contrasting qualities and advantages of a satellite view of the world (as proposed by Doreen Massey to see a city, say, as the trajectories through it) with those of the closer, embodied and immersed approach proposed by Tim Ingold going layer by layer deeper into the space. Find a site that you can view from high up, and from right on the ground. Make a performance that links the vertiginous viewpoint with immersion in the layers – perhaps use walkie-talkies, flags, beams of light, balloons or similar to connect the two parts of your site.

Exercise

Engaging with strangers as you go is a good preparation for when, later, you may need to negotiate with 'gatekeepers' or numerous members of a community for access to space or for information about a place. You may want some pretext for approaching strangers. You might borrow from Nobutaka Aozaki who, for his 'From Here to There' project, approaches strangers in New York, asking them for directions and provides them with paper and pen to draw him a map, later adding them to a giant vernacular cartography he has assembled. Aozaki, who moved to New York from Japan in 2005, sees his city through the eyes of both local and stranger – a doubled walking persona you might want to cultivate along with your doubled satellite/layer looking. Aozaki's work is informed by a concern with place; in his film *The Life in Underground* (2011) he re-imagines everyday scenes in the New York subway by overlaying them with news of the Tokohu Kanto earthquake and subsequent Fukushima nuclear power plant disaster; another way of double-looking: laying associations from a distant place over the immediacy of a present one.

Exercise

An effective way of shifting or 'making strange' your viewing of familiar streets is to walk with a new persona. Don't perform or imitate this persona, don't act it out, don't engage with passers-by 'in character', but simply view the world through this new persona's eyes, through their situation, through their narrative. Maybe ask a friend to choose a persona for you, and you choice one for them; barter and extend your use of personae. Ones that have proved to be effective are a fox, a ghost, a detective investigating a crime in a town where everyone is a suspect, a recent arrival in heaven or hell (you have to discover which one), a creature underwater, a cupid matching strangers and, most popular, the last human survivor of a zombie apocalypse (Smith, 2016, pp. 85–98). Driven by the erotic enthusiasm of Cupid, the paranoid flight narrative of a survivor, or the investigative zeal of a gumshoe you may find your way to places you would not usually go, to sensations you might not usually have, the possessor of information you have not heard before.

Idea

Is there a particular *kind* of place that you are looking for? While it might be best for specificity that no such preconceived idea figures at all, perhaps it is more honest and effective to own up to yourself that that is what you are ready to see. Maybe you are looking for something that has some of the features of a designated theatre space? A possible playing area or vantage points for spectators? Somewhere that 'an existing institutional arrangement of watchers and watched … can be annexed' (Pearson & Shanks, 2001, p. 111)? Or are you looking for a vista that can play as a backdrop to your performers' actions? Or a labyrinth to thread a narrative through? Are you looking for a lair or a haunt in which to confront a beast or a ghost or a history? Owning up to your preconceptions may help you to be surprised, and notice when an unexpected opportunity presents itself. It might help you to turn your assumptions around or inside out, before you gratify them: so, rather than 'how would this space behave like a theatre?', ask 'how could the unique affordances of this space reshape what theatre can be?' Equally, once you have established in practice the necessity for a 'particularity … to be lived-in, felt, and respected' and learned not to impose your own ideas on a site, there is more leeway for the unfolding of your performance as it is 'possible sometimes to make just a few modifications to a found space so that a performance may more effectively "take place" there' and how, often, a 'reciprocity occurs … spectators arrange themselves in unexpected patterns … these patterns change, "breathing" with the action' (Schechner, 1994, p. xxxvi). Not just spectators, but patterns of other elements of the performance can productively rearrange themselves.

Exercise

If you are exploring for sites for a group performance, then you might adapt the model of Forced Entertainment's *The Travels* (2002). Here the actors/researchers chose, or were given, particularly resonant street names – Hope Street, Achilles Street, Rape Lane – and then travelled separately to where streets with these names were located (at least that is the story; with Forced Entertainment one is never quite sure about any of their narratives, on stage or otherwise). In the performance, based purportedly on these journeys, the Forced Entertainment company members presented their findings in a formal manner, somewhat like a press conference after a public inquiry. Seated along one side of a long table, facing their audience, the different 'drifters', with microphones, recounted stories and moments and impressions and the interpretation of symbols from their streets. The different strands of individual narrative wove around each other. So, choose your own means of navigating – by geological features, by altitudes, by thematic names, by heritage landmarks – and make your separate journeys, or make them in small groups, returning to present your findings in a formal presentation style using text and projected images; either as a means of research for a performance site, or as a performance in itself.

Readings

There are numerous books of tactics and instructions that you can draw on for prompts to initiate your exploring or to give it structure. *The Fluxus Performance Workbook* (Friedman, Sawchyn & Smith, 2002), which is available online, has numerous elliptical and gnomic scores that either directly describe the model of a walk – 'Walk out into a forest and wrap some drab trees, or yourself, in tinsel' – or that can be adapted by you as the suggestive dynamics of a walk. Similarly with the instructions on the cards of Brian Eno and Peter Schmidt's *Oblique Strategies* (1st edition, 1975) or the poetic tactics in Yoko Ono's *Grapefruit*; her 'scores' sit somewhere between thought experiments and practical commands – 'Carry a stone. Go on carrying heavier stones until they become so heavy that the whole city starts to look lighter' (Ono, 1964, n.p.).

Many of the tactics in the following books come from artists with a performance practice and potentially feed directly back into one: Emma Cocker and Sophie Mellor's (2011) series of texts for *Close and Remote's Manual for Marginal Places* is a 'guide against guides' that can be mined for prompts to 'skirting', 'working the situation well' and 'making do with what has been left'. Directly realisable, poetic and funny are the counter-touristic tactics in Rachael Antony and Joel Henry's *Lonely Planet Guide to Experimental Travel*, Wrights & Sites' *An Exeter Mis-Guide* (2003) and *A Mis-Guide to Anywhere* (2006), WAN's *Ways to Wander* edited by Claire Hind and Clare

Qualmann (2015), and the handbook sections of my own *Mythogeography* (Smith, 2010), *Counter-Tourism: The Handbook, On Walking and The Footbook of Zombie Walking*.

Then there are books that are less like toolkits and more like descriptions of practice, but that can also be adapted or adopted for exploration. Anna Best's (2003) *Occasional Sites* recounts numerous 'drifts' in London and exposes the methodology of its project; exploring the convivial possibilities of psychogeography and shifting it away from literary solipsism. The second chapter of David Haden's (2011) *Walking with Cthulhu* describes an array of transferable techniques used by the horror writer H. P. Lovecraft while exploring the streets of New York at night in the 1920s. Dancer Simon Whitehead's *Walking to Work* and *Lost in Ladywood* collect together some of his explorations/actions, including carrying a kitchen table along country lanes, arranging for the shoes of 'holy men' in Birmingham (UK) to be available for anyone to walk in, following feral animals and walking in the company of a Shire horse. There are many more. …

3

Journey Performances

One sunny afternoon in the early 1990s I joined an audience for a performance of Frisch Théâtre Urbain's *Mephistomania* (1992–2010) on London's South Bank (Illustration 3.1). As we moved through the precincts of mid-twentieth-century architecture around the Royal Festival Hall we were at times chasing the action and at others encircled by it. The performers carried burning torches, waved giant flags, paraded in exotic, elaborately detailed, broad-skirted costumes and striking headwear, occasionally settling to perform short, melodramatic scenes from the story of Doctor Faustus: his temptation, magical empowerment and fall. The performers wore stilts, which raised them high above the spectators and made them visible for everyone in the crowd, as well as amplifying their athletic and violent dances. The actors were accompanied by a hand-pulled truck from which came a loud soundscape, huge clouds of smoke and other pyrotechnic effects.

Although our active participation in the theatrical action was not invited, the experience of moving with the performers was one of involvement, of being part of the spectacle of figures rolling along in a swirling red cloud to explosions and a thumping musical accompaniment. There was a toughness about the performance, as much circus as theatre; it was daring and dangerous (later I was shown the large burn sustained by one of the actors during this particular performance). It was far more of the streets than of the study; the Faustian myth was presented not for intellectual contemplation or psychological empathy, but as a source of overwhelming sensation and spectacle. The unremarkable pedestrian areas we travelled became abstracted and at times hidden by the clouds of coloured smoke and the billowing flags and skirts; the performance at times engulfed its audience in movement, sound and colour. The different resources drawn upon, particularly of sound and smoke, had created around the performance its own transient and diaphanous 'site', blowing along past the buildings, over the flat pedestrianised surfaces and around the actors, their truck, and us.

Mephistomania was not *about* a journey (except in the weak metaphorical sense of roughly following Faustus's moral adventure), but it *was* a journey. The selection of, and site-responsive preparation for, the route by the company's directors, Sarah Harper and Pascal Laurent, facilitated a smooth flow of action; the performers used the shapes of the spaces. The staid and blank concrete of the route and the exuberant and demonic supernatural qualities of what was performed were discordant, but not irreconcilable. The architectural environment re-emerged from the smoke and whirl of the performance as something more like geometrical forms than buildings. The terrain became more like consciousness than like matter; an environment in which concepts could manifest. Evil and magic could be here, and be modern. The smoky transit of the performance transformed the ambience and affordance of the existing site into something more transient: a testing ground of ethical choices.

Illustration 3.1 *Mephistomania*, Friches Théâtre Urbain, 1992.
Photo: Yannis Alevroyiannis.

You may, now, already have all the materials you need for just such an entangled performance journey, capable of engaging with and transforming its route. Not necessarily at the level of spectacle or with the literary embeddedness of *Mephistomania*, but if you have experimented with the walking and exploring discussed in Chapter 2, you may have gone beyond using your journey as an instrument for finding a site, or gathering emotional and physical information about it. Your journey may already have the form and content of a performance.

There are many different modes of journey-based performance. Sometimes these modes involve, just like Frisch Théâtre Urbain's theatre of the streets, the 'carrying' of a performance on a journey, stretching a narrative over a terrain. At other times, however, the journey itself can be the performance. The exploratory and improvised 'drift' often has performance-like qualities (spontaneous or planned); however, there is a more formal journey performance in which the route (the geographical line of a journey) is set and mapped, the score refined, the action rehearsed and then an audience is invited. At other times only a concept of a journey is set, the destination is uncertain, the route unplanned and the audience consists of strangers encountered at random.

If the performance is porous enough these accidental encounters may be full of chances for understanding. But the mingling of rigorously instructed audiences with passers-by at a disadvantage can lead to an uncomfortable privileging of those 'in the know' or an unhelpful misreading by the chance witness. With Willi Dorner's *Bodies in Urban Spaces* (Paris and subsequently numerous other cities, 2007 and ongoing), where the route is set, the performers rigorously trained and inserting their bodies, with extraordinary skill and choreographic elegance, into the affordant spaces of the city's buildings and a well-briefed formal audience racing to keep up with their unfolding of human sculptures in little noticed and unvalued void spaces, there is less for the encounter of performers and accidental audience. The latter may be far from 'accidental' in their understanding of what performance is, but they have not themselves been rehearsed into the 'correct' reception of the event; while the formal audience is usually 'particularly keen to take photographs of the sculptures, which [are] later widely circulated through social media sites' (Lawrence, 2015, p. 265). Dorner's defamiliarisations of public space (not always personally directed, but contracted to deputies) and their body–street relations are open to being misread (or perhaps perceptively understood, depending on your point of view) as the tableaux of a commercial street performance or a flash mob appropriated for a commercial advertisement; even Dorner comments: 'Myself I feel very *ambigue* on all the photos of bodies' (cited in Scopio, 2017).

There is a lesson here. The multiplicities of the street are such that too strict an address to them, or too simple and formal a dynamic, can generate complex and unintended meaning-making, though the resulting performance may achieve considerable success in terms of popular attendance or media reach and acclaim. The intentions of *Bodies in Urban Spaces*, according to Dorner's website, are to 'point out the urban functional structure and to uncover the restricted movement possibilities and behaviour as well as rules and limitations' in order to 'provoke a thinking process and produce irritation' (Dorner, 2017). However, the connectedness of urban with virtual space, and the dynamics of 'restricted' space when animated gymnastically by trained dancers, dissolve the 'rules and limitations' of ordered architecture as still images of the site, via the audience's phones, and flow into the web. Like all such unexpected dynamics, there is an opportunity curled up inside the unintended result: for such an agentive and influential audience can become partners in meaning-making with a performance company, if the latter can embrace the unexpected dynamics of their show.

In 2001, in the wake of 9/11, Donna Shilling walked from her college in Devon, UK, to her home in London, asking the people she met along the way: 'What is important to you?' While a journey like this might serve to gather materials for a presentation, book or blog, it was also already performance enough; the questions and answers became sufficient dialogue, the encounters constituted a score that did not require repetition or representation. However, such resonant acts are often porous ones, with more resilience than their apparent ephemerality might suggest; so when the controversial announcement was made in 2008 that Shilling's *alma mater*, Dartington College of Arts (an institution where many contemporary site-based performance makers trained) was, effectively, to close, Shilling recreated her walk. She followed the route in reverse, from London to Dartington, accompanied all the way by fellow alumnus

Timothy Vize-Martin, and occasionally by other former students and teachers, as a farewell to their college.

Bram Thomas Arnold's work *Walking Home (Again)* was initiated by a walk in 2009 from his home in London to the house in St. Gallen (Switzerland) where he was born. Rather than an end in itself, Arnold used the findings of his walk as the material for an exhibition, embedded within which was a two-hour performance. This piece, *Fondue* (2014), was both a dinner party and a documentary enactment; a convivial event within which Arnold could share the insights afforded to him by his journey, 'finding the universal in the personal and the personal in the universal, narrating a sense of loss that is widely felt and desperately hidden in contemporary Western society' (Arnold, 2015).

It may be significant that the journey performances cited above, on and off the road, are characterised by a gentle political engagement; an argument with borders and property that arises from the restrictions of a route, a dialogue with conviviality and strangerhood that emerges from the walk's encounters, and an enquiry about the nature of identity and transformation that comes with the pilgrimage-like experiences of many ambulatory performers. These qualities are chosen, however, or specific to their route; they are not inevitable and quite different qualities are possible. For example, in September 2006 the Chinese performance artist He Yun Chang walked from the hamlet of Rock in Northumberland, UK, to the nearby beach at Boulmer where he picked up a sizeable rock and proceeded to carry it on his shoulder around most of the British coastline. When the walk was completed the following June, Chang returned the rock to the beach where he had found it. *Rock Touring Around Great Britain* developed very little real dialogue with its route; it was a performance of an ordeal originally scheduled for the island of Manhattan. The terrain was largely incidental to the heroic task. On his walk, He Yun Chang cut a phantom figure, sometimes accompanied by followers, and photographs of his walk were shared online; but most witnesses to his ordeal – designed to 'represent the iron will of an individual' – were accidental and as likely to be bemused as informed.

Monali Meher walks backwards. In *Visiting Pearl* she walks backwards to the river in Guangzhou (2011), in *Visiting Marmara* (2013) she begins at the Istanbul Museum of Modern Art and, backwards, leads her audience to an unannounced point on the Bosphorus (Illustration 3.2), and for *Visiting Brooklyn Bridge* (2016) in New York she crosses the bridge and drops down to the waterfront. By walking backwards, Meher meets the eyes of the audience following her. She carries incense sticks in her hands, the smoke dispersing to the terrain, impregnating the scene, dissipating quickly; a symbol of the affect-led transience of her performance. For Meher, this ephemerality is a statement about a time of political insecurity, threat and upheaval; the precarity of her walk feeds a similar impression. In her *Facing Vooruit* (2014), made for the Sustainability Fair in Ghent in Belgium, while walking backwards she fixed her eyes on the building she was moving away from: the monumental Vooruit (Forward) building that had served Ghent's socialist and labour movements as an arts centre during the 1920s and 1930s. On arrival at her destination, she turned around to face a temporary bamboo structure made for the Fair.

Illustration 3.2 *Visiting Marmara*, Monali Meher, Istanbul, 2013. Istanbul Modern Museum and International Performance Platform (IPA).

Photo: Rob Sweere.

While Meher's journeys carry broad and paradoxical political metaphors about uncertainty for the future and more stolid traditions from earlier and equally unstable times, a hopeful backwards looking and a sustainable precarity (beginning at institutions and ending at rivers), and a positive connectivity (crossing a bridge, linking past and future utopianisms, meeting her audience's gaze), there is also something political in the corporeal mechanics of the walks themselves. By walking backwards Meher sets her body at the mercy of the obstacles and surprises of the route, but by facing her audience she can partially navigate her way by observing where the audience's eyes' focus, how they respond to what they see ahead and how they react to each step that she takes. She turns the audience's gaze into a collective and shareable mapping of the street ahead, a human mirror for what she cannot see. A dynamic of reciprocity and collective action emerges. The formally passive role for the audience, by its incorporation into the performer's perilous negotiation of her journey, becomes active, real and metaphorical.

During a brief stay in the Alumni Guest House at Carleton College, Northfield, Minnesota, USA, I looked out of my window and was surprised to see on the pavement (sidewalk) below three people walking backwards and facing four people who were following them. I discovered that this is how students of the college conduct tours of the campus for prospective students and their families. As well as being quirky and encouraging a friendly face-to-face relationship, the visitors are immediately drawn in to taking some responsibility for the welfare of their hosts and, in some sense, take a step to becoming part of the shared life of the campus community.

This transformation of an audience from spectators into active guides and witnesses (not simply observing but, in the broadest sense, testifying to, or accounting for, what they see) is something that the journey-performance lends itself to. In Fiona Templeton's *YOU – The City* (1988–1991, 2001), first performed in Manhattan, a single audience member becomes part of a play in which they are repeatedly greeted by characters with much to say about 'you' (the audience member); every sentence includes the words 'you' or 'your'. For two hours the audience member walks or is driven around the city; they are the one unifying and central presence at the heart of the play. Combining the hypersensitisation of certain kinds of walking with the asymmetrical prompt of Blundell Jones's *Tumbleweed*, the city, at least as now freshly and strangely perceived by the audience, can begin to change and perform. *YOU – The City* activated what Fiona Templeton calls 'the *unintendable*' (p. vii, emphasis in original). These are moments, for example, when passers-by interrupted or challenged the action: such as an audience member following a homeless person who had attempted to 'panhandle' from them, mistaking them for a performer (p. 14). As an audience member remarked:

> It was like these children's books where parts of it pop up, I was in the middle of the city and all of a sudden that two dimensional world … became three dimensional. Like if you look at a painting by Rauschenberg … you have painted parts and then you have a real broom stuck in, and you think, what is that doing there? (p. 54)

The association of site-specific performance with painting's escape from the frame is here made explicitly!

Despite their linear quality, and perhaps because of their association with such repeatable transits as pilgrimages, journey-performances lend themselves to re-enactment. Sometimes there is an element of criticality or humour in these; sometimes the copy intensifies the intentions of the original. Esther Pilkington walked only one half of Richard Long's *Crossing Stones* walk (1987), in which he took a stone from Aldeburgh beach to the shore at Aberystwyth and back again, turning Long's documentation of his walk into an instructive score, and adding an autobiographical warmth (Pilkington joining her home town to that of her grandparents) to Long's simple, dour text. Han Bing's series *Walking a Cabbage* in Beijing (beginning in 2000) is a comment on the upturning of traditional values in contemporary Chinese society; cabbage, formerly prized as a sign of affluence and sustenance in winter, is increasingly snubbed, while trophy dogs are paraded by many of the newly wealthy. So Bing walks a cabbage. When this performance was re-walked in Srinagar by the anonymous 'Kashmiri Cabbage Walker', the performer defined its aspirations differently, still satirical but more provocative, as 'demilitarization, de-occupation, decolonisation and even de-nuclearization'. In both cases, the walkers are challenging passers-by to question their (often extreme) responses to their performances' minor absurdities, while all around them, unremarked, what passes for normalcy is skewed by consumerism and military oppression.

In 2002 Peter Bodenham and Simon Whitehead, in a partial re-enactment, pushed a stuffed goose in a cart along old drovers' routes from West Wales to Smithfield Market in London 'In an attempt to be faithful to the original routes' (Whitehead, 2006, p. 10) As they went they wrote about their impressions of the journey and then distributed these reflections by text mail, voicemail, postcards and videos posted to the Web. On arrival in London they offered an informal account of their *2 mph* walk to those attending the 'Nightwalking Festival' by 'inviting delegates to enter our tent and read our notebooks' (p. 10). There was a certain irony to this sequence: when their performance was in progress their audience was absent; by the time an audience was present, their performance was over.

With a theatricality to match Frisch Théâtre Urbain's, Odin Teatret's *Anabasis* (1977–1984) obliquely invoked the fifth-century BCE journey of a mercenary army of Greek soldiers. Recruited to fight the army of Artaxerxes II – before whose tomb *Orghast* was performed – their victory was rendered meaningless by the death of their 'employer', Artaxerxes's brother Cyrus, and of all their senior commanders. With an improvised leadership they fought a long retreat home and back to safety. (Walter Hill's movie *The Warriors* [1979] is drawn from the same source.) Odin's actors/characters arrive on the street, on 'alien soil', mixing with the public until they are called into a group and begin their journey. At times they lure and herd the audience around them in a circle, at other times pushing the crowd before them with swinging sticks and stilts or driving the spectators apart by forming a wedge, as if in a battle. Performers descend on ropes from neighbouring buildings and climb spires and neighbouring monuments. They use the shape of the terrain like a military force might: 'taking the heights' and raising their flags on prominent roof tops.

Unlike the pilgrim quality of the presence of some journeying performers, *Anabasis* emphasises the theatrical-specialness of its performers. Three of the characters, including the skull-headed Death character 'Mr Peanut', are performed on stilts; two actors are at times carried on the shoulders of others while drumming furiously; several are masked. The actors' displays of aesthetic and athletic skills set them apart from their audience. The audience stands in for the chasing, surrounding and harrying army of the Persian king until the performance sucks this conflict into itself and the giant, black-costumed and stilted characters face off with the rest of the company who are fronted by a diminutive clown-leader. This comic figure, walking on his haunches and wielding a walking stick, brings the giants' leader crashing to the ground only for the tyrant to be resurrected by the rebels' own flags. The rebel mercenaries flee through the streets until they are captured under a giant black sheet and guarded by Death; the rebellion based in violence carries the potential to raise up its own form of morbid oppression.

Unlike, say, the explicit re-enactment of historical droving in *2 mph*, the performance of the historical narrative in *Anabasis* is an oblique one. Erik Exe Kristoffersen has described the performance as multilayered, as a 'story of "immigrants", of an army of actors … advancing through the unknown, occupying the town' (p. 64). There is always something more than the military 'back story' at work: the rebels may heroically prevail against the odds, but War itself is resurrected. The martial trumpets and drums of the rebels are made questionable by comic squeakers; the ambiguities of the characters and of the costumes they wear – ranging from business suits to an androgynous mask and a long feather boa – point to another, 'ahistorical' aesthetic: a Symbolist one.

In 1982 I saw *Anabasis* performed in Cardiff (Wales) city centre as part of Odin Teatret's brief residency in the city. Watching their recruitment of numerous passing shoppers, their confident command of a big, popular audience with a far from simplistic narrative, and their physical and sonic impact in a large, windy space, I knew I was witnessing something qualitatively different from (and superior to) any previous street performance I had experienced. The Odin actors demonstrated their fluency in a language of street presence; they were quick to snuff out or enlist each *unintendable* as it arose, assuredly marshalling a quickly willing audience. The evidence of a decade-long engagement with making processions was striking; but after attending a fortnight of workshops with Odin's director Eugenio Barba, and watching their indoor performances of *The Million* and *Ashes of Brecht*, it was equally clear that *Anabasis*, while tailored to the street, was also grounded in a more general Odin aesthetic that worked by the Symbolist juxtaposition of deregulated symbols to produce a mystery for further contemplation rather than any straightforward representation or iteration easily or immediately grasped.

An 'acid test' (not the only one) of performance is what remains; not so much in the documentations of critics and historians as in what 'stays' with those who were there: I still feel the visceral thrill of 'marching' with *Mephistomania*, but what I still see are the spectral shapes of the ghost-faced giant, 'Mr Peanut' and the tasselled drummer lost far from home in the sea of spectators' faces. While many street performances struggle to get beyond the mechanics of their own spectacle to a subtler aesthetics, there is the possibility of profound affects and intriguing indeterminacies beyond the battle for sustained attention. Ecstatic or numinous, the street and the road need not be blunt instruments. The exigencies of journeying offer a range and volatility that push beyond the limits of buskers' 'spots' or showpeople's 'pitches'. The route may be too extensive and detailed to research for any intense specificity; there has to be a flexibility, some imposition perhaps, and certainly improvisation. Thus the retail spaces of Cardiff city centre, with their canyon-like qualities, or the South Bank's concrete brutalism emerged, retreated and re-emerged in these performances, but always as the junior partners of the journeyers themselves. The specificity is to the *unfolding* of the path, route or vector, not the path, route or vector itself. Such an indeterminable independence is compared by the Spanish performance artist Esther Ferrer (whose '*Walking Is the Way*' unfolds under her feet a trail of sticky tape across politically resonant terrains) with a kind of anarchism: 'IT PROMISES NOTHING! Wow! What joy! It gives us no model of pleasure … at the end of an authoritative road. This is because, among other things, there is no road … "caminante no hay camino, se hace camino al andar"' (Walker, there is no road, the road is made by walking).

Such flexibility and autonomy welcome to the performance journey a range of specialisms and everydayness; it shifts back and forth between acts that emphasise the rough materiality of terrains and those that embrace the airy ambiguity of the spaces of non-representational performance. The *Walking Interconnections* project led by Sue Porter and Dee Heddon used an expanded and de-normalised walking (including numerous journeys made by wheelchair users) to challenge the absence of disabled people's voices from debates around sustainability. Bill Aitcheson's *The Tour of All Tours* (Beijing, Stuttgart, London, 2013 and ongoing), in which he collapses the many tours in a city into one tour, is just one variation on a range of 'mis-guided' tours that challenge the dominant discourses of the heritage and tourism industries. While *The Great White Way, 22 Miles, 9 Years, 1 Street* (2001–2009), William Pope.L's crawl dressed in a Superman costume (though not 'in role') along Broadway – the 'Canyon Of Heroes' – is a protest about and through degradation; an agitation around the spaces of race, power, dignity and fantasy.

In a non-mimetic walking, yet in a nod to some sort of role, Jess Allen, for *Drop in the Ocean* (2013; Illustration 3.3), shoulders a yolk with two pails of water along rural footpaths and through towns, 'sharing thoughts about water, interaction, swimming, life, fluidity, relinquishment, pain body, light body, and much more' with those she meets, valuing these encounters as a nourishing 'currency in its own right' (Anon., 2013). In some cases, the encounters – like those of poet Simon Armitage's *Walking Home* (2010), journeying along the Pennine Way in north-east England – are ones of barter; the travelling artists trading their performances, poetry readings in Armitage's case, for food and shelter; a nod to the historical (or imagined) troubadour.

Illustration 3.3 *Drop in the Ocean*, Jess Allen, 2013.
Photo: Sara Penrhyn Jones.

Dispensing with role altogether, different aspects of walking are some-times taken as performances in themselves. Trisha Brown's *Walking on the Wall* (1971, with revivals) uses rope or wires to transform the space of an otherwise unremarkable walking, with its dancers perambulating down the side of a tall building. In Sara Wookey's *Walking LA/(Sur)facing the City* (2008) two years of walking in Los Angeles, and framing the city through the 'lens' of pedestrianism, also turned to walls; photographic images, taken in the streets and projected onto the walls of a gallery, became frames for the performance's dancers. The anarchistic freedoms of walking performances on an unfolding road move in tension with their potential sublimation to the frames and wires of 'specialised' or spectacular performance space.

Fiona Wilkie in her groundbreaking book *Performance, Transport and Mobility* (2015) challenges the bias to ambulation in site-specific per-formance and disperses the archiving of performance practices to those realised by car, rail, boat and air travel. Coach travel, perhaps because of the precedent of a performance tradition on coaches (on board tour guide commentaries and entertainment) has been particularly popular. These have included Hayley Newman's *MKVH* (2006) in which she hired an intercontinental vehicle to transport herself and seven local volunteers around the road grid of the utopian 'new city' of Milton Keynes, UK, until it ran out of diesel; her documentation of the journey comes in the form of a film script (Newman, 2008). While Forced Entertainment's *Nights in this City* (Sheffield, UK, 1995; Rotterdam, Netherlands, 1997) drew more explicitly on the tour guide model, beginning in Sheffield with the words of a performer over the coach's PA system: 'ladies and gentlemen, welcome to Rome.'

KagranKollectiv's *Suburban Safari: or Who Can Find the Mountain Goat?* (2007), a walking tour of the Donaustadt rubbish dump on the edges of Vienna (Austria), led by performers dressed in 'Heidi' and mountain-guide dress, climaxed in a jeep plunging around the tip in search, successfully when I saw it, of the herd of Pinzgau mountain goats that were living there. In 1998 Wrights & Sites began their festival of site-specific performances on Exeter's waterfront, *The Quay Thing*, with *Pilot Navigation*, performed mostly aboard a ferry on the river Exe and along the sixteenth-century Exeter Ship Canal, in which the boat, its facili-ties, capabilities and its crew all served as performers and agents rather than just as a floating stage. The ferry moved in relation to performers and audiences both aboard and on the banks (in contrast to Dog Kennel Hill Project's canal-based *TUG* [2010–2014] which divided the audience with some on board a narrow boat and some on the towpath listening to a synchronised sound score [Bissell, 2016, p. 178]); a company (once again) commandeering an existing PA system, with its vagaries and distortions, to narrate their performance within (and subversive of) the quotation marks of a recognisable authoritative discourse.

Ria Hartley's *The Train Project* (2011), despite its speeds and range, was closer to Jess Allen's *Drop in the Ocean* than some of the more theatrically inflected, vehicle-based journeys. Over 15 days Hartley travelled by train across the UK, asking fellow passengers, crowdfunding investors and online contacts to advise her on her routes. She travelled continuously across the UK (when not waiting for a connection on a station platform); she was overlapping the train network with online and everyday friendship and conviviality networks 'to address issues regarding mobility and connectivity, as well as to expand notions of what a performance can be'. The foci of the journey were numerous, including short-term connections made with strangers and friends, stickering for re-nationalisation of the railways, tracking down the whereabouts of a former police train, losing and recovering luggage, following strangers on stations, a re-enactment of Gillian Wearing's *Signs That Say What You Want Them to Say, Not Signs That Say What Other People Want You to Say* and leaving invitations on trains to meet strangers on stations (at least one of which was responded to), elements of all of which were shared through images, texts and videos on a Facebook timeline. The performance was an adventure and a making of a tenuous and transitory mesh of friends, strangers and online audiences.

Exercise

Rene Gabri described how in New York-based e-Xplo's bus tours the company 'worked to consciously create tensions between what one is hearing and what one is seeing ... [to] produce a conscious listening (vs. hearing) and looking (vs. seeing)' (Thompson & Sholette, 2004, p. 43). Create a performance journey in which, in turn, each of the five senses is stimulated with information that is contradictory to what the other four are receiving.

Exercise

In *KabbaLAmobile* (1984) Rachel Rosenthal mobilised seven cars and their drivers from a Precision Driving Team to perform a mechanical ballet to an audience seated on bleachers in the car park of the local authority's utilities department in Los Angeles: hence the 'LA' embedded in the title with the echo of 'Kabala', a Jewish mystical tradition that mediates between an unchanging and shrouded Infinity and the material 'creation'. In *KabbaLAmobile* Rosenthal chanted mystical poems and texts about automobile engineering from motoring magazines to a musical accompaniment, weaving together the material and the spiritual, while the choreography of the cars followed patterns deduced from the Kabala tradition. Rosenthal emerged at the beginning of the performance from an underground space and climbed to a high platform, 'Face painted like a warrior, in billowing robes, Rosenthal chanted ... and danced shamanically' (Mock, p. 72); 'her movements seemed to cause the strange movement of the cars' (Chaudhuri, 2001, p. 8). Find a site and create a choreography for machines, piloted or robotic, maybe drones, that blends the abstract and the material, or two other such opposites.

Idea

I have been teaching undergraduates on site-specific performance modules in the UK for almost 20 years; over those years, whatever the context in which students are asked to make their first micro-performances (with a minimum of guidelines) – whether a field, campus, city plaza or park – I have never yet witnessed one that escaped the approximate measurements of an Elizabethan stage. Without explicit instructions – to work to the horizon or to bear in mind the sky (instructions which are about to arrive!) – the architecture of a theatre-designated building seems to prevail. Journey performances can go some way to challenging such assumptions, which can trap even experienced practitioners into reintroducing the dimensions, limitations and etiquette of the theatre studio or gallery to their chosen site. The dimensions and boundaries of a site are in flux in a journey performance; the site swings around the performer, rushing ahead of them or racing at them. It constitutes the unseen obstacles that are always likely to come quickly into view, demanding attention and response. The journey performance idealises a smooth space without borders; it spatialises the 'spatial turn' with its utopian, timeless and connected spaces of overlapping fields.

This is not without its own complications. Mobility, when conceptualised and idealised, particularly when by those who have access to rapid and unfettered transit, can make too much of the accelerations of its 'non-places' (Augé, 1995), globalised corporate spaces that are almost identical regardless of their location, and make too little of the frictions and obstructions experienced by others: by refugees, wheelchair users, transport employees or those for whom 'mobilities are often also about duties, about the obligation to see the other, to return the call' (Urry, 2007, p. 11). In representations of mobility that 'bring into question the apparent fixities of older forms of understanding' (Cresswell, 2001a, p. 9), little is made of inequalities of space and time experienced by those who work in, service or live around those places, failing to sufficiently acknowledge that 'different social groups do not move equally smoothly through geographic space' (Manderscheid, 2009, pp. 29–30; Massey, 1994).

Counterposed to the kind of ideal nomadism through 'smooth space' proposed by Gilles Deleuze and Felix Guattari (1987, pp. 419–23) or to the protean 'logic' of Manuel Castells's (1989, 1996) 'space of flows', pedestrianism can serve performance as a refusal, a 'go slow', a resistance to a general global dromology and its digital accelerations; a means to engage closely, even obsessively and critically with the textures and materials of the things and terrain to hand. This torque, however, can pull in different ways in different performances. In 'Suburban Safari' the audience were, discordantly and satirically, guided up the ziggurat-like waste dump by an Alpine Guide and a performer dressed as 'Heidi', but the motorised acceleration not only brought the participants, as planned, to the goats, but also unexpectedly found the herd ranged across remnants of the Reichsbrücke bridge which had collapsed into the Danube in 1976. The intended displacements (first to the Alps, then to an African safari) saw, in the end, the return of the specificity of the site. The acceleration of an intercontinental coach, which might be expected to break boundaries, was used in *MKVH* to turn a city's highly efficient transport grid into a mazy trap that was obsessively repeated. The journey can return us to the materiality of the route itself, exposing its obstacles and frictions, just as much as it can connect us to elsewheres.

Exercise

Nervousness around the safety of audiences as they move around, sometimes in large numbers, or attempts to enforce a certain kind of reception, can result in stewarding that borders on the aggressive. Audiences are hurried from one place to another, or strictly ordered where they should stand and how they can spectate. Ushers in hi-vis tabards can outshine the costumes of performers. Turn this to your advantage. Make a performance that is constituted of the moving of an audience by brightly coloured stewards; the encountering of the first 'performer', like the arrival of Godot, is always, and indefinitely, postponed.

Exercise

Make an instant procession with a large group. Divide the group into smaller ones. Each smaller group is to take responsibility for making or preparing different things (use whatever is to hand) – a chant, music/rhythm, a banner, flags, a ritual action for being performed once, prepared interactions with bystanders, a large burden to carry and so on. Give yourself about 20 minutes, then set off and see what happens. ...

Exercise

Devise a performance for four people sitting around a table in a railway carriage (not all trains have this); you decide on the combination of performer/s and audience member/s. Work from Michel de Certeau's idea of train travel as a 'travelling incarceration. Immobile inside the train, seeing immobile things slip by'; how can you animate both the pattern of immobility in the carriage, in which 'everything has its place in a gridwork' and the few moments of viewing of each vista (de Certeau, 1984, p. 111) as they pass by outside? By text, by a second framing, by bringing small objects from outside onto the table? De Certeau believed that the window of the train carriage separated and silenced what was outside, but also transformed it into something 'necessary for the birth ... of unknown landscapes and the strange fables of our private stories' (p. 112).

Readings

When the film critic Lotte Eisner fell seriously ill in Paris in the winter of 1974, the German movie director Werner Herzog decided that if he walked from Munich to Eisner's bedside he could somehow save her life by the act of making the journey. *Of Walking in Ice* is Herzog's diary of his walk: partly an act of delivering healing, partly a pilgrimage to his own inner loneliness within the isolation of dark forests; a 'dreaming on foot'. Herzog's directorial eye vividly picks out the organised qualities of different spaces as he skirts angry dogs, suffers from the intense cold and breaks into summerhouses for shelter. An artist who so often depicted the extremes of experience and people at the very edge of endurance, for whom art-making was often conducted in a state of desperate struggle against mounting odds, Herzog's account demonstrates how such melodramatic creativity can be transferred onto such a simple act as taking a walk. Watching young moped drivers, Herzog observes that they are 'moving toward death in synchronized motion'; he raises details to meaningfulness: the most innocent of actions is balanced at the edge of an abyss. Herzog took the decision to walk spontaneously, grabbing a duffel bag of belongings; he demonstrates that even a noble and excessive quest can be entered into with ease and little preparation, but not without risks.

'Dance as a form engages in the measuring of time, just as music does, just as muscle does, remembering the kinaesthetic memories and rhythms driven into the body.' *The Pennine Way: The Legs That Make Us*, Tamara Ashley and Simone Kenyon's account of their journey along the 270-mile Pennine Way trail, asks 'What makes an epic dance?' and then answers its own question, describing this long and arduous dance-journey in fragments of observation, complaints, interruptions from temporary companions, and reflections on the dynamic unhuman all around them that sweeps them up in mists and winds, batters their feet and tries to steal their lunch.

Photographs show Ashley and Kenyon stretched out across small bowed stone bridges, lying down along the timbers of a cattle grid and threading themselves into fissures in rock. They measure out the journey with their bodies, the length and duration of the trail dwarfing their two human forms; there is distance even between their descriptions of reconciliation: 'sounds of Robin playing soothe wounds within and between us'; 'River and Robin's fiddle are the only things that can pull us together today.' Far less melodramatic and hubristic than Herzog's magical quest, Ashley and Kenyon make a dance of conviviality under pressure, of sore and pinched bodies feeling their way towards homely and unhomely landscapes, 'a search for the rejoicing that company brings in order to move on together'; it is an exemplary text of how, without sentimentality, so many layers of a journey can be drawn into a dance.

4

What is a Site?

Space is not a container; it is not an empty carton just waiting for us to fill it. The visual display on a GPS navigation device, the movie architecture of sci-fi cyberspace or the street maps of gridded cities may all suggest exactly that quality; but they are *representations* of space, not space itself. The word 'space' suggests emptiness: the 'wide open spaces' of deserts and landscapes observed from a distance or the vacuum of 'outer space'. These notions come together with a theorisation of space that is smooth and even and abstract. It is a theorisation, a 'sense of space as a practico-inert container of action' (Crang & Thrift, 2000, p. 2), away from which geographers and philosophers have increasingly moved.

In this chapter – and you may wish to skip it, and carry on the practice-orientated narrative at Chapter 5, and come back to this chapter later to reflect – I will dive more into ideas: theories of space, key strategies for activating sites (archaeological, *chorastic*, mobility and Deleuzo-Guattarian) and challenges to the very ideas of site and specificity. While these subjects may not immediately appear to offer very much for performance makers, given the range of spaces (and even the range of categories of sites), abstractions and a powerful personal vision may at times be all that stands between you and the demands of commerce, repetition and what Anna Lowenhaupt Tsing calls 'scalability': the making of products that are indifferent to the scale or texture of contexts and encounters (2015, pp. 37–43).

The problems with that famous claim of Peter Brook's that he could 'take any empty space and call it a bare stage' (1968, p. 7) are not confined to Brook's speech act after the 'and', but include his prior assumption that he might ever find such a place as an empty one. Space is never empty; there is always a history. More importantly, there is always an agency, or agencies, in and of space. Even at the most extreme of circumstances, in a quantum vacuum, particles, borrowing energy from elsewhere, pop up out of 'nowhere' and then disappear as they pay back their lender. The sea goes flat, but this may be a prelude to its drawing itself up into the legendary 'seventh' and giant wave.

Doreen Massey, geographer and activist, in her book *For Space* (2005), a work that has been influential among a number of performance makers and theorists, argues for a three-fold replacement of 'empty space'. She proposes that, firstly, space is 'the product of interrelations', it is made by the meetings and assemblages and exchanges of people and things; secondly, space is a combination of unlikes, a multiplicity, and without that unevenness there is 'no space'; and, thirdly, space is 'always under construction' (p. 9), it is never completed and never 'virgin'.

If we take these propositions seriously, then, there is never a neutral zone or blank slate for a performance artist to write magisterially upon. There is, instead, a seething and volatile set of changing layers to shift with and respond to in order to write anything legible at all. Space does not give us sealed envelopes to which the choice of a performance site can conveniently, sympathetically, admirably and ecologically concur. Instead, there are difficult entanglements across borders, there are spills, evaporations, tides and gusts that defy and defile whatever limits we choose for them. A maker of site-based performance, then, may need to be a multivalent one, capable of engaging with multiple partners, human and unhuman, including the active presence of space itself.

At the same time as resisting the charms of purity and abstraction to be found in the idea of a dead and barren 'empty space', the Scylla to this Charybdis is to conceptualise place as 'closed, coherent, integrated as authentic, as "home", a secure retreat', and of space as 'always-already divided up' (Massey, 2005, p. 6). In the attempt to escape the empty and effete abstraction of philosophical space for the grittiness of locality and place, there is a danger in idealising the detail and roughness of the real with a single identity and a meaning that erects borders and excludes all others; performance scholar Dee Heddon has worried that there might be too much that is nostalgic in 'the lure of the local', that '[Lucy] Lippard's sense of place is really a sense of the past' (2008, p. 95). The political dangers may be obvious – the emphasis on borders and frozen identity likely to favour both petty and wider nationalisms – but there are problems for site-aesthetics too; for a place that is fixed and closed leaves little space for anything other than affirmation and repetition.

Over a few years of teaching on the Dartington Estate in Devon (UK) I saw how a space can be transformed profoundly in meaning, while changing little in appearance, and as a result of the most abstruse and distant influences. My teaching at Dartington coincided with the releases of the various parts of the movie adaptation by director Peter Jackson of J.R.R. Tolkien's *The Lord of the Rings*; when I first arrived, many of the students associated the woodlands and fields of the estate with the landscapes of Tolkien's book. Once the movies came out the landscapes of the book were re-interpreted as those of a mountainous New Zealand rather than of an English country estate. Dartington, if it had any literary lens for the students, was now closer to that of the novels of Jane Austen than the fantasies of Middle-earth.

Given this mutability in the quality of space, you might be sympathetic to Claire Doherty's suggestion to challenge 'site' rather than 'specificity', proposing an alternative category of 'situation-specific' in response to a 'state of flux which acknowledges place as … shifting and fragmented' (2004, p. 10), retaining rigour in response despite its shifting referent. While there has been some take-up of Doherty's suggestion in the visual arts, it has not yet had much purchase in performance practices or studies. Kris Darby (2013) uses it to more precisely categorise the ambulatory arts and performances of Wrights & Sites, but its relevance need not be restricted to mobilities. Indeed, it may be more relevant to other, but not all, site-oriented performances as a way of recognising how they give a precise and 'heightened attention to the paradoxical condition of being simultaneously situated and "displaced"' (Long, 2017, p. 5). This would apply to work such as Misha Myers's *Way from Home* (discussed in Chapter 8) or e-Xplo's *Picnolepsy* bus tour of Manhattan in 2002 which 'included fragments from an article by Robert Fisk reporting on the massacres in Sabra and Chatila … passing the site of the former World Trade Center, the only text relating to tragedy was of another event with a similar number of dead and missing' (Rene Gabri cited in Thompson & Sholette, 2004, p. 43); works that give focus to present sites, while empathic to those who have been displaced (corporeally or metaphorically) to them from elsewhere. These are performances that 'challeng[e] the perception that communities are place-bound … [and] refute the modernist perception that theatre is a neutral space … recognis[ing] that communities are plural and always in process' (Govan, Nicholson & Normington, 2007, p. 138).

Choosing any one place over another to be the site of a performance implies some concession to limits and a narrowing identification; even if it does not exclude 'multiplicity' and 'heterogeneous relations'. It may be complementary with, but is something quite different to, the rigorous affinity by which the performer gives their best attention – the 'attending to' and 'tending' identified and advocated by Melanie Kloetzel and Carolyn Pavlik (2010, pp. 6–7) – to their site, following that choice. It should be acknowledged that there has been some 'violence' in the setting of a 'site' and its boundaries, and that the choice may be of greater importance and impact than the performance in it: 'primacy should be given to this general attention to land. It comes before, and subsumes, *interventions* in the land' (Pearson & Shanks, 2001, p. 37).

On the other hand, this choice, to make the site unique, or – better – to acknowledge its uniqueness, is not necessarily an elitist or exceptionalist articulation of the place (though Miwon Kwon has argued that it contradicts site-specific art's original 'refuting originality and authenticity as intrinsic qualities of the art object or artist' by transferring them to something 'integral to the site' [2002, p. 53]); Doreen Massey argues that, although some critics have 'castigated' the idea of the uniqueness of a place as a kind of de-politicisation, 'mean[ing] that one could not reach for the eternal rules … "politics" in part precisely lies in not being able to reach for that kind of rule' but instead unlocks 'a world which demands the ethics and the responsibility of facing up to the event; where the situation is unprecedented and the future is open' (2005, p. 141). Embracing this conditional uniqueness – acknowledging that an ethical 'attending to' and 'tending' is at least partly obliged by the violence of site-making itself – may help a performance maker avoid undermining their otherwise vivid work, at least for the more attentive among their audience, by a crass spatial illiteracy.

I recently attended a conference on 'between spaces' at which a site-artist, involved in staging collaborative performances that engaged with the politics of derelict sites, rather casually dropped the information that in order to protect their performance 'props' overnight, they had sealed off a shortcut used by homeless people. Given the tone of the rest of the presentation, this did not seem to arise from a callous disregard for other users of 'their site', but rather by the panicky pragmatism that can kick in if one approaches a place as needing to be controlled rather than co-operatively engaged with. I have seen, and been the 'victim' of similar misunderstandings. In Vienna I attended 'dry runs' of two performances. On the first we were confronted by a snarling guard dog (the artist was behind schedule and his contact on the security staff was no longer on duty); on the second 'dry run', on the theme of escaping the city, after some five hours we were still extricating ourselves from the tunnels of the Wienfluss and had many, many miles yet to travel. Assumptions about the passivity and benignity of space, and its subservience before the authority of the performing presence, can easily coalesce into the belief that territory will, and should, fit itself to the art. This is an attitude that will, almost always, come back to bite a performance maker. While those who allow the volatility of the site to predate upon their own work – like Monali Meher, carefully and precisely putting herself at the mercy of uneven ground while surrendering a part of her capacity to control it – are often those who the site helps most.

Exercise

Create a variation on the carrying of objects and the delivering of gifts by carrying a script or score collected from an audience to take to and perform to another audience; once delivered this audience must give you a new script or score and identify a further audience to whom it should be delivered; and so on.

In many years of watching, making and teaching site-based performance, I have never seen a piece that was well-prepared in its attending to and tending of its site and yet was negatively disrupted by an unexpected intervention or interruption. Indeed, they are sometimes offers to add to your work at a profound level: 'Accidents and contradictions contribute to the complexity of the work – if they are embraced rather than ignored, they may satisfy … idiosyncratic and deep-felt structures' (Taylor, 2004, p. 19). At the same time, even the choice of the most apparently benign and ordered of spaces seems to afford little protection to productions that are not performed intelligently and thoughtfully with their sites: the dialogue-reliant piece I attended in the quiet garden of a pub was drowned out at crucial moments by trains passing on the tracks nearby, the presence of which the performers appeared oblivious to; the costumed period piece I saw in a country park (with no particular association to the 'period') did not survive the attentions of a Royal Navy helicopter. On the other hand, in what were far more volatile sites, I saw a piece concerning loss and departure on a beach enhanced by the unexpected sailing into view of a nuclear submarine; while a performance rather precariously staged at the edge of a road only increased in focus and intensity when, having reached the point where one of the participants knelt in the road and chalked the shape of a body onto the tarmac, a police car promptly drew up, parking its front wheels over the chalked corpse, and its occupants ran into an adjacent building.

So, if you are fortunate enough to find an affordant and attractive site for performance – whether that be a busy market square, an elevator, a whole major city, the road to Damascus, a field (quantum or full of cows), a website or sewers – and want to bring audiences or participants to it, before you move swiftly on to your performance ideas, it may serve you well to think about what exactly this thing, this place, this site is that you want to perform in and for you. What is it that you want to make a performance of and from? Rather than advocate any one particular or conglomerate version of what that understanding should be, I will list below some approaches, terms and debates and let you judge what seems most meaningful, apt, truthful and useful to you. Later you can test them against your own practical experiences.

Be warned, though: the so-called 'spatial turn', in just about every academic discipline going, means that an ambiguity has entered into much writing about ideas and places, and I do not pretend it is different here; writing slithers between spatial metaphors that stand in for ideas and ideas that seem to be more about real places than abstract concepts. To give you an example of just how difficult it is, as a performance maker or a researcher, to draw practically, helpfully and accurately on the ideas that have formed around site-specific practice, or been influential upon it, here is an example of just one idea: that of 'unfixing place'.

Idea

The idea of 'unfixing place' comes from the architectural historian and inventor of 'site-writing' Jane Rendell for whom '"unfixing" a place' encourages 'site art not only to access a place's potential for change, but also to cast place into the network of larger social relations' (cited in Kloetzel, 2015, p. 244). Rendell describes her use of 'unfixing' as having been taken from a tendency in recent spatial theory to critique writings 'that had emphasised the special qualities of particular places as if they were somehow pre-given and not open to change' (Rendell, 2009, p. 19) and she specifically cites a 1993 collection of essays edited by Michael Keith and Steve Pile as her reference point for this tendency. In their collection, Keith and Pile had described a new theorising of place that was 'no longer passive, no longer fixed' (1993, p. 5), drawing on the work of the thinker and activist bell hooks to suggest that such an unfixing might generate what hooks called a 'radical openness' and quoting her describing this openness spatially, as 'a margin – a profound edge. Locating oneself there is difficult but necessary. It is not a "safe" space. One is always at risk. One needs a community of resistance' (pp. 4–5). Here the particular context re-enters the discussion of the general and conceptual, because these lines of hooks's come from her 1991 book *Yearning: Race, Gender, and Cultural Politics* and in the passage cited by Keith and Pile, hooks is specifically describing a 'space' particular to black scholars from low-income families who 'passionately [hold] onto aspects of that "downhome" life while simultaneously seeking new knowledge and experience, invent[ing] spaces of radical openness' (hooks, 1991, p. 149).

Just as the places we encounter are not 'pre-given' and are always 'open to change', similarly our ideas about place and space have also been on journeys; they carry some of the dust of those journeys with them, but they are also missing parts of themselves. So, a transferable agency of change – 'unfixing place' – comes from somewhere and is founded in precarity and risk, and rising on a very particular and profound 'edge'. The efficacious taking of fixed place, unfixing it and making it into liberated space becomes possible to imagine because of struggle in a zone of risk and precarity by a specific community of black scholars from low-income families.

Theories of place and space, it turns out, rather than providing clear or neutral analyses of, and strategies for, uncomfortable and contested sites, actually themselves constitute other sites of discomfort and contest. So, the above theoretical unfixing of 'place' for a more fluid 'space' was all emerging at the same time as, Jane Rendell notes with some irony, 'those in the art world were specifying "site"' (2009, p. 19). Perhaps the artists were not entirely wrong to grab on to specificity against a fluidity that could work not only for change, but also for the dissolution of the agents of that changing.

In Chapter 12, I will come back to some of these issues of place, space and specificity; but, for the moment, having inserted this 'health warning', I will present some useful, if not always compatible, praxes: practico-theories with which to approach sites in general terms.

Archaeology: Mike Pearson, well known for his site-based performance-making with the Welsh companies Brith Gof and Pearson/ Brookes, has been instrumental, both in his practice and in his collaboration with the classicist archaeologist Michael Shanks, in drawing attention to different ways that site performance and archaeology interleave each other, from the documentation of performance's remains to the more subtle overlapping of processes. He proposes that the most intense connection of the two might be in relation to what is sometimes called the 'contemporary past', the present that is already passing (see Graves-Brown, Harrison & Piccini, 2013). He identifies how, in response to this passing, people are making their everyday spaces archaeological, how they 'engage in small acts of *curation* ... Juxtaposing today's milk bottle with flowers bought last week with a photograph taken twenty years ago with a family heirloom' (Pearson, 2010, p. 42).

By 'looking … in oblique ways, observing texture and detail' (p. 43), Pearson argues that we can recognise how, even in apparently mundane places, there are traces of the immediate and ordinary that constitute 'an archaeology of us' (p. 43); from these marks (and our recovery of the marking that made them) we have access to an existing score of how the place is being, and very recently was being created and performed. By close attention to the apparently mundane and its juxtapositions, a site can be articulated by a performance that is neither historical nor heritage-based, but is more like our everyday curations – made up from the assembling, arranging and rearranging of ordinary spaces and objects – to create 'a present that is itself multitemporal' (p. 42).

Exercise

Set a grid over your site, or a part of it. In some cases it will be possible to set up a physical grid with strings and stakes and sometimes only possible (or best done) as a digital or analogue mapping. Collect and log objects found in the squares of the grid. Chart the variations of texture, materials, numbers and so on between one square and another. These objects might be stones and detritus taken from a dry beach; they might be stories collected from passers-by in different squares transposed over a city centre. Where the act of collecting is in a strong dynamic relation with the site – I have seen this exercise attempted on the bed of a river – the collection may be the whole of the performance. Or, as part of, or at the conclusion of your performance you might display your findings, drawing on the performative procedures of museums and archaeology: labelled vitrines, field reports, lectures, documentation, reconstruction. Work out different systems and procedures to categorise, catalogue and exhibit your finds. Again, the choosing and labelling and displaying may constitute the whole or part of the public performance. Or you can extrapolate out from your limited findings and create an 'artist's impression' of your site's hidden world, perhaps as a visualised Neolithic village, a lost Modernist city centre, the ruins of a vanity project and so on. Choose an unlikely site for your pseudo-archaeological dig: a public library, a supermarket, a farmyard. Just as a professional dig must carefully preserve what is valuable in the site, devise your own means of extracting without damaging what others may value; privilege what is left over. Is there something existentially powerful about those materials that are left after the privileged artefacts have been separated and cleaned?

Chora: Certain spaces, often regarded as tawdry, undistinguished or even abject by casual observers, are regularly seized upon by performance makers as having a certain magical affordance for generating experientially intense or immersive performances. There is some objective evidence that certain kinds of sites share a similar quality, given that they have attracted site-artists, including parks, redundant industrial spaces, museums and so on (see Wilkie, 2002).

The idea of *chora* and of 'chorastic space' as it was described by Stephen Wearing, Deborah Stevenson and Tamara Young offers a positive spin to these predilections for qualities of 'fantasy, creativity, liminality, reordering and enchantment' (2009, p. 10), constituting a space of instability, a kind of pre-place or space of apprehension. While some of these places might wear the marks of aging or nostalgia, or display traces of history, wear and tear and abandonment, there is also something dynamic and utopian there.

Taken from Plato via Elizabeth Grosz, *chora* is a space where multiple possibilities are not yet closed down in resolution or synthesis, a 'space that engenders without possessing, that nurtures without requirements of its own .... a space that evades all characterisation including the disconcerting logic of identity' (Grosz, 1995, p. 51). It describes a space that resists exchange, commerce and the oppressive obligations of gifting and reciprocity. It works by an *evasion* (rather than a violent dissolution) of identities and hierarchy, suggesting that what is being found by performance makers in these places is a temporary space where things are in suspense and meanings can be performed before they are understood or recognised.

Chora is not just about spaces, however. It also applies to the participants' self-conscious reconstitution of their site-making selves. The freeing of artists and spectators from the conventions and obligations of commercial exchanges and consumption, characteristic of the earliest site-specific art of the 1960s, is there in chorastic sites, when participants are conscious, or made aware of, the invitation in these spaces to re-make their meanings. *Chora* is an energy that presages things, perhaps because chorastic spaces are often in some form of disruption or dis-assemblage through redundancy or closure or repurposing; an energy which develops new kinds of what Raymond Williams called 'structures of feeling' (pp. 133–34): common values and experiences that have not yet reached expression in the form of works of art or institutions, but have enough in the way of structure to be experienced and repeated.

Mobility: In the years around the millennium, particularly in the social sciences, there was a turn away from places and towards the connections and journeys between those places as subjects of study and research. There was a growing emphasis on spaces of travel and tourism, on the in-between places, and on how – for example, through the idea of the 'non-place', globally homogeneous sites such as airport lounges and hotel receptions (Augé, 1995) – places were themselves transformed and smoothed by all the motion through them. This trend was popularised by the sociologist John Urry (2000) as a 'mobilities paradigm' and idealised as the possible advent of a more communicative, more mutually understanding and heterogeneous global community. It represented a move (literally and metaphorically) away from 'the sedentary logic of state, science and civilisation' (D'Andrea, 2006, p. 107) and towards increased mobilities not only in critical discourse but in everyday life.

In terms of site-specific performance, the 'mobilities paradigm' re-addressed site as a bundle of trajectories and changes, not as stasis, fixed things, boundaries or hierarchy. Given that its metaphors 'bring into question the apparent fixities of older forms of understanding' (Cresswell, 2001a, p. 9), the mobilities paradigm challenges specificity as a conservative anchoring of meaning to fixed and located things. In my chapter on journey-performances I opened up some questions about how valid the ideas of site and specificity are in relation to performances that, with the exception perhaps of *2 mph* (see Chapter 3), import fictions and missions that are not specific to anything presently or previously occurring on their routes; now here is a paradigm of global character that offers the dissolution of any such fixed and located meanings as an unseating of sedentary thinking. It is an invitation to make work that frees specificity from site, and vice versa; instead, affirming performance as an expression of transition and velocity, of the ideal of nomadism in 'smooth space' advocated by Gilles Deleuze and Felix Guattari (1987, pp. 419–23).

Expressed in those terms, the mobilities paradigm sounds a little like the Futurists' glorification of speed and transport in the 1920s. Indeed there *are* concerns that it advocates a reactionary perspective in progressive terms in a way comparable to the Futurists. Some scholars have challenged the reality of the paradigm itself, with evidence for an opposite tendency in the global community. Yes, there is more travel, but it is increasingly restricted and loaded with obligations and responsibilities. There are inequalities of space and time – 'trajectories have ... very different rhythms' (Massey, 2005, p. 158), in how 'different social groups do not move equally smoothly through geographic space' (Manderscheid, 2009, pp. 29–30; Massey, 1994), and in imbalanced reciprocity in trajectory: neo-conservative policies moving in one direction and refugees in the other.

The paradigm's subversive, disruptive, liberating and multiplicitous qualities are susceptible to reactionary and frozen ideas that commandeer the same qualities that 'mobilities' proposes to set free: 'a rich terrain from which narrative – and, indeed, ideologies – can be, and have been, constructed ... conveyed through ... film, photography, literature, philosophy and law ... mobility "becomes synonymous with freedom, with transgression, with creativity, with life itself"' (Cresswell, 2006, pp. 1, 3). The case of the mobilities paradigm is a cautionary one that suggests that smooth space, acceleration and travel are not always reliable contexts for efficacious disruptions of fixed sites, but practices that may themselves require disruption. A wary performance maker needs to respond in turn to 'mobilities, immobilities and moorings' (Hannam, 2009, p. 106), giving the same careful attention to each one.

Exercise

Walk with a burden. It might be one like the telegraph pole carried for Lone Twin's *Totem* (1998 in Colchester, UK; 2004 in Brussels) that requires the assistance of strangers to even lift, let alone move. Or like Lonnie Van Brummelen's chalk statue of Hermes, it might shrink the further you take it, leaving its mark. Or like Monique Besten's, it may be a burden that grows as you go. Walk, like Donna Shilling, with a question to ask everyone you meet on your way.

Exercise

Find a site and create a short performance for it; perform it at the same time each day for a week. Be your own audience. Each time perform as exactly identical a performance as you can; how does the site change?

Smooth, Striated and Holey: The main thrust of the work of the French philosopher Gilles Deleuze (and I am already doing it a disservice by referring to it in the singular) was to bring to the ways that we talk about and do psychology, politics and arts the dialects of apparently alien discourses such as geology, biology and metallurgy in an undifferentiating articulation of life 'that goes beyond any lived experience … [that] has an overflowing and transformative quality which, through encounters, constantly opens up new possibilities … to multiply forms of life' (Crang & Thrift, 2000, p. 20). This 'life' is not limited to organisms; it spills over conceptual and material boundaries; it is an irreducible force.

Deleuze and his colleague Felix Guattari borrowed the terms 'smooth' and 'striated' from the composer Pierre Boulez to describe the spatial conditions – 'in the landscape, in mathematics, in music, in thought, in politics, in religion' (Bonta & Protevi, 2004, p. 144) – that either sustain or inhibit that vital force of life. Striated space is marked by stress and pressure, 'gridded and delineated, then occupied by the drawing of rigid lines that compartmentalize reality into segments' (p. 154); it fixes place as an immobile point, and it fixes people to that immobility, enforcing dwelling against wandering. Life, though, is a wandering force; smooth space does not so much facilitate that movement as enable life to sustain it in multiple and discrete (even contradictory) motions without collapsing all its differences into anything that would bring it all to a halt or a conclusion.

While 'Emergent properties, intensive becomings, occur only in smooth space' (p. 144), there is no simple correlation of smooth/good and striated/bad: 'never believe that a smooth space will suffice to save us' (Deleuze & Guattari, 1987, p. 500). For example, through global surveillance and the rapid transportation of troops, militarised states transgress the striations of borders and laws; this smoothing of space reciprocates by 'discovering ... "terrorist" enemies everywhere' (Bonta & Protevi, 2004, p. 145). Rather than smooth space, Deleuze and Guattari identify a third space, 'holey space', as the 'space of counter-action to striation' (p. 145); this space includes mines, sewers, caves, bunkers – places where those who oppose restrictions have often hidden out and organised. Others since have extended this to include cyberspace and forests. There is a considerable overlap here with the kinds of spaces that are attractive to site-specific performers, and to related activists such as urban explorers. As well as identifying holey-ness in virtual space, there is also a connection to the use of public space as a kind of hiding in plain sight; mapping the invisible and overground tunnel systems and blind spots that exist in everyday public places. Deleuze and Guattari might have been thinking of site-specific performance makers when they issued their provocation to 'Transpierce the mountains instead of scaling them, excavate the land instead of striating it, bore holes in space instead of keeping it smooth, turn the earth into swiss cheese' (p. 482).

What kind of performances and what kinds of sites might emerge from a theatre which, rather than expressing itself through its traditional expertises in exposition and display, burrows down, shelters, hides, camouflages and conspires clandestinely? A theatre – and one sees the beginnings of it in the 'invisible' elements of performances like Back to Back's *Small Metal Objects* (2005–2012, 2016), Begat Theater's *Hidden Stories/Histoires Cachées* (2010–2011) and Rotozaza's *Etiquette* (1998 and ongoing) – that is staged covertly and conspiratorially (with their dramatic decisions and plans) in translucent labyrinths, all in plain sight?

There are other approaches to space and place you might find it variably useful to read about and use, or carefully avoid. These might include a synchrony – a slice through time – as understood by structuralists, which prioritises the atemporal space of relations and interactions over their movement and disappearance in time. In the 'Geopoetics' of Kenneth White there is a direct address to place as part of the cosmos, for which mimesis in all its forms – 'reproduction, representation, reflection' – is inadequate, requiring a turn through 'fluctuation, irregularity, complexity' to 'presence-in-the-world, experience of field and territory, openness of style' (2003, pp. 32, 25). Or you might look for networks and meshworks, maybe follow Manuel Castells's notion of a 'space of flows' where 'the network of communication is the fundamental configuration' by which 'places do not disappear but their logic and their meaning become absorbed' (1996, p. 443), or, perhaps, the meandering vision of place and space for which Tim Ingold, against the network's lines connecting *a* to *b*, proposes instead lines without destinations or nodes, 'interwoven lines, not a network, but a meshwork' (2007, p. 80).

You might immerse your performances in Michel De Certeau's tactics: tiny and everyday acts of resistance at street-level that compromise the blank space of power (1984, p. 95). Or use an idea of 'landscape' (see Daniels, 1993; Matless, 2016) which collapses a place into a single viewpoint to it; a combination that has 'provided a basis for locating new communities of nationhood in a kind of collective cultural memory of belonging' (Pearson & Shanks, 2001, p. 39) while globalising a way of looking 'generated from the same aesthetic and pictorial models established by a select elite and culminating at the end of the eighteenth century' (p. 40).

You might deploy a mythogeographical approach (see Smith, 2010), by addressing 'not only the individual's experience of space, but the shared mythologies of space ... the personal, fictional, and mythical on an equal footing with factual, municipal history' (Turner, 2004, p. 385). Or you might want to shake any complacent ease you have detected in these pages, any sense that little is at stake except for careers and egos, and make performances in spaces where 'stability of geography and the continuity of land ... have disappeared ... [where] identity is confined to frightened little islands in an inhospitable environment'. Edward Said (1978, p. 95) is writing there of himself and fellow Palestinians, but it could apply to many for whom any performance on any ground might require an act of decolonialisation.

Exercise

Devise a simple action or ritual of entering your site as your selves and then gradually transforming your selves into your performance personae. Each time you perform this transition allow the site to influence it a little more. You might notice how it becomes increasingly difficult to 'be' yourself; so – if you experience this – reverse the process and devise a simple action or ritual for returning to yourself.

Exercise

Create a dramaturgy based on a ritual (or set of rituals) for a particular space. Make sure your actions are sufficiently striking and symbolic (in the broadest sense) as to imply a heightened and possibly sacred meaning, but not so explicit as to resolve their meaning. (If you borrow, as Elia Rita did [see Chapter 8], an action from a particular existing practice, be careful to select one that is sufficiently obscure or common as not to narrow down or resolve its meaning.) Then, when thinking of the abstract and developing space of the performance, consider how you create different layers of performance from those that are least accessible to its audience (chance or invited) to mediating layers that draw the audience into engagement and interpretation. Consider how these layers work, in terms of both space and function.

Exercise

Create a dramaturgical structure based on the temporality of illusionists' tricks: that misunderstanding that audiences have about when the trick begins, the 'magic' having already been put in place by the illusionist before they announce that they are going to do it. Prepare a site as a series of faux-spontaneous reveals (unveiling the mechanics of the tricks as you deliver them); the effectiveness being not in a trick itself, but in how its mechanics represent their own processes or entangle with the processes of the site. I saw an effective use of such an (eventually) openly dishonest frame in a performance piece that began as what appeared to be a live stream from a ferry on 'la Manche' (the English Channel) projected for an audience in a lecture theatre; in the middle of the showing the performers entered the hall (the 'live stream' had been recorded) and completed the performance live and present. For a moment, the performers seemed to be both here and there, afloat and on dry land; the distance between them and the location they had performed was, in the same moment, measured and collapsed.

Idea

Not everywhere are site-specific art and performance, or the ideas that underpin them, celebrated. There are fundamental criticisms of the category of 'site-specific', challenging its legitimacy as a meaningful category, particularly as one that is happily 'embraced as an automatic signifier of "criticality" or "progressivity"' (Kwon, 2002, p. 1). Two assaults on the category are those mounted by Miwon Kwon in 2002 with the publication of *One Place After Another: Site-Specific Art and Locational Identity* and the accumulated criticisms of critical theorists assembled for the 'When Site Lost the Plot' symposium at Goldsmiths University of London in 2013.

Kwon argued that what might have been 'vanguardist, socially conscious, and politically committed art practices' had inevitably ('always') 'become domesticated by their assimilation into the dominant culture' (p. 1) and that, in the case of site-specificity, this was at least partly due to the weakness of the category itself. Rather than the disparate genealogies articulated above for site-specific performance, Kwon located site-specificity's origin in the art world and in a minimalism that was 'based in a phenomenological or experiential understanding of a particular location, defined primarily as an agglomeration of the actual physical attributes of a particular location', but had subsequently liquifacted until 'site can now be as various as a billboard, an artistic genre, a disenfranchised community' (p. 3). Kwon challenged the idealisation of the 'nomadic' in thought and art – by which 'The "work" no longer seeks to be a noun/object but a verb/process' (p. 24) – as facilitating this change; under pressure as a result of the 'demand for singular on-site projects in various cities across the globalized art network ... site-specificity is being reconfigured to imply not the permanence and immobility of work but its impermanence and transience' (p. 4). 'Site' was no longer a place, but had become a 'discursive vector' (p. 29). Smaller site-specific artworks started to be moved around; ironically, nomadism had led to greater commodification, an art responding to 'actual physical attributes' had to become mobile to be exchanged and part of an effective commercial market.

These arguments (and the historical account) are legitimate ones. However, in the process Miwon Kwon makes a categorical assumption about site that establishes a dichotomy between location and mobility and limits her thesis to a set of art practices that mostly do not include performance. For example, many of the journey performances I have described above are as obdurately unmarketable, uncommodifiable and tied to their particular routes and the 'physical attributes' of them as any of the early site-specific artworks that Kwon describes. Rather as Augé's reflections on 'non-places' fit a little too well with the outlook of an international academic, Kwon's concern that 'for many of my art and academic friends, the success and vitality of one's work are now measured by the accumulation of frequent flyer miles' (2002, p. 156) also places her in a particular milieu to which many, perhaps most, site-specific performance makers are not aligned. Worrying about a general being 'out of place too often' (p. 157) throws the onus for specificity onto the artist and away from the site; after all, can a nomad not attend to the specificities of wherever it is they arrive? Are we only ever specific to where we are 'at home', where we dwell?

Despite, these problems and qualifications, when applied to particular cases within theatre and performance, Kwon's criticism of how repeating the same processes for different sites leads to diminishing returns and 'render[s] methodologies of critique rote and generic' (p. 47) has force and significance; not only for some of the 'headlining' companies and individuals in receipt of invitations from large global capitals, but also for artists who operate across limited local or regional terrains.

Doreen Massey struggles with something similar to this in her book *For Space*, where she tries to keep life in both 'space' and 'place' as meaningful categories, steering away from the essentialism in statements like Edward Casey's that 'To live is to live locally, and to know is first of all to know the places one is in' (1996, p. 18) while also avoiding any general lauding of placelessness and acceleration. Both extremes are at odds with Massey's idea of space as a multiplicity; one a vapid ideal, the other a frozen identity. Instead Massey argues for the validity of the *unique* features of particular places, but resists any 'notion of place [that] remains too rooted, too little open to the externally relational' (p. 183), referring directly to the (still very influential) phenomenologist Martin Heidegger, whose essentialising of a practical being and care in the world (through a concern with people being authentic to their 'thrownness' into existence) led him to prioritise dwelling over doing (with a resonance to Nazi politics of identity and land, and a romanticisation of the German farmer, that Heidegger variously supported and accommodated himself to).

Miwon Kwon, in turn, provides a useful corrective to any idealisation of a 'reconnecting to uniqueness of place – or more precisely, in establishing authenticity of meaning, memory, histories, and identities as a *differential function* of places' (2002, p. 157, emphasis in original); in other words, as a function whose derivative exists at every point in its domain and turns located meaning, memory, history and identities into value-added exportable entities, equivalent to the problem of performance and gentrification noted above. Kwon's objection, then, is not to 'specificity' and 'location' as such, but to their transformation into mobile categories applicable to any place in general and none in particular.

Kwon's criticisms were, ironically, followed promptly by a surge of international popularisation for site-specific theatre. Rather than marking the end of site-specificity in art and performance, the years around 2002 instead marked a shift *within* its popularity towards the performance arts, and a shift of power within performance practices to an immersive visual/literary theatre with much (characters, fictions, texts and narratives) still in common with its immobile building-based precedents.

Just over a decade after Kwon's book, philosopher Robin Mackay and other participants at the 2013 'When Site Lost the Plot' symposium tried again; repeating some of Kwon's arguments – 'site-specificity … now runs the risk of being assimilated into a capitalist logic adept at transforming specificity into reproducible symbol and immaterial value' – but turning them on their head; rather than mourning the loss of contingency they sought to 'secure an escape route to wider horizons' (Mackay, 2015, pp. 1, 2). Rehearsing ideas not dissimilar to the anti-theatrical high modernism of the likes of Clement Greenberg and Michael Fried, curator Matthew Poole argued that a work of art was itself a site and therefore could not be specific to any other site outside of itself (Mackay, 2015, pp. 85–87), while Robin Mackay similarly struggled with the practical relation of artwork and site, complaining that 'an artwork claims to be related to a site … claim[s] to be an image or map of that site, often while becoming a new part of it' (p. 221), putting a negative spin on what might be a model outcome for Victoria Hunter or Mike Pearson.

In the documented discussions of the 'Plot' symposium, the artists are often at odds with the theorists (mostly associated with accelerationism and geophilosophy), some of whom stage an argument against site-specific art and performance for daring to occupy the same ground as ground itself, proposing instead that space is already occupied and – here the argument is tinged with ecological apocalypticism – is antipathetic to human occupation; a cosmic version of postmodern 'placelessness'.

While some of the questions and issues raised above may seem to you as more appropriate for specialist philosophers, and unlikely to give much pause to many performance makers, they inflect the question 'what is a site?' with an obligation to look at what kinds of sites are chosen and how they are chosen. Are you choosing sites that are conducive to, even protective of, human performance? Is the escape from the theatre building or gallery a step sideways to spaces outdoors that offer something comparable to the facilities of theatre buildings, or an escape to wider horizons that avoid a sedentary audience's closer attention to script and theme? Do these choices, when taken together, imply a proprietorial understanding of the world as benign, inhabitable, consistent and welcoming of the performers' presence; or of a terrifying world at odds with human presence? Is your site trying to kill you?

Considering performance in the face of swarming, swamping jellies and on a ground antipathetic to performance, should you be preparing for a site-practice that addresses what Dona Haraway (2016) calls the Chthulucene, in which, partly but not exclusively by our own actions, humans face, and not for the first time, the monstrous on and in and of this planet?

Exercise

The performance artist He Yun Chang was dangled above the Liang River (Yunan, China) in 1999 for his performance, *Dialogue with Water*. He had asked a local butcher to make a small cut in each of his arms; then used the same knife to cut into the waters as if attempting to divide the river in two, his blood dripping down his forearms and into the flowing river. As a result of this 30-minute performance, Chang believed he had cut a wound of 4,500 metres into the Liang. Devise some equally futile or impossible tasks – for example, washing a river to clean it of pollution or malign associations. These failures (or maybe even an unpredictable success) may illuminate the nature of the site.

> **Idea**
>
> I've been using the word 'disruption' in the chapters above to describe the break made by an exploratory walker into the hyper-sensitised state of the drift. Also, as something that a performance intervention can do. When this act of disrupting entangles with a site that is equally disrupted and disrupting, we can borrow from Anna Lowenhaupt Tsing's (2015) book *The Mushroom at the End of the World* and describe that double disruption as a 'disturbance'. Tsing uses the term to describe a quality of spaces where living processes and human agency combine to challenge a conventional separation and translation of life worlds into units to be scaled up or down in the interests of asset accumulation and commercial distribution. Her key example is how the commercial devastation of forests in the USA has created its own anti-capitalist economy of outsiders and migrants harvesting and collectively trading the mushrooms now growing in the remnants of the forests.

Any 'disruptive' performance intervention might shift into 'disturbance', entangling its own disruptive capacities with a space that is itself disrupted. A common example of 'disturbance' when exploring for a performance site on a 'drift' is the discovery of ruins: ancient or recent. The attractiveness of these places, particularly when they are recent industrial ruins, is often described, disparagingly, as 'ruins porn', as decadent romanticism. I think that is a mistake. Yes, there is a neo-gothic thrill to be had at the abjection of these sites, but there is also the re-entangling of alienated and separated units with life worlds; so, why not uninhibitedly celebrate such 'disturbances'? For example, dreamthinkspeak in their *Before I Sleep* (2010) for the Brighton Festival (UK) – a performance attended by over 21,000 people – combined the temporal ironies of a long-redundant department store in the town with themes from Anton Chekhov's *The Cherry Orchard* (1903), so that the dreams and hopes of the play's bankrupt aristocrats would, after promenading scenes led the audience through the disused building, run up against a hauntological space with remnants of a later, but now ruined, world's idea of 'modern', 'happiness' and 'future'.

In contrast to shock capitalism's tendency to exploit natural and unnatural disasters in order to 'wipe the slate clean' or 'start again from scratch', an attentive and considerate site-practice can embrace and conserve the creative possibilities in a 'disturbance', as the opportunity to celebrate and engage with old knowledge and old materials, exploring and tending ruins and their decay; not because of heritage's subservience to old property, but because these are materials that were once deployed to make a future, and may be recoverable for making something else: new, or anew.

The idea of 'disturbance' theorises something more radical than a simple intervention in a place, or a reform of its processes by a new practice. In these sites, the existing conditions and relations have been destroyed; they are not coming back. What comes next grows from the ruins of the previous system, rather than by either the repair of old ways or the wiping clean and starting from scratch; it is an alternative to gradualist reform, the brutal shocks of the market or the dialectical leap and rupture.

Exercise

Find a place of ruins, a place where all previous relations and processes have wholly broken down. Devise a performance that acts out a new and future set of processes for this broken place – not necessarily a healing or a mending, but an innovative bending. Use what opportunities have been opened up by the dereliction itself... What has been released by it? What has been revealed? How can you repurpose the wounds and holes?

Part II

Generating Performance

5

Visiting Your Site

The Sri Lankan writer Vajra Chandrasekera has explained how 'I find it difficult sometimes to read exploration as other than a euphemism for empire and exploitation' (2016, p. 106). In the chapters above I have used the word 'exploring' to denote a hyper-sensitised wandering about, looking for performance sites. Indeed, the first draft of this particular chapter was originally headed 'Exploring your site'; 'visiting', however, suggests something closer to the relationship of a guest to a host than that of an invader to an unwary local. As Chandrasekera points out, even haphazard wandering may be inflected by privilege and plunder: 'Thoreau comes up with ... folk etymologies for the word to "saunter" ... to be "*sans terre*", without home ... "equally at home everywhere". But of course, Thoreau is not talking about the peoples who were systematically displaced from the land that he and his ilk consider empty and free to be experienced' (pp. 105–106).

So, what happens if you consider yourself a guest rather than an explorer? What if you consider yourself not as a privileged arrival, but as a compromised visitor with something to prove or redeem? Someone with an obligation to respect another's hospitality? What charge or price might you pay? What gift might you bring? What kinds of exchange should you prepare for? Are there conventions of greeting and welcome that you would extend to a human host to which you can find an equivalent for a geographical host? How will you announce your arrival; it might be a knock on a door or a ring on a bell at the home of a human host, but how might you address your site before you enter? Or will you wait for the site to invite you in? Perhaps, rather than dashing to its centre, you might work your way around its edges, slowly. Or is that too furtive? Maybe you need to allow the site to 'see' you, allow it time to move to include you.

Who has most power in the exchanges between you and the site?

Exercise

Cliff McLucas, a director of Brith Gof, was the first to use the terms 'host' and 'ghost' to describe the relationship between the site (the host) and the transient performance (the ghost): 'The host site is haunted for a time by a ghost that the theatre makers create. Like all ghosts it is transparent and the host can be seen through the ghost' (2000, p. 6). Prefiguring your performance, how ghost-like can you make your first visit to the site? Subsequently, can you haunt the site? Does your persona give you permission to 'walk through walls', to enter places and follow routes you might otherwise hang back from in a more solid character?

Exercise

Think with your feet. Roll, nudge, gently kick the things of the site. Walk it barefoot.

Exercise

Every day around 60 tons of cosmic dust from meteors and comets and other astral bodies land on the Earth's surface. Some of it comes from Mars. Get down on your hands and knees. Visit Mars.

Just as a site is not a blank slate, neither is a performance maker; we all carry our own baggage of associations, accumulated skills and past experiences. Finding an efficacious way of relating the different qualities of both sites and artists may be usefully thought of as a search for the best arrangement of voids, in order that things (objects, ideas, information, emotions, connections) flow back and forth between site and artist.

Cathy Turner has described this relation as one of porosity in relation to 'deep dramaturgy', borrowing from Heidi Taylor the idea of 'a need to "embrace" accidents, contradictions and signs in the performance space that offer independent meanings', and then interpreting this 'embrace' as 'an encircling movement, opening to and then holding ... An attention to the relationship between inside and outside. The possibility of reciprocal movement or resistance' (Turner, 2014, p. 199).

In geology, 'porosity' means the number and arrangement of voids in a rock. As Turner herself points out, this concept is not simply about flows of actions or ideas, but about a certain kind of structure or architecture that is built by the relation of artist to site; one that 'might be considered in relationship to a civic need for that encircling "embrace" (space and holding) of what is incidental, frictive, contradictory, or of that which produces meaning in unforeseeable ways' (p. 200). While the flows may be what form the content of your performance, the architecture around your void may be what remains to shape the future of the 'new space' of the site you leave once the performance is over.

Given the flow, or permeability, that a generous porosity generates, there is a natural favouring of an embodied research which is located to the site itself. This might work as an effective dynamic for any particular site-based production. Research then might constitute something like an embedded ethnographic study; and you may well find that there is much to be gained by learning about some of the procedures – interviewing, participant observation, surveys, taking field notes, case studies – and the principles used by cultural geographers and anthropologists in the field. Martyn Hammersley and Paul Atkinson's *Ethnography: Principles in Practice* (2007) is a good starting point, not least for its morale-boosting suggestion (for a lay researcher) that 'as a set of methods, ethnography is not far removed from the means that we all use in everyday life to make sense of our surroundings' (p. 4).

Exercise

Lie down in your site; in a public urban site perhaps only you, small animals and homeless people ever have this perspective.

Exercise

Unfocus your eyes and fuzz your vision of things close up; allow your focus to slip into the far distance, or towards things to the side of your vision.

Exercise

Use composer John Cage's principle of 'considered improvisation': having found a site, before you devise anything in the way of a performance first collect together a list of tactics for making performance (time sequences, velocities, a focus on particular colours, a spectrum of atmospheres); then work 'freely' in the site using only the tactics listed.

Serendipitously, the aesthetics of performance making mesh with a common approach to ethnography which emphasises the subjective and unstable quality of findings, acknowledging that 'it is possible ... to operate with knowledge which is less than certain' (Taylor, 2002, p. 4) and defers the immediate re-organisation of intuitions and affects into an 'objective' state, skirting 'Quibbles over the ontological status of the truly true and ... the primacy of one discourse over another' in favour of 'finding ways ... to report experience to others and ourselves' (Mitchell & Charmaz, 1998, p. 243).

Given the support of ethnographers and academic geographers for sincere everyday and subjective engagements with a field of research, you might interweave with these a limited theatricality (any organising narrative, character or psychology mostly bleached out). Such a methodology (used by Simon Persighetti and myself for gathering materials for our ambulatory performance, *A Tour of Sardine Street* [Exeter, UK, 2010]), generates a de-characterised performance-like presence, in the guise of everyday, if somewhat eccentric, personae, and allows one to engage directly, but reflexively with the people and living materials of a site.

Exercise

After an hour of your visit, turn around; reflect on what has happened so far. How have you changed in that time?

Exercise

Over three years (2007–2010), Simon Persighetti and I prepared our journey performance *A Tour of Sardine Street* on one street in Exeter, UK, visiting the route once every couple of weeks (see Crab Man & Signpost, 2012). From the very start of our devising process, by carrying various objects like cases and sticks, wearing unusual symbols like sardines, and by our obsessive attention to the details of the street, we drew attention to our visits. Many times we were asked about what we were doing and our subsequent explanations sometimes led to offers of information and invitations to the less accessible parts of the street: a chef led us down to the basement kitchens of a large hotel to examine the remnants of the eighteenth-century prison on which the hotel was built, a shopkeeper invited us in to hear Bach played on the instruments he had for sale, and we shared in one passer-by's flight from a poltergeist. Performance scholars Jennifer Parker-Starbuck and Roberta Mock reflected upon our methodology for this project, described how by performing ethnography and then 'acting' as ethnographic performers we were not only sharing our 'fieldwork' in our everyday encounters and aesthetic constructions, but that 'the embodied knowledges gained are disseminated experientially through presentations to and interactions with other people on the street… "that will initiate its audience into the methods of exploration and intervention and into the narratives and patterns that have been found"' (Parker-Starbuck & Mock, 2011, p. 227); in other words, the 'new space' generated by this kind of site-visit/site-performance includes a new space of procedures in which audiences are not only experiencers but are initiated into the practices of a lay performance-ethnography. Begin your performing at the very start of your research; that way you can draw the people of your site to you, encouraging them to unselfconsciously share their information in response to your quest. Kathleen Irwin, co-artistic director of Knowhere productions, has described how, working in a new space, her company not only conducts a 'thorough investigation of archival records' but makes their presence public by 'Boarding in people's home or bunking down in empty buildings'. From the start the company's presence is 'closely monitored' and quickly the locals become 'accustomed to seeing the costumes, puppets, and props'. Although the company members remain outsiders (and do not pretend to be anything else), their immediate presence is a means of encouraging invitations such as neighbours hosting barbecues for them 'where we gathered gossip and shared stories', as well as 'sidewalk conversations' the contents of which are often at variance from official narratives (Irwin, 2012, pp. 89–92). Prepare a sustained visit – or series of visits – to your site, by choosing some material, or particular objects, ones that you think might figure in your performance, and parade these, offering them as a medium of exchange and a conduit of information with local residents and passers-by.

Embodied research seems suited to a preparation for site-specific performance, particularly one matching Thornton Wilder's description of a certain kind of dramaturgy, 'not a story read from ... beginning to end, but a thing held full in-view the whole time ... a landscape' (cited in Fuchs, 1996, p. 93). However, it seems unnecessarily puritanical to insist upon it as its sole form. If we think of sites as meshworks of connections then to understand any particular one it may be necessary to track and trace movements to and from it that cross its horizons and borders. This may involve searching for documentation about a site; some present in the site, some available online to a researcher working in the site. Sometimes, though, it may be found among newspaper clippings or on microfilm in a distant museum, or from witnesses located far away from the site. Anything from gleanings from online chat rooms to extended oral history recordings might be helpful.

Exercise

Try not to over-prepare your visiting. Rather than set up formal interviews through official organisations, the company devising *The Last King of Devonport* (Plymouth, UK, 2008) went from pub to pub around their site, engaging locals in conversation, hoovering up stories and testing the temperature of feelings about their proposed performance site. If there are no obvious communal meeting points, go from person to person, asking at the end of each conversation for a recommendation (and maybe an introduction) to the next person you should meet with. If you use interviews or chance conversations as a means to gather texts or narratives, consider what kind of obligations you might have to those who speak to you. What expectations have you triggered? How far is it OK to 'sample' another person's life? And what of those whose reflections never make it to the final script; 'these real people are doubly "voiceless", having been initially courted, but then passed over in favour of other voices' (Heddon, 2008, p. 136)? Can you search out discarded interviews? Recorded but never published stories? Can you mine a seam of materials that have been suppressed, forgotten or discarded from which to shape a performance?

It is rare that lack of information about a site is a problem; more often, it is a case of how to deal with the incoherent avalanche of disparate forms and contents. This is exacerbated for those performance makers who have only a narrow window of time in which to prepare. They can benefit by deploying the same process of prefiguring in their desk-based research as for their embodied on-site presence. Rapid searches, intuitive leaps, shortcuts and sideways connections necessary for time-poor research may directly and indirectly inform the unfolding structure of your performance. You may trace the same narrative (up and down) through a multitude of layers; or you may find that different kinds of information spiral outwards from a single narrative to gather multiple thematic or associational threads, so your performance spreads simultaneously in different directions, like Wilder's 'landscape'.

I recently visited, on a research mission, the site of a famous nineteenth-century crime near my home in Devon, UK; on the face of it a clumsy and murderous assault by a disgruntled servant upon an employer. The numerous accounts, contemporary and subsequent, that I turned up, as well as associated artworks that include a silent movie of 1912 and a 1971 'folk-rock opera', suggest a far more complicated web of different suspects and a complex set of relations between the local middle classes and their servants. Research that at first seemed to get deeper and deeper into the same precisely located story actually dispersed its meaning across many stories and various sites around the region and beyond. I experienced something similar in the site itself, where I was misdirected and misinformed by various well-meaning locals and visitors; there is no signage about the events there, and the building itself was long ago demolished. These very instabilities, however, are now a potent dramaturgical 'offer', for a performance chasing characters around a car park at the foot of a wooded cliff with 'hidden ruins' and the unlikely promise of evidence surviving within the trees.

All of which begs the question – if misinformation and misdirection are also to be admitted to a site-specific work, what exactly does the specificity in 'site-specific' mean? How much can it contain? In popular journalism, the term 'site-specific' is often used to describe *any* kind of theatre or performance not in a studio or a theatre-designated building. If, however, we assume a more rigorous and comprehensive understanding – making a performance that is not only enacted in your site, but devised in the site and *about* the site – how much of the materials assembled by the visiting described above can be contained in that 'about'?

Here is an extended example of that 'about', testing its boundaries: since the rise of the 1960s counter-culture (but with roots from earlier movements), a combination of disparate forces and discourses – 'radical feminist' Goddess worship, occult psychogeography, deep ecology and James Lovelock and Sidney Epton's idea of Gaia (1975), among others – has assembled to cast a certain spiritual 'air', an aspiration to the numinous, around some site-based performances. Such works, from the extensive repertoire of visually striking rituals and intercultural actions created by Red Earth (Europe, Java, Japan and Mongolia, 1998 and ongoing) and Antenna's forest-set and masked *Pandemonium* (Fort Barry, USA, 1987–1988) to the vernacular and localised theatre of *The Walthamstow Mysteries* (London, 2014 and ongoing), share a common romanticism bolstered by the resilience of the 'earth mysteries' movement, sending echoes and replications of common themes drawn from across cultural and temporal borders.

Such an assemblage is neither a guarantee of, nor a death knell for, specificity. Caitlin Easterby, co-artistic director of Red Earth, commenting on their production of *CHALK* (2011) on Wolstonbury Hill on the Sussex Downs, UK, is very clear that what they made was 'not historical re-enactment, neither is it an attempt at "authentic ritual". We are creating a contemporary performance' (2011, p. 27). A genuine listening to and amplification of the ambience of a space may begin with a desire for the numinous. At the same time, a knee-jerk, 'spooky', generic categorisation of a space may throw up a veil of obfuscating ambience to mask a site's peculiar qualities. 'The Weyburn Project', in the former Saskatchewan Mental Hospital (Canada, 2001), embraced and critiqued this and turned it to specificity's advantage, with its ghost-tour tropes and stereotypical visual elements of the feared asylum repeatedly subverted by unexpected elements like the accounts of the staff's experiments with LSD (as a means to empathise with patients' conditions) and its precise autobiographical reflections: 'when the hallway's a bit dark, we get a sense of hope, down the end of the hallway there, because there's light' (Diener & Wolfson, 2004).

Seeking the root meaning of words is very rarely productive, but the ambiguities of 'pagan' *are* useful here. Sceptics about claims for a coherent pre-Christian 'pagan' religion in what is now Europe will often cite the root of the word 'pagan' as meaning nothing more than 'rural' or 'country-dwelling', and as having no religious significance. That is mostly correct; however, the word *was* sometimes used in relation to religious beliefs, and when it was it defined no particular faith, but rather the quality of a faith that is tied to a specific locality.

Today, a performance in Glastonbury, UK, which sought to animate its mounds and hills as sites of magical or spiritual presence would have specificity (and paganism, in the sense of a religion at least partly based on locality) on its side (Chryssides & Zeller, 2014, p. 261). For these sites are already marked by their role in Goddess-oriented beliefs manifest in sacred dramas performed in the 1980s and 1990s by Ariadne Productions, written and directed by Kathy Jones, with large casts of locals involved: *Inanna and Dumuzi* (1985), *Green Tara* (1988), *The Shining Ones* (1989) and others (see Jones, 1996), reviving a tradition at Glastonbury that dates back at least as far as Alice Mary Buckton's processional drama *The Return of Bride* (1914).

A Goddess-oriented performance might be efficacious in its own terms, though there is nothing very convincing by way of documentary evidence for its roots in any pre-Christian tradition nor for the kinds of interpretive claims made upon the landscape. These are probably impositions on complex spaces every bit as egregious, ideological and appropriating as the heritage industry's 'country house' narrative. There is, however, an evident contradiction in my scepticism; at least as far as the issue of site-specificity is concerned.

The archaeological and geographical bases for Kathy Jones's performances – that idea that a Great Mother religion spread westwards from the Near East early in the Neolithic period (from 4800 BCE to 3800 BCE), along with its stone tombs and earthen long barrows, and established itself in a tradition of millennia-old Goddess worship in the Glastonbury landscape – was partly inspired (along with reverence and intuition) by a now largely discredited academic archaeological orthodoxy. In the 1970s, as more accurate dating of prehistoric sites was upsetting this orthodoxy's narrative of a steady spread of these architectures, as if by travelling missionaries, and as a reassessment of the few female figurines from the period suggested that they were as likely to be toys as religious objects (Hutton, 1993, pp. 36–41), so a popular counter-culture almost immediately revived the discredited orthodoxy, re-characterising it as a brave, novel, alternative and anti-establishment narrative. The ironic and contradictory tension that ensued is part of what, at Glastonbury, is now specific to its locality.

Specificity, then, is not a reductive process of authentication based on the latest stage of academic learning; instead 'It can overlay the documentary, the observational and the creative within a given location or architecture without laying any claim to accuracy or historical verisimilitude' (Pearson & Shanks, 2001, p. 159). It, at best knowingly and openly (but just as likely to be incoherently and opportunistically), embraces the inauthentic, fabricated, wilful, nonsensical, paradoxical and criminal where it is particular to a place. In that sense there is nothing that is necessarily, in any other terms, efficacious in a genuine site-specificity except the care and integrity (Kloetzel and Pavlik's 'attending to' and 'tending' [2010, pp. 6–7]), with which it addresses what is present there, in the site, whether convenient or inconvenient, consistent or inconsistent. It is not a form of hyper-realism; rather, a site-specific performance can be best judged (for its specificity) in terms of the intensity of its attention to what is both natural and fabricated in its localised space and to how all the elements of the site entangle in the conditional uniqueness of a performance. No 'site' has an original, permanent base or real identity to authenticate and be authenticated (that is the work of popular historians and nationalist poets); the site-artist has the more complex, if less heinous, task of making a meshwork-sense of the multiple eddies of materialities, sufferings, dreams and memories, documentations, diaries and monuments, fauna and flora past and present, architectural revenants and planning applications, pub chat, local 'urban legend' (how local is that, ever?), administrative structures, trash, informal markets, dignities and indignities ... and so on.

In the face of such a challenge, to maintain both multiplicity and specificity, there is arguably only one real error – to think that there is ever a single or simple explanation of a place – whether that be historical, spiritual, supernatural, political, aesthetic, anthropological, psychological, scientific or otherwise. Like good science, a site-specific piece of work moves forward by a fascination with what it does not know or what it can barely even imagine a meaning for, but that begs the investigation:

What is this place? What is happening here? What does all this mean? How could this be? The paradox of site-specificity is that, if genuinely pursued, it brings us to an uncontainable and promiscuous multiplicity of possible 'heres' – 'the local is always heterogeneous' (Pearson, 2010, p. 57) – and it is the judicious combining of those possibilities that constitutes the litmus test of the art.

In the above senses, although, say, Punchdrunk's shows are more site-sympathetic than specific (they usually begin with existing texts or narratives rather than ones generated for and from their site), such is the depth and detail of their attention to their sites that Punchdrunk's work may be more specific to its sites than, say, a performance generated entirely about and in the site that fails to attend carefully to it. When I saw Stephan Koplowitz's site-generic *Liquid Landscapes* (originally Los Angeles, 2008) in the Tinside Lido swimming pool in Plymouth, UK, in 2009, with its performers dancing against the backdrop of the bay of Plymouth Sound, the choice and adaptation to the shapes, colours and textures of the Lido and its surrounds – creating lines of danced movement that reflected the stripes on the pool's floor and the railings around the pool, ending with a slow and ominous exit from the pool (evoking the deathly presence of the nuclear submarines in the Sound) – exceeded the connection to site of other more literally specific works that I have witnessed.

So, perhaps you should ask not only what it is that is specific to the site that your exploration is looking for, but also if there are particular and appropriate principles that can guide your way of sensing for or feeling for or looking for in your particular site? Are you seeking well there? Are you seeking responsibly? Are you seeking beyond the surface, beyond first impressions? Are you seeking what you can use or control or are you surrendering something of yourself to the site in the process of your seeking? Are you after things which the site puts beyond your control? Are you after things that reach out to entangle with you or things that dwarf you, scare you, repel or flee from you?

If you are seeking for a backdrop to your performance, then you may be after the most passive elements of the site. In which case, you had better judge well, because you are unlikely to enjoy it if the dozy and co-operative site abruptly 'wakes up' in the middle of a performance.

Idea

Are there 'gatekeepers' (security guards, landlords, caretakers, residents) you need to negotiate with to gain access to your site? It may be easy to see these people as barriers to your work – and, indeed, they may be obstructive, that is their prerogative – but they can also be participants and partners. If you need to repeatedly go through them to gain access then you will probably *need* to establish at least a working relationship with them; the 'gatekeepers' may also help you with far more than just access. Preparing to make a performance with live artist Nicola Singh in a very small Devon, UK, village, consisting of a single street built for workers at a nearby quarry, I called with Nicola on the local councillor, a biker it turned out, to ask about permission to use the local gardening allotments. Though helpful, the councillor was clearly a little nervous about what a performance might entail and if and how she could help at all, so she took us to see another villager who was responsible for the village's water supply (this is sometimes called 'snowball sampling' in ethnography, being passed from one contact to another, allowing those on the ground to at least partly shape the researcher's narrative). The village, we were told, had its own tiny reservoir and filtration system, which this second villager was happy to demonstrate for us; in a few minutes a wealth of themes (climate, purification) and things (water, bottles, filters), all of which were to become central to our performance, were offered and gathered up. So, on the days of the performance – *Fabulous Walks* (Teign Village, UK, 2008) – there would be communal drinking and washing of wounds and the watering of Nicola's character as if she were a plant in the allotments (Illustration 5.1).

Illustration 5.1 *The Fabulous Walks*, Teign Village, UK, 2008. Performers: Katie Etheridge and Nicola Singh.

Photo: Mike Tooby.

This may not always be the best way: to seize on first impressions and first stories as the basis for your performance. Certainly you should note any immediate ideas you get from a newly found or newly visited site, but you might want to put them aside for a while and give yourself a chance to fully explore your site before moving on to ideas about how it can be performed. This may help you avoid losing sight of the space in your enthusiasm for a striking performance idea. Nevertheless, though it is not the only way, a powerful organising performance idea can emerge very quickly.

Exercise

Find the gatekeepers to your site. Make a performance with them.

Exercise

Work to the horizon. Take a deep breath and exhale along the line of the horizon, turning gently in a circle. In terms of vista, that is how far your site stretches. Create a short performance where you use that scale. In Plymouth, I watched performers on the top of a car park, while others performed on the balcony of a nearby tower block and others still were far away on a hill on the other side of the Hamoaze estuary of the Tamar River unfurling a giant banner in the mists. One way of connecting audiences to such distant performances is to use audio recording or live broadcast, with spectators listening on earpieces. Certain kinds of performance that can easily become drowned out by everyday sounds or dispersed by distance and wind conditions become possible once again through technology; subtle live dialogue or quiet soundscapes can accompany performers who may only be visible in the far distance. For their multi-form artwork *Broadcasts from the Edge of the Horizon: The Beacon* – centred upon a locally iconic tree silhouetted on the very edge of the horizon and visible from the centre of the city of Exeter, UK – Volkhardt Müller and Dawn Scarfe created a walk from the city to the beech tree, a middle of the night radio broadcast that was partly a live audio stream from the tree and a performance viewed by spectators in the city through binoculars (Müller & Scarfe 2017, pp. 26–31). The spectators were able to instruct, by walkie-talkie, volunteers on the hillside around the tree to manipulate two large white discs that moved about the green fields like errant moons. This kind of work can take advantage of both a seemingly impossible intimacy and a sense of spatial dislocation, amplified in effect by what we hear set at odds with what we see, and vice versa. Create a performance, using either recorded or live broadcast sound, for spectators observing performers working on the horizon, incorporating elements of both intimacy and dislocation.

Idea

Just as performers draw upon ethnographic research practices (as described earlier in the chapter), so researchers – in the social sciences particularly, but also in other disciplines – have begun to deploy performance strategies and 'mobile methodologies' in their work: putting into play the bodily presence of the researcher as part of the research itself. Given the specialised nature of certain sites – for example, where you might need some technical understanding of the mechanics of a heavy industrial process, of complex ecological issues around re-wilding or of arcane medieval church symbolism – you may choose to work with, or be partnered by, experts whose knowledge-gathering may turn out to be as performative as yours.

This reciprocity – between persons and processes – may extend beyond the research period. Some performance makers, particularly those inspired by 'relational aesthetics' with its move away from performance in 'independent and private space' to 'artistic practices which take as their theoretical and practical point of departure the whole of human relations and their social context' (Bourriard, 2002, p. 113), have drawn on scientific, bureaucratic and technical processes as the sources for their dramaturgy. Mark Dion's *The Thames Dig* (1999) mimicked something very like professional archaeology, Gillian Wearing's *Signs That Say What You Want Them to Say, Not Signs That Say What Other People Want You to Say* (1992–1993) was something like a journalistic 'vox-pop' with the artist giving passers-by in the street sheets of paper on which to write their first thought and then taking their image holding their word or statement, while Christian Nold's *Bio Mapping/Emotional Mapping* projects (2004 and ongoing) in numerous cities including Paris and San Francisco, use a combination of GPS and a sensor like that of a lie detector to monitor people's excitement levels as they encounter different spaces.

These kinds of crossovers can have their pitfalls; when Christian Nold's projects were first covered by the mainstream media, he was eagerly approached by 'estate agents in California wanting an insight into the geographical distribution of desire … advertising agencies wanting to emotionally re-brand whole cities' (2014, p. 4). His experience flags up a danger that while an appropriation of other technical processes can be very fruitful, these techniques carry their own meanings and associations along with them that may not be consonant with or identical to their practical operation. This can lead an unwary performance maker – thrilled to discover the theatrical nature of specialist practices, from casting letter shapes in concrete to interviewing suspects – to something that is more like a low-level social science project (with little contemporary disciplinary provenance) than a performance. This can leave experts disappointed that there is no transcendence of their techniques, and 'lay' audiences disappointed by the softness of the 'hard science': a lose-lose hybridisation. Nold's response to the misreading by corporations of his work is instructive, maybe even exemplary: he turned his work on its head. Rather than sell his data to commercial companies, he shared it freely with his participants, encouraging them to re-encode it with their own associations and stories and so 'generat[e] a new type of knowledge combining "objective" biometric data and geographical position, with the "subjective story" as a new kind of psychogeography' (p. 5).

Exercise

Approach your site as if it were (and it may be) a crime scene. Play detective or forensic scientist. 'That incidental object left behind may witness the absence of an event now passed. Things may not be what they seem... significance depends on context' (Pearson & Shanks, 2001, p. 61). Put your site on trial. Conduct a public inquiry into things done there. Map the generic spaces of criminal hurt. In 2015, I pointed out how recent revelations about the abuse of vulnerable people, mostly young and mostly female, by celebrities, politicians, 'care' officials and organised gangs in the UK, had often identified a particular kind of space of abuse; a space that seemed to go missing, to become invisible or meaningless. This space was largely unacknowledged in the public, legal or institutional discourses about the abuse, but had been consistently exploited semi-explicitly/semi-covertly by the abusers (Smith, 2015b, pp. 10–15). This space was rarely a public place, but it (and what happened there) was often known (or 'half known') to, and even administered by, public institutions and communities that the abusers operated within. These were not places of confinement or concealment, but inversions or inlets of semi-informal and semi-official space: dressing rooms, changing rooms, recreation rooms, private rooms on wards, curtained beds and so on, made 'safe' for the abusers not by complete secrecy or by the incarceration of their victims, but by the knowing or half-knowing acquiescence of authorities who did not want to know and did not act, or others who 'half-knew' and did not know how to respond. Site-specific performance has confronted recent sites of abuse and exploitation; such as Nhlanhla Mahlangu's *The Workers Chant* (2017) in a former migrant workers' hostel in Newtown, South Africa, herding its audience like de-individualised labour, using the lavatories to call up those who died in the compound and were disposed of like waste, shining a light on 'a dark but underreported blot on SA's [South Africa's] conscience' and challenging 'the present-day complacency of "born-frees"' (Kennedy, 2017).

Street-based performance has challenged ongoing situations, such as comical disruptions by the Clandestine Insurgent Rebel Clown Army, entering Army Recruitment Centres and bringing the work there to a halt by their bungling and calamitous attempts 'to help out'. Consider how a site-specific performance might respond by exposing or opening up a space of ongoing abuse or exploitation, how a performance might address and confront such behaviour; treating your site as a 'crime scene' does not have to be a game of metaphors, it can be a raw and direct response with consequences. This raises some daunting issues and prospects. This is not the kind of project to take on lightly, without knowing the sites well and establishing reliable allies and safety nets for your performance; so, ask yourself, should that not be the default setting for every work of site-specificity?

Exercise

Consider how you can apply the practice of 'authentic movement' to a site visit. Ignore anything you might know about the site and attend only to how your body – drives and feelings – responds through its movements to this one place. Work with a colleague who can operate as a witness, 'holding the ground' for you (warding off intrusions and malevolent gazes) while attending to their own feelings and associations as you respond to the site. At the completion of your responses, ask the witness for their observations.

Idea

A place is already a performance. There is an argument that says that if we can identify a space as a place, then we are recognising something that is already there, that is already in process; that in it are not just the shapings of, and tools for, performing itself as a place, but that that performance is in progress. A place is not a collection of materials, but an action. In other words, what can be said of a prehistoric long barrow or a stone circle can just as easily, and just as appropriately, be said of a supermarket, a city square, a suburban back garden or a park: 'they mark out, mark off and set aside space. They are the transformations of space through objects: linear and circular configurations and constraints which affect and regulate the way space is experienced and interpreted... where the human body is framed and observed' (Pearson & Shanks, 2001, p. 121). Given, then, that there is already in these spaces an agency or intention, explicit or implicit, a performance maker might at least consider first the existing agencies and affordances in their site, and before imposing their own agency submit to how 'the space may act directly upon the body, causing irregular movements and orientations, channelling the eye, regulating patterns of visibility and hiddenness, controlling the spacing and timing of encounters' (p. 121); only after that, choosing where to conform and where to defy the place's performance of itself.

Exercise

In the graphic novel *The Theory of the Grain of Sand* (2016), part of the 'Obscure Cities' series by François Schuiten and Benoît Peeters, numerous uniformly white stones of the same shape and weight appear mysteriously in the flat of an elderly man. His living space and the safety of the entire building are thrown into question. Can you use a similar device to help uncover the wrinkles and vulnerabilities of a site? Find a source of readily available and identical objects and place them in different arrangements – evenly, clustered, and so on – throughout your space. What stands out from the site now, what is highlighted by the uniformity? What patterns, other than your own arrangement of the objects, have been highlighted? You can animate this exercise further by blowing soap bubbles into your space and modelling the air flow, or launching numerous small rubber balls into it and tracking their trajectories within it. If there is a group of you, use your own bodies as the equivalent of the rocks or rubber balls, seeing what patterns emerge from your collective shapes or progresses around your site; what happens when you speed up or slow down, when you move in close proximity to each other and when you move spread far apart?

Exercise

Chart. Chart your life, chart your journeys for a week, chart a prospective performance site and then set it in relation to a chart of your everyday life; use the relationship between the three charts as your score. How can you perform those relations; of your connections to this space, of the site's relation to the ordinary and routine, of one space to a whole life?

(Each of the exercises in this chapter can be used as data gathering about your site, but also, in themselves, they might constitute a performance action or some part of one.)

Readings

Tim Edensor's *Industrial Ruins: Spaces, Aesthetics and Materiality* (2005) is a very personal piece of writing. It rests on years of wandering around in derelict foundries, rusting factories and trashed warehouses. Attentive to what has gone, to the almost-warlike gladiatorial conditions of heavy industry and the relentless passage of materials, Edensor's method is bodily; he understands these spaces most by being in them, to some extent putting himself at their mercy, using his body and its senses as his research methods. Edensor conveys the stickiness and stinkiness of finding your way through the ruins of what were places of work, production and profit-making; but he also conveys feelings of 'uncertainty about what went on' there (p. 15). Edensor respects their pasts, but he visits them in the present as places that are 'ripe with transgressive and transcendent possibilities... in which interpretation and practice of the city becomes liberated from the everyday constraints which determine what should be done and where' (p. 4), as places that inherently bring into 'question the persistent myth of progress' (p. 14). Edensor rejects the idea that these industrial ruins are ugly or worthless; for him they are playgrounds and thinking places. They are places where there are 'possibilities of confronting that which is repressed', but they also 'represent the fecund' (pp. 13, 14), the power of materials to oxidise and change, of nature to reclaim, of humans to repurpose useless things for raves, intimacy, performances and illicit exchanges.

As well as good advice on keeping safe, and an exemplary sensibility to all the resources of a particular place – its smells, colours, textures, the crunch of glass underfoot, the change of temperatures from one space to another, the effects of dampness – *Industrial Ruins* is also a template for how to turn the fragments of observation and experience into a blueprint for a totality, a kind of pre-dramaturgy, the sort of guiding and spectral idea of what a performance will be about that comes before the means and structure. Edensor's blueprint is a plan to 'confound the normative spacings of things, practices and people ... [seizing] opportunities for regulated urban bodies to escape their shackles in expressive pursuits and sensual experience' (p. 18).

Readings

Nan Shepherd was a visitor of mountains. A published novelist, her book *The Living Mountain* (1977) was written during the mid-1940s, but rejected by publishers and put away in a drawer until it eventually got into print through a small academic press. A now acknowledged classic work of land-scape writing, it is also a handbook for exemplary presence in natural sites of any kind. Shepherd's visiting is self-conscious and self-reflexive. She is careful not to cloud the space with her own preoccupations: 'often the mountain gives itself most completely when I have no destination, when I reach nowhere in particular, but have gone out merely to be with the mountain as one visits a friend with no intention but to be with him' (p. 15).

Shepherd gives us some simple tips for disrupting immediate and super-ficial impressions, such as 'changing of focus in the eye, moving the eye itself when looking at things that do not move, [this] deepens one's sense of outer reality. The static things may be caught in the very act of becom-ing. By so simple a matter ... as altering the position of one's head, a dif-ferent kind of world may be made to appear' (pp. 10–11). *The Living Mountain* also explains how you can let a site help you, even when it at first appears to be hindering: 'Haze, which hides, can also reveal. Dips and ravines are discerned in what had appeared a single hill: new depth is given to the vista' (p. 43). Nan Shepherd's self-reflective sensing is never a solely technical matter. More than help you gather any particular under-standing of a place, reading her book is more likely to change the quality of your relationship with places, if you accept her invitations to 'Lay the head down, or better still, face away from what you look at, and bend with straddled legs till you see your world upside down ... Details are no longer part of a grouping in a picture of which I am the focal point, the focal point is everywhere' (p. 11).

6

Site Aesthetics

There is no right or wrong way to make performance in any site. Or to put it another way – there are only relative and contextualised right ways that will not apply to everywhere. The universe, it has turned out, is not made of smooth and even matter, but is uneven and wrinkly, obeying different rules at different scales; at the most basic level, rather than harmony being the driving principle of the cosmos, it is the imbalance between matter and antimatter that provides a reason for there being any universe at all. The art of site-specifics lies in the choices (intellectual or intuitive) you make about which wrinkles to exploit, and how wrinkled your exploitation should be.

When teaching on the 'Site Projects' module at Dartington College of Arts, the students had access to much of the woodlands, fields, tracks and river on the Dartington Estate (Devon, UK). A minority of the students each year would respond to the invitation to create performances in these spaces in a combative fashion. Fridges would be suspended in trees, cabarets staged in the river. There was an immediate and powerful effect to be had by 'trashing' the existing landscape-aesthetic of the site. The problem that then arises is not with the trashing itself, but where to go from there; repeating the outrage is likely to produce diminishing returns.

These occasional provocations (both of the site and of the teachers) generated an immediate energy, a sharp juxtaposition, an indictment of being asked to address a soft and idyllic landscape; yet they were incredibly difficult to sustain. Despite the incongruity, the impact faded quickly. A more careful looking at and working in the estate revealed that there were existing incongruities in the seemingly idyllic setting and odd intolerances in its policing (for example, it was fine to harness and dangle performers from trees, but not for them to walk backwards on a pavement) every bit as sharp and absurd as that between oaks and freezers. It was only necessary to identify, identify with and highlight the existing tensions to create an uncomfortable exposure of contradictions (in the terrain, and in the institutions that managed it) and these did not so easily fade away as they were not imported outrages, but immersions in what was there; an approach articulated by choreographer Stephan Koplowitz (1997) to the *New York Times*: 'I'm interested in becoming part of the design and rhythm of the site and amplifying that.'

An example that married extreme incongruity with social and geographical precision was artist Maurizio Catalan's installation of a copy of the giant 'HOLLYWOOD' sign above Los Angeles, in 2001, above a waste dump on the edge of Palermo in Sicily, a city with high unemployment and a declining population. Just as a performer in a swimming costume entering a swimming pool empty of water might evoke the missing water so Catalan's installation evoked the wealth, power and glamour missing from the suburban Palermo landscape.

Koplowitz's aspiration suggests an element of self-denial, but that is not necessarily the case; the mechanics of amplification can overwhelm its original subject. If the performance maker draws upon elements of theatricality, heightened behaviour or narrative and dialogue, it has to be with the acknowledgement that these practices have an energy of their own that can 'force a pause in the flow of audience movement and collapse the sense of simultaneity into a single moment of action … to place a focus on the performer, rather than on the space, which becomes relegated to a background' (Turner & Behrndt, 2008, p. 196).

This chapter will address how for a rigorous site-specific approach, the aesthetics of each performance intervention are forged in a tension between the qualities of the site and the predilections of the performance makers; the latter always to some extent (because they are mostly nomadic) threatening to lose touch with their raison d'être and obscure the object of their desire: the site. At the same time, there is another tension at work in site-specificity; for the associations and aesthetics brought into the site by the performance makers (just like those of any other agentive presence there) become a part of that site; there is always an entanglement to be finessed and never a simplicity to be returned to. In that spirit, I am offering below three overarching aesthetic approaches to site-based performance in the knowledge that they are necessarily generalised, not necessarily discrete and open to whatever adaptation and traducing the specificity of any use will subject them to: transparency, camouflage and symbolist.

Transparency: These are light, self-effacing and non-invasive performances *through which* a site can be performed and witnessed. This approach will suit the less-busy site, places that will not 'drown out' a subtle approach. It is likely to suit performances where less dominant and more delicate senses are required. An example of such a transparent performance, with three contrasting presences within it, is *On the Scent* by Curious (London, 2004). Here, in different parts of a domestic dwelling – offering the raw scents of food in the kitchen, unguents in the bedroom and flower-flavoured chocolates in the lounge – the three performers are distinct in their manner, but never imposing or psychologically complex; they address the small audience directly, always generously and sometimes intimately. They are like embodied memories, wearing 'character' lightly; their roles – 'cook' or 'brusque researcher' or 'invalid' – are more like functions than personalities; they articulate more than they dramatise.

The performance is further diluted by the fact that although it is 'performed "at home" … the home in which it takes place is not the performers' (or spectators) and, in this sense, the picture of "home" that we are offered is made strange' (Heddon, 2008, p. 120). In the last room visited, where the smells of medicines dominate, the performer speaks of lies and deceptions and the phantasm of nostalgia that holds a person in a forever-present that has long gone. Departed objects of desire are evoked by fading but persisting perfume, hundreds of thousands of victims killed at Hiroshima and Nagasaki by burned hair. By these transparencies, *On the Scent* invokes and evokes stark and sometimes apocalyptic memories hovering somewhere between the authenticity of real history and real feelings and the confection of sweets, perfumes and medicinal drugs.

Escaping from the usual agencies of 'character' adds to the spectral and uncertain quality that *On the Scent* gives to usual certainties: 'When the children leave home, does the home/mother/self cease to exist?' (Heddon, 2008, p. 123). What is always real is what seems most vulnerable; the scents are like a subconscious for the performance, replacing and expelling the usual objectives and super-objectives of personae.

In her 'earth body sculptures' (1973–1980), Ana Mendieta's presence is almost overwhelmed by the terrain; mud, clay and water cover and hide her body. Sometimes the artist disappeared altogether, leaving only a mark made by her body in marsh grass or riverbank. When she remained bodily there, her presence was often precarious, barely supported. Sometimes Mendieta used fire, giving the materials of a place an agency, just as the release of odours animate *On the Scent*. In Mendieta's performance-sculptures the land 'plays' the artist's body as if it were a score or text, approximating and simplifying its shape, almost – and cruelly – universalising it; a very partial escape from oppressive categorisation.

Rather than the immersion of an audience in their own overwhelming experiences, in a 'transparency' like Mendieta's, spectators are invited as active witnesses; not to their own affects, but rather to the effecting of things (including people) by other things (including people). Mendieta's audience have obligations, to be attentive; in this 'transparency' the focus has moved away from the human 'act-er', whether artist or audience, and is displaced to the material consequences of things, and to the 'other' human experiencer, an 'other' that has to be imagined, a challenge that can only be properly met by empathy.

Performers and performance in a 'transparency' are not necessarily 'absent' or self-denying; they are something more like bright photographic transparencies projected onto a screen. We very much see them, they are very much there – they have colour and shape, very bright and very sharp perhaps, they represent stuff – but they do not hide the site that is both behind, supporting, but is also through, penetrating, their presence. Through the performers and their performance we can see the texture of their site just as we might see a wrinkled unevenness in a screen through (and highlighted by) any projection upon it. This kind of 'transparency' can be realised in different ways. For example, the voices of performers who are unseen can overlay a space in the same way as a projection.

Disembodied voices invite the audience to imagine who might possess them, imagine or deduce what the speakers might be doing, how they move, how they appear, what they might wear, what they mean or symbolise. Such imaginings are transparent ones; there is only the site to test them against. Through them the audience sees the site as meaningful, as values.

Invisibility, transparency or the marking of character by scent or tactility, light or shadow, rather than psychological acting, does not imply, let alone require, the absence of performers from your site, or a lack of 'performance presence' or competence on their part. In 2001 I was working with young school students on a site-specific performance (*Church*, Exeter, UK); twice, once in rehearsal and then just before a performance, the students' drama teacher encouraged them to 'stay in character!' Even though none of the students had a character to stay in, they understood. They were to maintain their focus, not to distract from the quality of their presence by exposing or performing their own self-consciousness, nerves or egos, but to remain self-possessed. That would be enough to be 'character' in a transparent performance.

Eugenio Barba of Odin Teatret (Hostelbro, Denmark) has written about a similar kind of presence as being that of a 'dilated body'. For Barba this is a default mode for the actor. It is 'a way of moving in space [that] manifests a way of thinking ... the motion of thought stripped naked' (1985, p. 14); character and psychology are displaced in favour of the embodying of an idea (or rather the thinking of the idea). This is achieved, at least in part, through the application of a 'negation principle' whereby 'the actor negates an imminent action before carrying it out, by executing its complementary opposite' (p. 19). To extend this idea to the examples above, this might be the absent body of Ana Mendieta leaving its trace in other materials or Lois Weaver's 'researcher' distractedly talking to recording equipment while addressing the audience at the start of *On the Scent*; this is a thinning out of attention that would probably be accounted disastrous in a stage drama. In a transparent performance, however, it strips down to the work's (and site's) 'way of thinking'.

Barba's aim for his acting method is not to create a meaning from any 'idea' or share the actual thinking, or psychological state, of the actor, but to reach a state of '"pre-condition" ... which prepares the void in which a sense, an unexpected meaning, can be captured' (p. 20). In our preparing for *Church* we had used simple exercises to a similar end – exploring the site blindfold, each student with a non-blindfold helper, walking from one end of the deconsecrated nave to the other, moving in and out of the energy and posture of an expressive body. The displacing of their senses and the extroverting of performance and behavioural modes that the students might usually take for granted, was a way to their knowing by only partially knowing, expressing by only partially performing. By allowing the young performers – trained to fill their performance with their fulsome energies and emotions – to thin out their presence, they had the invitation to stay open, sensitised and ultra-responsive to all the 'others' in the site and to changes of agency; in their case, on one performance day, to the sudden and unusual strengthening of the wind that blew violently across the graveyard.

Unencumbered by the melodrama and individualistic psychology of contemporary naturalism, renegotiating their own roles in relation to the stories, roles and myths familiar to them from the media and the street, a 'transparent' actor, fully engaged with their site, 'plays with ideological figures, subverts and humanises them and keeps them moving and changing, perpetually recreating them as fluid living presences' (Soule, 2000, p. 183). These 'transparency' skills are not unique to site-specific performance; elements can be gleaned from various acting disciplines. They, rather than any imported score, are the writing of performance by its site; but, within which, the 'transparent' performer is no passive amplifier or mirror, but argues, jostles and wrestles the site's own script. At the same time, a 'transparent' performance not only illuminates, but also changes and re-sites (as well as recites) ignored, difficult, ambiguous or abused sites.

Camouflage: This means creating performance that is as variegated and demonstrative as its site, integrated by its theatricality and noisiness rather than its unveiling and illuminating by restraint. By excess and showiness a camouflaged performance flattens itself into the unevenness of its space. This approach will best match a place that is rich in detail, a place that threatens to overwhelm any human presence no matter how histrionic, a place packed with existing 'performance' and narrative, florid in materials and design. After choosing such a site, making a performance with exaggerated and baroque qualities can be an entanglement with, and (paradoxically) a disappearance into the space that changes its nature: it can make 'new space'.

In 2008, I attended a performance of *The Last King of Devonport* given by one of the three larger companies assembled by Part Exchange Theatre for their Hidden City Festival of site-specific theatre in neglected spaces in Plymouth, UK. *The Last King of Devonport* was centred on, in and around the Devonport Guildhall, an early nineteenth-century institutional building built in Greek Doric neo-classical style that had largely fallen into disuse. This was a decline that had begun as long ago as 1914, when the town of Devonport lost its administrative independence as one of three towns amalgamated into the city of Plymouth, for reasons of military convenience (constituting a significant naval port).

By 2008, the Guildhall building had accumulated the marks of a rich jumble of former uses, including a large and crumbling mural painted for the *Challenge Anneka* TV show and the disused cells of former law courts. At first, and perhaps this can be put down to my predisposition towards the more 'transparent' approach to site, I was put off by the cabaret-style introduction staged between the giant columns of the building's facade. By the end of a journey through the building's labyrinthine corridors and anterooms, I was wholly ready for the story of 'boxing metaphor and fighting hero, Rocky Devonport, who stands up against every setback the centuries throw at him' (Aspinwall & Mitchell, 2010, p. 29). This climactic part of the performance was staged in the main hall inside a boxing ring, reviving one of the Guildhall's more recent functions and objects. The exotic costuming and make-up, the high, but unpredictable emotionalism of the performances and the picaresque dialogue all served to identify the performers/characters as integral parts of the enhanced rooms, hall, corridors and portico; they neither revealed nor illuminated the site, but rather had become extrovert parts of its history and architecture of crime and punishment, popular performance and pugilism, local pomp and low life. There was no pretense that the performers were creating organic and realistic individuals (even the main figure of Rocky was so obviously un-individuated and symbolic); there was no modulating of their expressionism in concessions to a more accessible behaviourist naturalism; instead, the actors wore their artificiality defiantly, swirling fragmentariness and grotesque detailing as if they were invoking the precise dreaming of the site.

This overheated assemblage of rough music, folk-theatre performance styles and populist themes (e.g., of a much-beaten fighter making a last stand), because of the specificity of the accumulation to such a much re-used and re-purposed space, and to a much abused, ignored and deprived wider community, was wholly appropriate and attentive to the dynamics of the Guildhall and its locale. If the acid test of a transforming of the site into 'new space' is applied, then the subsequent re-appropriation of the building for community events and its conversion to use by various agencies (with all the ambiguities that such redevelopment, including gentrification, can bring) suggests that it was passed by *The Last King of Devonport*. The last time I walked by (in early 2017), a large and jubilant wedding party was emerging through the neo-classical pillars where *The Last King of Devonport* had begun.

Watching that 2008 performance in the Devonport Guildhall, a strange and rather wonderful misunderstanding occurred; a testimony to the efficacious operation of chance and randomness that can work in a site-specific performance's favour when it is in touch with the perverse dynamics and multiplicities of its space. In this case, alongside some university colleagues in the ambulant audience, I had emerged into one of the anterooms of the Guildhall, following the performers from the basement corridors. In the anteroom – to my colleagues and me, at least – a scene was in progress, a large-scale staging of a communal social event, with numerous members of the local community performing; there was laughter, pranks, food was being served, drinks poured. Our focus shifted from group to group, as small moments of engagement, greeting and hilarity rose and subsided. This was all going on under the strange mix of communal creation and media concoction that characterised the *Challenge Anneka* mural; more than a little dream-surreal in its content. We stood and marvelled at the subtle skills of the community actors, so relaxed and yet so precise in their seamlessly interwoven interactions, impressed by the fine detailing of tiny gestures and tensions, and the interplay between this particular performing of a local community and the cock-eyed representation of it on the wall behind. After about ten minutes of this, it dawned on us that what we were watching was not a performance at all (at least in the aesthetic sense) but the other half of the audience enjoying their interval refreshments (the audience had been split in two at the top of the performance and the two parts re-united in readiness for the final boxing ring section in the adjacent large hall). What we were admiring as performance was everyday life. Wholly unintended by the production, it was, nevertheless, a striking and unforgettable experience of defamiliari-sation, wholly consistent with the rest of the camouflage.

Another example of camouflage, though very different in style – these categories are not defined by the techniques deployed, but by their tendency towards some general dynamic – was *My Word Is My Bond* (City of London, 2002) by FrenchMottershead. In a bar of the Throgmorton restaurant in London's financial sector, 25 performers mingled with 50 paying audience members and an indeterminate number of accidental participants/witnesses who wandered in from other parts of the establishment over the duration of the evening. The performers would periodically but seamlessly break into micro-scenes, devised from interviews with locals – from bankers to bar workers to people who had slept, homeless, on the streets there. The audience members occasionally became drawn into 'scenes' of their own, not always able to tell who was who, improvising with other audience members (each under the impression that the other was a rehearsed performer); it was sometimes unclear where the line was drawn between a formal performance of city-boy bad behaviour and over-enthusiastic audience participation. As low-key, everyday, aggressive and absurd actions orbited each other, 'audience members closely scrutinized each other's behaviour, on the look-out for "actors" staging "micro-performances" ... The distinction ... made deliberately unclear' (Turner & Behrndt, 2008, p. 197).

The impact of *My Word Is My Bond* was less formalistic than ethical; the challenge to the audience less about identifying a 'distinction between "authentic" behaviours and "performance"' (p. 197) and more about how they moderated their own behaviour or responded to the temptation to perform to, and 'out-perform', others, whether audience members or performers. One reviewer recounted how she found herself falling out with a friend as a result of her behaviour/performance in the bar, the two of them engaging in a bitter shouting match outside the London Stock Exchange after the show was over: 'it was not so much "we are all performers" as "we are all wankers in a bar" – but of course it's up to us to choose how much of a wanker' (Kimball, 2002).

Just as in a performance of transparency no absenting of the performer need take place, so in a performance of camouflage there is no need to absent character; rather the actors can comfortably deploy conventional stage strategies of naturalistic performance at some times, and the more abstract techniques of populist theatre at others; never quite a behavioural imitation of a person – whether because of an excess of theatricality or the lack of any 'distinction between "authentic" behaviours and performance' – but an illusion in circulation among other illusions. In that sense, 'camouflage' is every bit as transparent as 'transparency'; both dynamics working to enact their sites, 'transparency' tending towards the materials and textures, 'camouflage' towards the historical traces and contemporary social relations.

Symbolist: The philosopher Slavoj Žižek describes the three levels of the Bates's house in Alfred Hitchcock's movie *Psycho* (1960) as three parts of a symbolic space; the ground floor where activity is socially conforming is representative of the ego, the bedrooms are the domain of the super-ego (where the voice of the dead mother chivvies away at the son, demanding obscene behaviour) and the cellar is the place of the id where desire is uncontained (Fiennes, 2006). This way of describing a place is drawn from some larger corpus of symbolism; in Žižek's case one drawn from Freudian and post-Freudian psychology. It can come from philosophical, biological, geological, psychological or other organisations of categories. In relation to a particular site, this ordering can be explicit and an integral part of the space's design – as with, say, a Freemasons' temple or with the interweaving of liturgical script with the histrionic platform of a medieval cathedral's layout – but it can also be imposed; in the case of the house in the *Psycho* movie, it is arguable whether there is an integral Freudian order there, or whether it has been imposed by Žižek's subsequent interpretation of the location.

Any such distinction – between design and interpretation – is mostly irrelevant to Gaston Bachelard's 'poetics of space'; he articulates spaces phenomenologically, according to the effects of the architecture or natural place upon its resident or visitor, not according to the histories of the place. Any one space is always both reminiscent and symbolic of another. Bachelard cites the story of a deep-sea diver who becomes lost in a desert, quoting the diver's account of how, in his imagination, 'I flooded the space around me while walking through it … I moved about in the heart of a fluid, beneficent, dense matter … the memory of sea water'; from this Bachelard extracts 'a psychological technique which permits us to be elsewhere, in an absolute elsewhere that bars the way to the forces that hold us imprisoned in the "here"' (1958/1969, p. 207). The metaphorical leaps and leaping metaphors of Gaston Bachelard are something more than arbitrary graspings. When he generalises the space of any 'corner' as 'a haven that ensures us of one of the things we prize most highly – immobility … a sort of half-box, part walls, part door' (p. 137), he also illuminates the qualities of specific corners. It is not precise enough for Bachelard's generalising to simply associate a woodland with the stories and fairy tales of ancient forests; instead it is necessary 'to know how the forest experiences its great age' and Bachelard's way into that impossibility is by another knowing: 'that my grandfather got lost in a certain wood … This, then, is my ancestral forest. And all the rest is fiction' (pp. 188–189). To create work in symbolic space is a process that blends the subjective with the real, the personal with the historical, in order to firm up its abstract meanings with precise, local materials and effects.

An example of this combining of a subjective affecting by a particular space (or set of spaces) and its entangling with a symbolic order is manifest on an epic scale in Matthew Barney's *The Cremaster Cycle* (1994–2002), a series of five lengthy filmed performances, apparently intended only for private viewing (a handful of DVD sets of the films have been sold and exchanged for astronomical and exclusionary sums of money) or for occasional gallery exhibition alongside numerous other materials including still images and installations (though the complete films occasionally escape onto YouTube). The overarching theme of this epic 'cycle' seems to be the role of a state of potentiality that, in human anatomical terms, occurs prior to the emergence of any sexual differentiation; within that theme the films enact various interplays between sexual and anatomical reactions and among other resonances – for 'this is "The Waste Land" for a generation that grew up with "Star Wars"' (Jones, 2002) – a postmodernist mystical version of Freemasonry.

The only section of *The Cremaster Cycle* on general release on DVD, 'The Order' (2002), is performed and filmed in the Guggenheim Museum in New York. Barney, in the role of the Entered Apprentice (one seeking entry to the first and lowest degree of Freemasonry) attempts to climb up to the roof of the central part of the museum, in an action comparable to that of a character in a computer game with numerous levels. Barney clambers and leaps up the famous spiral layers of the Guggenheim. He encounters various tasks and provocative or antagonistic figures; embracing and then slaying his ego in the form of a shape-shifting Entered Novitiate/Cheetah Woman played by Paralympian Aimee Mullins. Close to reaching his objective, Barney 'plunges' slowly back down to the very bottom of the building, into a pool of half-naked dancers (a banal sensualism), before making a final and transcendent ascent; the symbolism of an initiate – or any creative individual, seeking something beyond their selves – needing to first plumb the depths before being able to reach for transcendence is explicit.

This seems (and is) a long way from 'transparency'. There is, however, a relation between a symbolist and a transparent aesthetics and that is their (and camouflage's) testing by specificity. The transcendental modernism of Frank Lloyd Wright's Guggenheim design, conceived in response to a request by the museum's first director for a 'temple of the spirit' and the building's authoritative (some might say authoritarian) accretion of meaning and value-making in the contemporary art world – from its cancellation of a Hans Haacke show critical of New York landlords in 1971 to its mounting of exhibitions of designs from fashion houses that sponsor the museum – all seems to be explicitly engaged by Matthew Barney's athletic striving for upstanding behaviour and elite creativity as he climbs up through the layers of temptation, task and gloop in 'The Order'. The hierarchy of forms, followed by the transcendence of forms, the secrecy and defence of the institution and the precarity of the human body (no matter how athletic) in sustaining a creativity that repeatedly returns to its inspirational genesis (even if that is in the most degraded layer) are all there in a space every bit as exotic as Matthew Barney's confection. The extreme openness of performance styles and personae – gymnastic, 'hardcore' musicianship, chorus line dancing, symbolic ordeal and contest, mystical icon – disperses any 'tendency to place a focus on the performer, rather than on the space' (Turner & Behrndt, 2008, p. 196) as the centre of meaning, leaving gaps for the presence of the site to re-emerge.

Exercise

In 1981 the sculptor Richard Serra (a performer in Matthew Barney's 'The Order') placed his artwork *Tilted Arc*, a large and tall curving metal strip, across Federal Plaza in New York. Some hailed this as a welcome and assertive return to specificity; rather than blending in or disappearing within the space, as some critics felt was becoming the fashion for public art, *Tilted Arc* disrupted the look and everyday uses of the Plaza. Among those disrupted were local office workers who found that they had to adapt their usual trajectories to navigate around the sculpture. It was too large and too obstructive to be ignored or enjoyed as decoration. It had agency. The installation was controversial and in 1989 it was removed, with Serra claiming, famously, that 'To remove the work is to destroy the work' (1991, p. 38). Create a physical installation or a performance intervention in a public space, which, by a tweak or a reorientation can shift between an aggressive disruption of everyday uses and an embroidery around them. Play with this oscillation, changing the balance of discomfort and delight, to discover what those uses are, what are precious and what are disposable, what an audience will embrace and what they will find intolerable.

Idea

In the last four decades of the twentieth century, artists from disciplines like painting and sculpture turned away from the networks of exchange and purchase by which an art world of objects and representations was sustained and turned to their own bodies as the raw material for their work. To share that work the artists often encountered their visitors, viewers or audiences in live events; indeed, the term 'performance art' would be almost subsumed by that of 'live art'. Given that the emergence of site-specific art and performance was at least partly inspired and motivated by similar rejections and embraces, 'liveness' has continued to figure powerfully, but ambiguously, within site-specificity. After all, it could be argued that to be specific to a place is also to be specific to it as a space-in-time; so that rehearsing and fixing a performance too rigidly is not to be specific to the site if over that time of rehearsal the site changes (in however small or subtle a way).

At the same time there may be an assumption, perhaps inherited from live art, that there is something especially, even essentially, subversive about liveness. That by being:

> open to the moment-by-moment of the live's happening before applying the rules through which we might presume to understand what is taking

place around us … 'being live' displaces, if only for an instant, the constellations that bind knowledge and representation together to fashion the narratives and structures that presume to describe and organise phenomena into concrete formations. (Quick, 2004, p. 93)

Along with this potential to disrupt, there comes something like a moral imperative in live art-influenced site-based performance to 'stay in the moment', to be 'fully present' in the space and to be 'tuned in' to it. This hyper-concentrated focus upon a spatial essence – a presence and present-ness of things, informed by a privileging of affect in common with a phenomenological approach in other fields – rather than a series of broken-up encounters with discrete objects and consequently variable feelings, can lead to a kind of self-hypnosis: a fixation upon a singular affect as representing the base essence of a site. When the effort and mechanics of focus overwhelm the doing of the encounters with the objects, those who are happy to accept this essentialism can seem self-deceived; they blur the particularities of their site by their hypnotic focus upon it and their heightened feeling in it. This 'liveness' itself – rather than live differences and dynamics – can be, absurdly, fixed.

Directing 'Project 3' in the orangery and conservatory spaces of a large eighteenth-century former 'stately home' (Bretton Hall, UK, 2007), the choreographer Victoria Hunter noted that an 'ebb and flow between the dancers' sense of connection and disconnection with the site was an important and significant element of their site exploration' and so she introduced a 'pedestrian rule' that allowed the dancers to acknowledge that they had become unfocused and disconnected, and to 'walk, pause, observe and take time to reconnect to the site and the other bodies' (2015a, p. 190). Although Hunter tends to configure this 'pedestrian' state as secondary to, and less efficacious than, the focused and connected state, there is an argument to be made – particularly in relation to understanding the things of a site as equally active as the performers – that a shifting from different levels of focus is as, if not more, helpful as seeking a single level of heightened intensity.

In the blanked and super-controlled conditions of designated theatre-space and studio, there is often a uniformity of heightened focus throughout a performance, both among performers and between performers and audience, particularly but not exclusively during the performances of narrative-based plays. This heightened state, essential in order to follow the complexities of plot or the subtleties of psychological characterisation, may not be appropriate to site-specific performances if we acknowledge that their sites are rarely smooth and blank, but may be so exaggeratedly conflicted and uneven between their discrete parts that different levels of 'connection and disconnection' are appropriate across a performance, both for performers and audiences.

Exercise

Gaston Bachelard describes the meditational and self-reflective qualities that can accompany and colour household chores such as polishing and washing (1958/1969, pp. 67–71). Choose a small site, or define strict limits within a larger one. What happens if you wash and/or polish the objects and the surfaces of the site? What new site is unveiled? What else is reflected?

Exercise

Explore what ordering of symbolic forces you think is appropriate for a range of sites that you find. For a labyrinthine site you may perhaps choose an anatomical order, your performance entering inside the organs of a symbolic body. Once you have settled on a symbolic order, create a performance driven by your categories. Inside the anatomical labyrinth are you surgeons or killers, viruses or antibodies, food or thoughts?

Exercise

For her 'Two Hotels' project (2000) Geraldine Pilgrim created site-specific performance at two former Midland Hotels; *hotel* in the Midland Hotel in Morecombe, UK and *dreamwork 3* in the Midland Grand Hotel at St Pancras Station in London, both empty and suffering some dereliction at the time. Both were promenade performances and both engaged a large number of community and youth performers. They were also united by a common aesthetic that took advantage of the abject and melancholy affordances of the depredated architectures of the two buildings. The seaside hotel in Morecombe is made in a version of Art Deco, the one in London is neo-gothic. In Morecombe, Pilgrim used sand that covered the floors of the hotel's verandas, as if the beach were encroaching into the hotel, while inside protective white sheets over furniture created ghostly shapes. Characters in evening dress, lost souls, the ghosts of long gone guests, brass music played by a uniformed band; all nostalgic but in decay. At the Grand in St Pancras, if anything the decline was even more pointed; images of incarceration, loneliness, suspension, isolation, disembodiment, unconsciousness and routines detached from reality predominated. There is a melancholic romanticism at work here, a sensitivity to and aestheticisation of the trappings of ruin. The closure and decay of formerly grand buildings provoke a kind of dread or awe; but is a melancholic interpretation a reactionary return to an aesthetics of the sublime and the picturesque, previously torn up by the modernist formalism of site-specific performance's origins? Is there a space in the tension between openness to the ambience of ruined place and resistance to the return of a picturesque space in which to make a performance? In a ruined site, create a short scene or action or tableau/installation that combines a rigorously researched history of the site with a melancholic romantic picturing; a critical not an ornamental romanticism. Can you push the nostalgia so hard it becomes something else?

Exercise

Find a homogeneous site, somewhere dominated by few materials or by a single overarching design – for example, a clay quarry or a football field. Borrowing something from Ana Mendieta's methods, create a performance that leaves a subtle, but developing trace capable of upsetting the homogeneity or skewing the pattern.

Exercise

Find the busiest place you can. Create a performance there that is equally busy, busy enough to disappear, to become part of the busyness and business of the space.

Exercise

Find a small picture frame with nothing in it; use it to isolate and play with picture-making and the picturesque, accidental or designed, in the landscape. (This was employed to great effect by Cathy Turner in her section of

Wrights & Sites's *Pilot Navigation* [1998], where it was directly related to the work of an imaginary landscape painter, the audience being encouraged to use their frames to picture and select the subjects of his paintings from the surrounding canal-side terrain.) Use a small frame to identify a tiny or distant site within which to set your performance. Create a tiny performance very close to an audience who are using frames through which to view the event; or make a very large and spectacular show to be viewed through frames from far away. Give each of your audience members a 'Claude Glass' (black mirrors) in which to watch a performance in curved reflection, highlighting the central subject and abstracting it from its surroundings.

Readings

There are so many 'kinds' of space, so many places that a performer might find themselves choosing, or having chosen for them, as a site; yet there are no technical schools, not even much in the way of manifestoes for schools, for producing performance in such spaces. There is no Stanislavski of site-specific theatre. Each company or individual either starts from scratch, or takes something from a practitioner they admire, or leans for a while on the teaching of mostly isolated individuals in academia. Although Rachel Rosenthal's 'The DbD Experience' is directed to preparing performers for small studio performance, its 'Doing by Doing' exercises are flexible, open and translatable to site-specific devising; whether for dilating the site-artist's body, releasing the absurd and juxtapositional in spontaneity and scenography/dramaturgy or developing a sensitivity to context. Many of the individual exercises and the guiding ethics of 'The DbD Experience' – an enquiry into a cosmos ('perhaps many') that is partly invisible, 'archaeology with ourselves as the digging sites' (2010, p. 25) – can be adapted and reapplied to working on site. From learning to put the everyday 'in brackets' (p. 27), cultivating 'No-Focus Focus' for opening up peripheral vision (p. 43), 'Seed to Tree' by which 'to begin to discover in [yourselves] the life and biology of non-humans' (p. 46), 'sculptor and doll' (p. 51), telling a story without human presence, the cultivation of 'Levels' (comparable with Mike Pearson's dramaturgical stratigraphy [see Chapter 8]), developing a light trance through hyper-attention to objects (p. 78), and so on. Rosenthal's acting exercises (pp. 91–100) aim for an expression of emotions without a linear psychological propulsion – 'you don't play a person who is "sad" … you play the "essence of sadness" or "sadness itself"' (p. 94) – an alternative to objectives and super-objectives without abandoning psychological or subjective presence altogether.

Making a Performance: Devising Histories and Contemporary Practices by Emma Govan, Helen Nicholson and Katie Normington (2007) is another useful resource, given its blend of ideas and historical accounts with descriptions of re-applicable and adaptable current practices. The entire book is potentially relevant to a maker of site-specific performances, dependent on their interests, and given that even some of the practices coming from building-based disciplines are sufficiently, like Rosenthal's above, malleable or transferable to other formats.

Of particular relevance is Part Three of the book (pp. 103–54), which addresses the places and spaces of performance making, starting from the liminal performance terrain mapped out by Richard Schechner (described in Chapter 1) and then working its way back and forward across the boundary between designated and found spaces of performance; a border on which, as the authors concede, 'it is difficult to maintain a close guard' (Govan, Nicholson & Normington, 2007, p. 107). *Making A Performance* then explores a range of approaches to making site-based performance both for found spaces and for theatre-designated studios, including Pina Bausch's research into everyday life and leisure performances; Grid Iron's stripping away of the decor of a large house divided into bedsitting rooms to an almost abstract space; the conviviality of Lone Twin 'heightening an awareness of the possibility of being both a stranger and an inhabitant of a place' (p. 125); the fluid subversions of Space Hijackers who are as active in changing the meaning of presence as in making a product of performance; IOU and the exigencies of creating performance in a functioning hospital; and Rona Lee's multi-form *The Encircling of a Shadow* (2001) on the Cornish coastline, UK, drawing in community performers for a singing to the sea of the women's names – 'Our Margaret, Jackie, Rose' – painted on the prows of local boats.

The breadth of the techniques, approaches and outcomes is instructive. Sometimes the same tactics (say, a devotion to participant observation as a research method, or the deployment of local contemporary 'legends') crop up across different working methods or stylistic performance products, perhaps informed by similar philosophies of space and place. While, in very general terms, some practitioners cluster closer to live art while others are more similar to a 'matrixed' theatre tradition, there is no orthodoxy to follow and little evidence of the usefulness of grouping companies and individuals together; instead, the account given by Govan, Nicholson and Normington is much closer to a variegated toolkit or palette from which a reader might borrow certain ideas, techniques or images without committing themselves to a holistic performance practice. There is variation not just from country to country, or region to region, but within localities; however, the absence of *formal* homogeneity does not imply that there are not cultural gaps or the privileging of certain assumptions about what is or is not suitable or valorised content, cultural voice or effective presence.

7

Personae, Presences, Characters

There is no generic right or wrong performance mode, style or discipline for a participant in a site-specific performance. Such is the argument of the preceding chapter, based partly on the almost infinite range of possible aesthetic approaches and the multiplicity of possible sites. However, there is also some sense, stronger perhaps outside of performance-designated buildings than within them, that a performer (no matter how masked or scripted) is always performing their personal presence, even their 'inner self', as much as any fiction, script or bare list of tasks. That, given their vulnerability as people – animals and citizens – in a less controlled performance environment, no matter how florid the characterisation or functional the action, the dislocation from an authorised performance space, somehow more pointedly exposes the performer's performance of themselves.

Erving Goffman's initiatory work in this area, published in *The Presentation of Self in Everyday Life* (1959), argued that any individual gives meaning to themselves in everyday life by how they 'present' a self to an audience of others. There is always an element of performativity, in the sense later given by Judith Butler (1990) in everyday life; an individual's identity is being created by, rather than simply represented by, their performing it.

Just as a place has a history, no human presence (no matter how deep within) is neutral, but is always unfolding as part of, and with, the space around it. The performer is also a landscape, or more correctly is threaded throughout, but not wholly coterminous with, one. Never wholly identical to their environment, nevertheless an individual practices 'an embedded and engaged being-in-the-world that comes before any thought of the world or of landscape as merely an eternal object. Body and environment fold into and co-construct each other' (Wylie, 2007, p. 144). In that engagement it may be that what you choose to perform in a site-specific work of theatre is not a character or persona, and not even, primarily, a presence, but, rather, the effects of what the site does to you by your being in it: 'collapsing, rising, falling ... the symptoms of ... engagement' (Pearson, 2006, p. 173).

If in your performance you attempt to adopt too rigid a portrayal of character and identity, as if these were fixed or given by forces independent of your site, there is a danger that you may light up a set of ideological dominances to delight an audience hungry to have its assumptions affirmed (assuming that they recognise your imposition on the space as matching the fantasies they have to do the same), but puzzle and alienate one that does not have access or sympathy to them. Taking the dictum of the Dutch planner Aldo Van Eyck (1959), that 'Whatever space and time mean, place and occasion mean more ... space in the image of man is place[,] and time in the image of man is occasion', you might consider what is the 'occasion' of your character, persona or presence. Van Eyck did not by 'occasion' mean simply an event, an isolated occurrence, but rather a 'participation in what exists' (cited in Lammers, p. 57) which oscillates in and out of a site through memory, given that an 'occasion-experience ... will tend to resist being exclusively tied in memory to the particular location where it took place. It may shift to quite another place ... it may shift back ... each occasion, each object is as it were transformed by other places, other occasions' (p. 58). While performers, like audiences, bring their own 'baggage' – mental and emotional – into a site, and become part of its 'occasion', their tricky challenge is to identify the arrival and returns of 'memory' for their performance persona and for their site, then choosing and embodying the points where these meet in their performance, thus participating in the 'experienced time' (p. 58) of a particular place.

Creating a genuinely site-specific performance presence, persona or character is, then, a performative act that emerges in the same way, and at the same time, as a performer's understanding of the margins and mesh-works of their space unfolds. Attempts to make personae for site-based arts have never been characterised by any kind of orthodoxy or consistency. While disciplines and individual techniques may serve well from site to site, even where there are categorical differences between the spaces, there is always the likelihood that imported performance skills will dominate, block, disappear or cancel out the qualities of a new site that do not 'fit' the imported skills; or, vice versa, the qualities of the new site will disastrously trip up the performance skills. A repeated style might help to 'brand' a company's identity, and gratify those audiences returning to see the company in a new site for 'more of the same', but it may also sit uncomfortably with the practice of specificity and at cross-purposes with the drive away from homogenised product and commercial packaging which inspired site-specific arts in the first place. It may not be bad, or wrong, but it may be becoming something else.

Paradoxically, then, there is, as yet, no specific acting or performance method, particular to site-specific performance. Instead, there are many practices upon which to draw, in different combinations and with different levels of intensity. So, instead of a discipline to master, this chapter offers different approaches to performance as examples along a continuum of further possibilities.

Autobiographical and autoethnographic presences

It might seem common sense that one of the most straightforward, literal and direct ways to perform the specificity of a place is to choose a site that constitutes a landscape of your own life story (or a significant part thereof). Yet it should be noted how few of the autobiographical performances that are described as 'site-specific' are ever strictly that. Bobby Baker's autobiographical *Kitchen Show* (1991), which makes reference to Baker's own kitchen, was staged in other people's kitchens; *On the Scent* (see Chapter 6) relied heavily on its performers' autobiographies (particularly on reminiscences about the older generations of their families and their homes) but was sited in the houses of other people (Heddon,

2008, p. 89). Carl Lavery's *Mourning Walk* crossing Leicestershire and Lincolnshire, UK, to mark the anniversary of his father's death was performed to audiences in theatre spaces in Lancaster, UK (2006/2008; Lavery, 2009, pp. 25–40). Mike Pearson's *Bubbling Tom* is a rare (and fleeting) exception to this side-stepping of literal autobiographical place as the site of performance.

Perhaps it is the doubled stress of presenting a self, directly, and then to underline that self-exposure in the raw space of the events narrated or re-enacted, that shifts performers away from the literal places of their autobiography. Scholar of autobiographical performance, Dee Heddon expresses discomfort at even the generic confinement of Baker's work: 'I … admit to resenting the constraints apparently placed on Baker's creativity which oblige her to so persistently transform her everyday into moments of aesthetic pleasure. (Oh, if she could only go for a walk around the streets of London)' (2008, p. 119). How much more uncomfortable, then, if the confinement were to the literal places of that everyday life? Such spaces are, perhaps, simultaneously too close and too distant; too unmediated in terms of their location and yet too distant in terms of the events there being now in a past that is not now there and therefore no longer present. Performers, by choice or instinct, seem to mostly avoid this tearing of space from time.

This suggests that performers exploring site-based work for the first time should exercise a certain wariness about the rawness or nakedness of their performance and its place. Space is never neutral, but the spatial host of autobiographical performance may be particularly loaded. Just as the sacramental bread of 'the host' in Christian ritual is simultaneously ordinary, magical and subject to horrific conflicts around and about its status, so the places of your past (or present) despite their apparent ordinariness (for most performers) may shelter revenants that will remain dormant until stirred by the intensities of performance. Unusual states of performance presence, or the consequences of re-enactment (with the possibility of, paradoxically, revealing more than the original events) may raise a ghostly host. Significantly, when Dee Heddon explains her concept of 'autotopography', the landscape of autobiography, she describes something that is as active and self-reflexive as a production of a new space in a familiar place: 'writing place through self (and simultaneously writing self through place)' (2008, p. 91).

Svetlana Boym described the doubleness of nostalgia as 'a sentiment of loss and displacement, but ... also a romance with one's own fantasy' (2017, p. 1) and there is no reason to believe that other non-nostalgic orientations to the past are incapable of being similarly doubled, self-reflexive and generative. The past might seem to be safest when most precisely, and with least fabrication, fixed to a site; yet in practice this seems fraught with dangers, in both success and failure. In the latter case, Melanie Bennett describes the process of memory recall in autobiographical performance as 'like an intensely nostalgic activity because it must always fail in its attempt to return to the past, to remember its desired object' (Bennett, 2013, p. 54), while in the case of the former, though hardly sinister, Pearson describes how the success of engagement and recall in *Bubbling Tom* became problematical, when despite his having 'learned a long text, in itself a feat of memory ... I can barely get a word in edgeways. I am constantly interrupted by others with additions to, and corrections and contradictions of, my story' (2006, p. 22) as his mother and other relatives and residents were empowered to remember and to share.

My own experiences in devising and performing autobiographical pieces, such as *The Crab Walks* (2004), were, like Bennett's, characterised by a failure to recapture memories and feelings despite revisiting places I had known well in my childhood and my inability (occasionally farcically so) to gain physical access to others (Smith, 2009, pp. 57–80). This abjection, and the new adventures that emerged as I became distracted from my original intention, constituted the narratives of my performance; the obstructions provided by grumpy hoteliers or my own loss of memory became the antagonists to my solo presence. It thus became possible to displace a potentially psychologically conflicted performance (about my relationship to my family) to the narrative contest; the struggle to make the performance, thanks to its reflexivity, became the dramatic tension it required. This released me (as a performer and a person) from an obligation to repeat intimate inner conflicts except as I chose to dramatise them metaphorically or allusively in the narrative. This is similar to Melanie Bennett's 'dramaturgy of failure ... that not only animate[s] the theme of failure (collapsed relationships, unsuccessful gender performance, broken families...) ...but performances that use a form of representation that falters, unravels' (2013, p. 47). With such a dynamic, the performer shares a certain 'practised amateurism' with the audience, owning up to their own uncertainty as both deviser and deliverer of the drama, doing battle with their own limitations and, at the same time, exposing the difficulties of the geographical and emotional territory they are attempting to navigate.

Through this kind of reflexive form, an autobiographical performer might create a theatrical displacement of the trauma of difficult emotional content to the more controllable fissures within art making. This shifty (hidden or non-explicit) and shifting self-protective strategy perhaps explains why there is such displacement in so many site-based autobiographical performances. Canadian theatre scholar Jenn Stephenson describes a similar strategy in TJ Dawe's *Totem Figures* (2008). Once again, the bounds and location of the site are fraught; although the show was performed in theatres and studios, Stephenson describes it as 'a rare piece of site-specific autobiographical performance' (2010, p. 53), for TJ Dawe is a well-known solo performer on the Canadian fringe theatre circuit, so these stages *are* his autobiographical sites when he deals with himself as performer, and the content of *Totem Figures* concerns his conflict around his continued presence there.

In each of the above cases, avoiding a fabricated or psychologically driven 'actorly' performance in itself did not bring their performers to a naked 'live art' rawness, but rather to a dramaturgical strategy around mistakes and inadequacies that hides the 'hidden self' and speaks in simple, yet oblique terms. In Dawe's case these terms were the totem figures of his show's title: key figures (a personal Mount Rushmore) through which, or in relation to whom, Dawe felt he had lived out his own life (including Jesus, his father, Luke Skywalker and Charles Bukowski). Jenn Stephenson contextualises *Totem Figures* in a celebrity culture in which for many 'it is the quotidian life of the actor that attracts our curiosity. Our desire is for contact with the real' (2010, p. 49); and yet (or perhaps this desire is driven by the fact) the usual relations of an artist or performer to 'home' or 'community' in the entire capitalist era have been ones of alienation, exile and displacement.

In October 1966 the slag heap of coal waste from the mine at Aberfan in Wales collapsed and slid down the mountain into the village, killing 144 people including 116 young pupils in the village school. I was ten years old at the time, living in an industrial English city 120 miles away, yet the news affected me and my friends sufficiently for us to stage an improvised performance in our garage, using whatever was in there as our props and scenery; the 'box office' takings from the audience, comprising parents and neighbours, were sent to the disaster fund. It was my first site-specific performance, and though I would return to similarly intimate and personal spaces (our back garden [*Bubbleworld*, 1999], my attic office [*Forest Vague Panic*, 2001]), and although much of my work has included autobiographical content, it is more usually, and in conformity with the general trend I am describing, performed distant from, or at least to the side of, the sites of that life.

In 1984, as a result of support work for striking miners in Wales, I met and became friends with Mogg Williams, a retired miner and poet. Still living in the pit village Ogmore Vale, where he was born, grew up and worked, Mogg wrote directly of his experience. In the 1980s and 1990s I attended some of his 'poetry readings' in local social clubs; these consisted of someone calling for order, someone else might sing a song and then Mogg – who would be there on other nights when he was not reading – would read his poems to a silent and intently focused working-class audience, defiant and almost defeated:

> While you spin remember blind wheel
> The dreams you crushed when I was young. (Williams, 1996, p. 45)

And then he would read of Aberfan. Finally, after the applause, the club members would return to their pints. There was no sense of Mogg's performance as an interruption in the life of the club; it was an intensification of the anger and experience already there. The individuals described in some of the poems were present in the room.

Although the 'community play' movement, beginning with the pioneering work of the UK's Colway Theatre Trust, established by Ann Jellicoe in 1979, has repeatedly established the capabilities of non-trained local performers to engage audiences with performances based on local themes and issues, this human resource has been, paradoxically, far less engaged by site-specific theatre and performance makers. It remains a possibility; for the meantime, most examples of autobiographical site-specific performance are more mediated; either by re-voicing or displacement.

The 'Womanhouse' project (Los Angeles, USA, 1972) is an example of performance makers' direct personal experiences mediated through a site, which though not the specific location of those experiences, was discovered, negotiated, repaired and prepared by the performers; and was at least generically significant in relation to their experiences. The site in question was an abandoned and dilapidated mansion in downtown Los Angeles, secured for a short time prior to its demolition for the use of the women students on the California Institute for the Arts Feminist Program led by artists/educators Judy Chicago and Miriam Shapiro.

There was a strong autobiographical steer at the heart of the project with 'Chicago and Shapiro emphasiz[ing] authentic art content: art that came from experience' (Crawford, 2016). By choosing an abject home that had been abandoned and left to rot, the students had entered a problematised generic space of domesticity, which, despite their repairs, was both ambiguous and gender-significant. Despite lacking either plumbing or heating, the students repaired walls and floors, added partitions to create new spaces and cleared debris for performances and the installation of mixed-media environments. Their interventions varied in their approach to the generic significance of the building: some chose to celebrate the domestic crafts and labour that might once have been practised there (the final resident had been an elderly woman living alone); some to satirise and protest the generic home's confining, trivialising and limiting of women to domestic roles; while others still were driven by an aesthetics of 'excess … the women asked themselves: [what] would it be like if a woman kept on crocheting, if she never stopped, if she crocheted a whole room?' with the strategic intent that 'it is in this excess that the gendered activities and roles begin to break down through humor and suffering' (Crawford, 2016).

The various performance pieces created for the 'Womanhouse' were devised during, and supported by, workshops with Judy Chicago, in which the student artists were encouraged to draw from their own experiences. The pieces were performed in the former living room of the partially repaired mansion. Three of these – *Cock and Cunt Play* with its display and manipulation of prosthetic genitals; *Three Women* in which real experiences slowly emerged through a facade of exaggerated costuming and stereotypical 'types' of hustler, hippie-chick and maternal young woman; and the choral movements of *The Birth Trilogy* – were extrovert in their theatricality and symbolism, deploying broad generic characters and energised but untrained physicality characteristic of agit-prop street theatre. For these performances, the living room functioned as much as a substitute theatre studio as a revenant of its previous life as a domestic space; despite a grotesque pertinence to domestic oppression.

However, in two pieces – *Waiting* and *Maintenance* – the relationship was quite different. There was a more direct and literal relation to the site of the mansion and to the room; the performances were restrained, allowing the performers to draw the space into their pieces and set it to work for them. For *Waiting*, artist Faith Wilding sat in a draped chair, its short back giving her very little support, before an exposed and fireless hearth, as she quietly and plainly recounted different orders of female waiting: 'Waiting for him to give me pleasure …Waiting for the children to grow up and leave home … Waiting to have some time to myself … Waiting for life to begin … Waiting for the struggle to end' (1971, n.p.). The slow aggregation of still intensity was such that 'the sense of a life deferred, leaves audiences stunned … everyone was deeply moved' (Gerhard, 2013, pp. 59, 62). The effect of the directness of the performance was all the more powerful for its siting in the derelict home of an absent woman owner, a house awaiting its own destruction.

In *Maintenance*, domestic tasks – the scrubbing of the living room's large polished wooden floor, the performer on her knees and with head bowed, and the meticulous and repeated ironing of large white sheets – were acted, more functionally than expressively. What was normalised and end-driven in everyday life was made critical and observably oppressive when enacted repeatedly within the hollowed shell of the former living room. The ironing action in *Maintenance* was reinforced in the site by the proximity of an installation in a linen closet made by the performer; behind the doors of this closet was a female figure attempting to escape a cupboard full of folded linen, striding out but restrained by shelves that still held her body by the neck, chest and waist.

Although these performances were confined to a single room within the 'Womanhouse', they were seen by spectators in the context of their negotiating the many rooms of the house, from a kitchen with a surreal ceiling of fried eggs turning into breasts through a collectively created sensuous and utopian dining room filled with images of consumption and pleasure to a 'menstruation bathroom'. The immersive experience of the spectators, often wrapped in the kinds of imagery associated with dreams, fantasy and excess, seems to have empowered female visitors and women-only audiences who felt they had 'walked into what was essentially their "home ground"' (Gerhard, 2013, p. 64) while troubling many of the men, when there were mixed audiences, who seemed to struggle 'to know how to show their response' even when they wanted to be supportive (p. 62).

During its month-long existence 'Womanhouse' was visited by audiences numbering many thousands; away from a conventional or institutional arts setting the project attracted women's groups, high school classes and other visitors who might otherwise have been discouraged by a formal venue. There were insufficient precedents to mark the choice of a derelict mansion as a 'cool' space solely for intellectuals and an 'art crowd'. Once the project was over, the installations were broken up and the house was demolished; the events, objects and sensations of the missing house made way for their repeated retellings in publications and documentaries, but most significantly by word of mouth in a form that Rutgers University archivist Stephanie Crawford has characterised as 'something akin to a feminist myth … passed from [one] feminist campfire girl to the next'; 'myth' here not in the sense of untruth, but a 'structure to understand something incomprehensible' (Crawford, 2016).

The project was not without its tensions between teachers and students, and between individuals. Despite detailed reminiscences and dissident re-tellings turning up significant wrinkles (meaningfully resonant with the ambiguities of space in *Mobile Homestead*, discussed next), the transformation into 'myth' of events in the physical space of 'Womanhouse' is highly significant for site-based performance in general. Given the innovative creative relations; the intensity and directness of the impact of the house's environments; the embodied witnessing of spectators; sensitivity to the mansion as a fluid space through which visitors could move impulsively; the tension between the generic and the specific in and between the performances; and the particular moment in the popular unfolding of second-wave feminism from which 'Womanhouse' emerged, any one of these elements might have seemed 'incomprehensible' to many people at the time and constituted a resource for making *a new imaginary space* (a 'myth', if you like). The women's assemblage of site and performance has retained an almost corporeal spatial coherence in many imaginations ever since, despite (and because of) the demolition of the site itself. While the 'new space' of 533 Mariposa Street, in the sense of its redevelopment for new residential dwellings, was unaffected by 'Womanhouse', another kind of new space was created: something imaginary, utopian and certainly prefigurative of other possible spaces, conceptual and material.

An autobiographical presence or motivation is no guarantor of authenticity and efficacy. Taking the autobiographical out of a private space may be brave, but it is not of necessity honest, nor straightforward. Mike Kelley's rigorously self-critical account of his installation *Mobile Homestead* is exemplary in acknowledging the sorts of difficult, sometimes painful, complexities that can arise once an artist chooses to express a 'simple truth' about their relation to the world. Kelley's *Mobile Homestead* (completed 2013, after Kelley's death in 2012) is a gesture of reversal of the white flight from the disinvested inner city of Detroit to the suburbs where Kelley grew up. Kelley, contrarily, re-sited a to-scale copy of his childhood suburban home back to the abject centre of the city as both a work of public art and a demonstration of the failure of public art; of the incapacity of public art to play the socially efficacious role it sometimes claims for itself. Rather than an embodied performance, Kelley created a space for others to perform and perform in.

Mike Kelley described *Mobile Homestead* in contradictory terms; it was 'Turning my childhood home into an "art gallery/community center" … [as] a sign for social concern, performed in bad faith' (Kelley, cited in Anderson & Haley, 2014). The installation's main building is open for community use; however, beneath it there is a labyrinthine basement – its tunnels and cubbyholes of autobiographical significance for Kelley given his childhood access to such spaces thanks to his father's work as a school janitor (see Miller, 2017) – access to which is restricted to the artist's friends and to other artists. It is a space described by Kelley as designated for 'private rites of an aesthetic nature' (Kelley cited by Miller, 2017).

The significance of *Mobile Homestead* for site-specific theatre and performance is worth consideration; in relation to both scenography and performer presence. On the one hand, in the installation there is a public engagement and an autobiographical entanglement of private experience with a grand (and pernicious) sweep of social change; this is staged in (and by) an everyday and, to all appearances, domestic space. In *Mobile Homestead* the space itself becomes the performer of its meaning; partly by its appearance and partly by its mobility and the social tension provoked by its shift of site, from historical to performative. On the other hand, there is the intimate and private space, a second or secondary stage, that is never fully or publicly revealed and yet is the more rooted or founded of the two stages; the primary public performing-stage being reliant on the secondary secret stage both for its structural integrity and for the bitter dynamic that generates the 'drama' (the doing) of the two spaces as one artwork. Kelley stages, but does not resolve, the displacement of artist from community within a drama of mass social displacement and division enacted in and by Detroit.

In some sense, are site-specific performers also 'mobile homesteads'? Is the dramatic impact of their performances, in their presently dominant modes, no matter how transparent, deadpan or downbeat their style, reliant as much upon the raw and inarticulate energy of inner and secret selves that we keep and, if we are to believe psychologists like Christopher Bollas (1987, pp. 246–47) and Josh Cohen (2013, pp. 6–8, 20) should keep, hidden, as on a wholly raw exposure of the performance environs in which an only ever partial and crafted revelation is enacted?

While an autobiographical presence seems a commonsensical, if psychically and spatially challenging, approach to making site-specific performance, there is an alternative that sits close to its subjectivity, yet is less closely focused to the theatre maker's self. This is auto-ethnographic performance; drawing on the (only recently generally acknowledged) virtues of this particular ethnography, in which the subjectivity of the researcher is the medium of the research, if not the subject of it; part of an ongoing experiment with 'what social sciences would become if they were closer to literature than physics, if they proffered stories rather than theories' (Adams, Ellis & Bochner, 2010, p. 1). The auto-ethnographer investigates their subject by exploring their own reactions to it through self-reflection and, often, in writing about their experiences. Often an auto-ethnographer, rather than seeking out unfamiliar situations to study, will investigate their own familiar groups or spaces through their experiences of and in them. This is not an exclusively mental reflection; auto-ethnography offers a way of expressing 'more fully the interactional textures occurring between self, other, and contexts … concentrating on the body as the site from which the story is generated' (Spry, 2001, p. 706).

While it has emerged as a practice in itself, auto-ethnography's characteristic features are present in more conventional ethnographies. Martin Hammersley and Paul Atkinson, who define ethnography as 'an integration of both first-hand empirical investigation and the theoretical and comparative interpretation of social organisation and culture', suggest the relevance of this research discipline for an autobiographical and subjective theatre, particular when sited, acknowledging how 'there is no sharp distinction even between ethnography and the study of individual life histories, as the example of "auto/ethnography" shows, this referring to an individual researcher's study of his or her own life and its context' (p. 1).

For performance maker Melanie Bennett, site-specific performances carry certain ethnographic qualities in their 'interdisciplinary approach and tendency toward animating the historical, social and spatial dimensions of an environment' (2012). She has described how in her *Garden/Suburbia* (co-created with Hartley Jafine Aaron Collier and Andy Houston), authorised and informal memorials in the Lawrence Park area of Toronto were chosen and then reinvented through the experiences of the performance makers, locals and audience. This ambulatory performance included recorded audio elements, live guiding and audience participation. At one point along the route, the audience were invited to wander off alone and make their own auto-ethnographic exploration of the neighbourhood, encouraged on their return to compare their experiences, contrasting Lawrence Park with their own home communities.

At the site of a small home threatened with demolition and replacement by a larger one, the audience's guides – Bennett and Jafine – clashed, drawing upon contrasting experiences of the nurturing capacities of smaller working class homes and the spacious houses of the wealthy. These associations were then woven into those expressed to the performance makers by local residents. So, for example, Bennett narrated an encounter with a local senior over a tree stump: the man valorised the obstruction as a welcome revenant of what had been there, while to Bennett it conjured abject associations with the protective canopy of the 'family tree': 'I just wanted someone to acknowledge that the tree wasn't as strong and protective as we thought. But they continued living as if the tree was continuing to widen with the years of memory' (2012).

Discordant elements in *Garden/Suburbia* – the contradictions of gentrification in Bennett's semi-utopian neighbourhood, frustrations turned up by her auto-ethnography, feeling unable to say certain things, and the collapse of the conventions of tour-guiding with her and Jafine unable to agree on the meaning of the place they are narrating – fit Bennett's aesthetics of failure (discussed above). In *Garden/Suburbia* the various collapses of conventions and assumptions were crises that opened gaps into which the site could perform itself and the audience enter more intensely into the space. Bennett, who describes herself as a 'failure aficionado' (2014, p. 126), has noted the efficacy of a kind of amateurism; how a certain open ineptness can serve a performance. Eschewing 'the prejudiced and narrow model of a "professional" theatre actor', a product of a '"country club" acting programme' (2014, pp. 128, 129), Bennett, empathises with inexpert, lay performance-making processes in which 'Human awkwardness and malfunctions are mandated' (2014, p. 129).

Such are the canny, yet apparently naive, tactics of Marcia Farquhar who leads and stumbles, combining authority and vulnerability, cheek and poetry, in her 2010 walking performance *To The Shelter* in Margate (UK). The performance marks the writing of part of T.S. Eliot's long poem *The Waste Land* in a large cast-iron beach-side shelter in 1921. Farquhar leads her audience towards the sea as she bumbles/declaims: 'Margate Sands ... th... it's obvious I know, but it's a marvellous ... I don't really want to get in your way here, but I can't help it.' Her audience are caught somewhere between engagement, amusement and embarrassment, and must think into the spaces that Farquhar leaves un-narrated.

Her stumbles are the moments where the audience must link her thoughts with their own intuitions of the meanings of the place. The studied awkwardness does not derail the performance, but jerks assumptions about how it should progress, interrupting the expected flow with hiccups and uncertainties ('I would imagine', 'allegedly') and a sudden reaching for an elusive idea; these are moments that draw the audience into the making as well as the consuming of the piece.

In such stutters, a performer tests the performance against their own experiencing of it. Marcia Farquhar tells the story of Vivienne Eliot, in a state of mental breakdown, pouring molten chocolate through the letter box of her husband's employers. She pauses and then muses aloud on the practicalities of preparing, transporting and pouring such a liquid; testing the story against her own experiences, expectations and associations. By making bathetic spaces – the venerated, but banal shelter, a public lavatory with a large sign for TOILETS (an anagram of T.S. Eliot) – the sites for her celebration of a modernist classic (which itself frames and samples just such everyday ordinariness), Farquhar creates a nervous comedy through which a narrative of breakdown catches the audience without supplying an easy way to process it. At the conclusion, Farquhar apologises: 'thank you, I must rush back to the next... ' and she struggles for what to say, then, 'congregation'. In a final word – whether intended and momentarily forgotten, or plucked from the air in the moment – she upsets both the audience's picture of themselves and the framing of her own event; cultural connoisseurs are jerked into rethinking themselves as spiritual devotees, on a journey not unlike a part of Eliot's own.

In an auto-ethnographic context, failures, malfunctions, cowardice or avoidance are differently significant from other more conventional disciplinary contexts. Because the auto-ethnographer must slide between their context, their research itself and their self, when things fail they still reveal, they still count as findings of significance rather than unproductive non-events or dead ends. Indeed, at times, they constitute findings that less reflexive disciplines find difficult to identify or collect. In site-specific performance, because a similar reflexivity (particularly in autobiographically inflected performance) applies, short of someone being hurt 'nothing can go wrong'; mistakes and accidents can be as expressive and precisely communicative as a smoothly run show. While in a building-based theatre, a carefully developed atmosphere can be broken by a sneeze, if a site-based performance is sufficiently porous, and structured to account for the agency of its site, unexpected disruptions, interventions, unravellings and malfunctions can further open the pores of the performance, and are as likely to add to and unfold the performance as damage or diminish it.

Ablative presences

Rather than any version of realism or mimetic representation (such as characterises even the most radical of the autobiographical presences, as described above), 'non-matrixed performance' steps *aside* from any such processes. In the context of site-specific art, this means to eschew tapping directly into the energy of a site, either by representing, reproducing or amplifying it. Such a sidestepping is considered in various forms by Mike Pearson who speculates on 'what might be the nature of performance prefixed with *clam*, unknown to; *ob*, in front of; *juxta*, close to; *penes*, in the power of? Or, in the prepositional *ablative* indicating rest: performance "in the presence of", "together with", "adjacent to" the site?' (2012, p. 81) Responses to such suggestions might range from a task-based 'stage-hand' presence described by Michael Kirby in 'happenings' to an abstinent or stoic disruption in a more conventional mode like that of TigerLion Arts' *Nature: A Walking Play* (2016, Lisle, Illinois, USA and touring parks and gardens), where a conventionally representational dialogue scene about a coming railroad between actors impersonating Henry David Thoreau and Ralph Waldo Emerson was interrupted by a train-like procession of percussion-playing performers emerging from woodland surrounds (Illustration 7.1).

In 1959 Allan Kaprow created *18 Happenings in 6 Parts* for the Reuben Gallery in New York. This projected into the public realm artists', choreographers' and composers' experiments with 'happenings' initiated at Black Mountain College (North Carolina, USA) in the early 1950s. From the start of this experimental work, creating these closely planned events with their contained improvisatory passages, striking visual actions and elements of specificity to their sites – empty houses, car parks, woods, and so on – their organisers and fabricators had problems with performers. Allan Kaprow tried to work with trained actors who were experienced in performing experimental theatre; despite their familiarity with

Illustration 7.1   The 'progress machine' from TigerLion Arts' *Nature,* a walking play about Emerson, Thoreau, and their mutual love of the natural world.
Photo: Winslow Townson Photography.

avant-garde performance, Kaprow found that many of the actors were uneasy about performing without 'parts' or roles, that they wanted to impress the spectators and that some wanted to 'star'. So he turned to his friends, painters rather than performers, and then to volunteers at art galleries and found these much easier to work with. Kaprow believed that painters were more suitable than actors because 'they sensed the origins of what they were doing in painting and felt they were almost acting out planes, spacing and images' (1965, p. 48).

Theatre scholar Michael Kirby characterised the most appropriate mode of performance for a 'happening' as similar to that of the stage hands who change scenery on stage and in view of an audience during a break in the action, or that of the wardrobe assistants who enter an acting area in view of the audience in order to help a performer change their costume (p. 40). Such a 'non-performer' is aware that they are being watched, but they are not trying to convey any message or motivation (other than completion of their task), and they certainly do not want to 'star'; they are organised, they have certain actions to carry out and they do these as efficiently as they can. Another analogy would be with an athlete in a competition who has things to do, is organised, is aware of the spectators, and yet focused more on carrying out set tasks than representing or considering their significance (Kaprow, 2003, pp. 63–64).

This approach affects more than just performance presence, serving as a means to developing a relationship with a particular site. Emma Govan, Helen Nicolson and Katie Normington note that the company members of Lone Twin, Gary Winters and Gregg Whelan, have acknowledged how 'the physical labour that they undertake within a place gives them a clear function within that setting and relate that to de Certeau's theorisation of a subject's agency arising through "ways of operating" within a space' (2007, p. 123) (Illustration 7.2).

Illustration 7.2 *Sledge Hammer Songs*, Lone Twin, 2005. Railway Workshops @ National Review of Live Art, Midland (WA).

Photo: Lone Twin.

One of the main (and continuing) misunderstandings about happenings is that they were mostly improvised. In fact, while performers were often given plenty of freedom in deciding how they were going to carry out the action-tasks set for them, these were contained within the 'compartments' (both spatial and temporal) of the happening's text; performers were rarely asked to make anything up during a performance, but were mostly expected to have prepared their contribution in some detail beforehand. Only in avoiding tripping up or hurting another performer, or in some engagement where one section overlapped with another, were performers expected to respond in a spontaneous manner to each other. Mostly, there was an attempt to keep the individual sections and action unconnected, even disconnected, from existing performance conventions of any kind; traditional or experimental. The separate sections were played out mostly *alongside* each other, in tune with Pearson's suggestions above, rather than in consequential sequences, thematic unfolding or an overlapping entanglement.

The makers of such happenings often favoured everyday activities, whether highly skilled or routine, or appropriations from more popular arts such as the use of aerial performance more common to circus than text-based theatre. Michael Kirby described these kinds of action and presence as 'non-matrixed performance' (1972/1995, p. 41). Unlike an actor in a theatre-based play, or even one improvising within conventions, such as in a Commedia dell'Arte improvisation – in which the actor performed within a matrix of texts, traditions and memories of former performances – the 'non-matrixed' mode involved the performer in carrying out actions that were indeterminate, actions that sat between conventions and were unconstrained by them.

Any subversion of the dominance of performance by a naturalistic representational or psychologically founded realism will chime with Bertolt Brecht's 'epic theatre' project (despite its repeated disparagement and misrepresentation) to demonstrate *what* happens and *why*, rather than impersonate the personalities in an event. Epic theatre disrupts any seamless weave of occurrences and psychology in order to uncover their contexts and represent their conditions not by recreating their appearance in everyday life, but by 'mak[ing] them strange … uncovering … by processes being interrupted' (Benjamin, 1973, p. 18).

While most realisms are passive, retrospectively enacting or reenacting and portraying the inevitability of events by a morbid invocation of the components of their pasts, epic theatre seeks to hang onto the instability and contingency of their former present-ness – the actor 'must be free, at the right moment, to act himself thinking (about his part)' (Benjamin, 1973, p. 21) – despite their transition to representation. By disrupting inevitability, the actions of the characters, more quoted than behaved, consist of the dynamic between their choice-making and the forces that bear upon them, with the possibility that change, from subjective to social-structural levels, might result in a different outcome to the one portrayed. In this sense epic theatre is dialectical; it should always contain the possibility of its opposite. This is exemplified in one of the building blocks of 'epic theatre', the street scene (Brecht, 1964, pp. 121–29) in which a performer impersonates a passer-by explaining the events, actions, motivations, meaning and consequences of a road accident to a crowd who may or may not have witnessed these events. Brecht was keen that this not be performed too well by the witness in case 'the bystanders' attention were drawn to his (*sic*) powers of transformation'; instead it should be a repetition without flourish, allowing the wrinkles, oppressive forces and contradictions at work in the event to re-emerge through the 'straight-faced' restraint of the re-telling. Augusto Boal and Panagiotis Assimakopoulos's 'invisible theatre' covertly generated such events for a street audience who were allowed to assume that the events unfolding before them were real and spontaneous, and were encouraged by the covert actors to debate the meaning of what they saw.

While this is not the place for a detailed exposition of 'epic theatre', it is worth noting that its technical elements are driven by an attention to their relation to space and to material (including bodily) processes. The well-known 'distancing' devices of titles, half-curtains, cartoon-like costuming or acting in quotation marks that serve to expose the mechanics of fabricating a drama (adding these to the constructed intensity of the emotional connection between actor and audience) also apply to the performers' and space's co-construction of their relationship: exploitative, aggressive, harmonious, cooperative, conflicted, or whatever. Thus the effect of making everyday things strange (the *verfremdungseffeckt*) includes disrupting any assumptions about any site/performer relationship as natural or inevitable.

Such contingency might at first appear at odds with the idea of specificity to a site, with its apparent implications for a certain homologous relationship of place to action: the performance channelling the site, the one equivalent to the other. However, in theories of space and place, like Massey's, portraying a site as un-made and unfinished, the disruption of epic acting can be an equivalence to the incompleteness of space. What seems inevitable, commonsensical and natural is subject to a crisis in which the possibility of its reversal, negation or transformation is imagined and performed being imagined.

In such a performance, the actor betrays and outrages their site; their narrative or projection of character or persona exposes the same contingency in the apparent material solidity of the location as in their own actions (which might partly explain the attraction of sites in ruin or of those in transition between different uses). An example of an epic and situated performance is *CauseWay* (2014) written by Victoria Bianchi; a performance in and around the Robert Burns Birthplace Museum and Cottage in Alloway (Scotland) that 'celebrated' the centenary of a failed attempt by two suffragettes to blow up Burns's former cottage with pipe bombs. Not only did the performance set out to destabilise the 'androcentric heritage narrative' (Bianchi, 2015, p. 55) perpetuated by and in the Museum site, but invoked the volatile qualities ('radical protest … terrorism' [p. 57]) of the narrative: failure, anonymity, secrecy, ambiguity, silence.

The audience for *CauseWay* followed performers impersonating the two suffragettes as if on the last stage of their journey to bomb the cottage; arriving at their target the two performers narrated the space ('including an exploration of parallels between Burns's work and the suffragette cause' [p. 59]) through an imitation of historical individuals who sought but failed to demolish it; reflecting on their own portrayal and on the constraints of the performance they inhabited. In this journey-narrative, the fate of the site in one temporal dimension hangs, unrealistically, in the balance, while in another its continuity, consistency and integrity is questioned by an indictment of the skewed and exclusionary dominant narratives still at work there. In 'eschew[ing] the hierarchy between the thematic and the physical' (p. 66), favouring 'a geometric or structural engagement' over a 'thematic' one (Wilkie, 2002, p. 155), the creative team that made *CauseWay* did more than make the site archaeologically meaningful; they rendered it, by their epic method, existentially contingent. Heritage (in the sense of the inevitability of the past) was hurt where it is strongest, in the seeming resilience and integrity of what remains; 'the performance worked against a notion of the heritage space as a static, "sacred space" and offered possibilities of how such a space can be constantly reconfigured' (Bianchi, 2015, p. 70).

One approach to making an ablative performance in a site is to use a flexible system for generating actions. Mike Pearson working with Lyn Levett, John Rowley and Richard Morgan developed just such a technique of corporeal improvisation which they called *In All Languages* and which consisted of learning ten 'languages' each of which comprised of ten movements or interactions: 'four solo, three in pairs and three in groups'. Pearson describes the first solo in the system as including 'the "words" wave, clap, point, beckon, hands through hair, rub face, sit, scratch, squat, push down and out', for none of which there was any prescribed gesture or action, but rather the individual performer should provide their own interpretation, stringing the movements together in an order of their own selection. The second duo in the system, consisting of 'words' such as 'mirror, copy, model, statue, shake, push against, pull against and embrace and collapse' are intended to be used by a pair of performers as constituents of a physical call and response equivalent to a liturgy or a conversation. The quality of this exchange is one that is negotiated between the performers rather than notated in the system, though they should subject their actions to ten 'procedures' (raising or reducing energy, speeding up or slowing down) and to ten 'orders of mediation' including 'spatial confinement or increase in environmental hazard' (Pearson and Levett, 2001, pp. 82–83).

Other methodologies for developing movement, action, gesture or dance might similarly function as a means to performance in the ablative, dependent on their flexibility, reflexivity and responsiveness to the specificities of site. There may even be a 'purist' argument for insisting on performance makers creating a bespoke system for any particular site, but for many artists a more realistic approach would be adapting a sufficiently flexible existing methodology. For example, a variation on Mary Starks Whitehouse's 'authentic movement' in which a mover simplifies their actions with the help of a 'containing' witness who holds the space for the mover in response to a more varied terrain or more complex interior than the flat floor of a secure dance studio. Or perhaps, Melanie Kloetzel's reflexive and critical engagement with dominant tendencies towards serialised site-adaption (discussed in more detail in Chapter 12), performing adaption while setting it to the side for critical examination, proposing how a 'dancing body could both exhibit adaptation and draw attention to the links between global and local sites' (2017, pp. 122–23). For this work Kloetzel developed a five-point system (see 2017, p. 116) of sensitisation to the site, physical integration through movement tasks morphing into choreographic figures, repetitions informed by the site, a forefronting of the body's adaptive process to one and many sites, and departure and leaving alone.

Given the 'non-theatrical' quality of site-specific performance, in the sense that it reverses the 'disappearing' of the stage in the interests of a fiction or a performance presence and seeks to intensify the manifestation of its site, the idea of a performance 'to the side', with the performer stepping aside to allow the space to 'take the stage' may have something to offer spatially to site-specific performance. In many non-theatre-designated sites, too deep an immersion in character or interiority can either be obtrusive or puny; without the focus and disciplined space of the stage or studio, the inevitability of the psychological back story can either become swamped in information 'noise' or embarrassed by its own clunkiness in contrast to the subtle multiplicity of its space. In these sites, a certain non-engagement of character, even a certain naivety (just the doing of things) can either be disarmingly and mis-directingly (in the magician's sense) powerful – so that the 'noise' begins to work for the intervention and through an artful artlessness, disparate elements accumulate around such a character – or the only thing that is possible.

Exercise

Devise a performance presence that neither follows the logic of 'information structure' (by which the actions and psychological development of an impersonated character are followed), nor the illogic of 'character' in, say, Surrealism ('the chance meeting of a sewing machine and an umbrella') which is designed to create an alternative reality as in dreams or fantasies; instead, attempt an a-logic. Lift things and actions from a meaningful situation in a particular site and then reintroduce them into their original space, isolated from the connections that made them socially meaningful. (Avoid the temptation to make them absurd or surreal.) Then, similarly, isolate and re-enact the materials of your own body rather than their social identity. First, identify a site and situation in which your appearance generates a particular identity; then remove yourself from the site. Can you perform your material body, returning to the site, but disconnected from the matrix of conventions? Observe how conventions will try to rush back into any non-matrixed space, demanding your identification. How long can you hold them off and perform in the respite? How can you trap the conventions racing back in, re-triggering them in their extreme and predatory forms, exposing their usually covert and unassuming everyday operations?

Exercise

Perform heavily clothed. Perform lightly clothed. Perform by changing body temperature. Play hot, play cold.

Exercise

Broaden the palette of a persona's private symbolism or a character's psychology; not by looking inwards, but by working with things and materials and agents themselves disconnected from meaning-making matrices: disarranged chairs, large flimsy structures, painting or projecting movie images on bodies, street games like Kick The Can, plastic walls, children's paintings, the sounds of a steam locomotive, placards, door chimes, car horns, crashing barrels, chicken wire, ice cubes crushed under car tyres, vegetables hanging from a mouth, beating a wall with tree branches, lawn mowers, smashed dishes, a body emerging from a building, the silhouette of a cloud. Find a space with some athletic or industrial connotation: a gym, a stand or a set of bleachers, a workshop, a production line, a quarry yard, a swimming pool. Devise two sets of actions, one referencing the painting/shapes analogy, the other using the stagehands/athletes analogy – not imitating individual painters or athletes, but imitating their approach to carrying out tasks and responding to shapes and materials.

Performing character in a site

The modern realist acting methods that developed within (and largely replaced) the repertoire of melodrama were all devised to train performers for theatre-designated stages and buildings and were largely coincident with the rise of the theatre director. Most of these methods – Stanislavskian use of affective memory, epic, the 'doing' of Sanford Meisner's techniques, the expressionist and ambient tendencies of Michael Chekhov's training – were founded in some kind of theory: psychological, somatic, political or mystical. They were often called 'techniques' and their use of exercises to prepare for and scaffold the making of character reflected how technical developments, particular in lighting but also significantly in theatre architecture, had made certain kinds of acting possible. Lamps that could be closely focused, bright electrical light, intimate studios and stages 'in the round' enabled and pre-empted a subtle and restrained psychological style that was to dominate TV and film acting.

This kind of technical specialism, when removed from the platform of the illuminated stage, can come over as overly contrived or, contrastingly, overwhelmed by the 'flat', immense or baroque and distracting qualities of a site. As a teacher, I have seen plenty of compensatory smuggling of extraneous character narrative into site-based performance by students confronted by challenging sites (as an artist I still see it in my own work). This contraband characterisation is often proposed as a radical break from restrictive site-specificity, but it rarely goes much further than an entrenchment of familiar norms of masterful human dramaturgy. I have seen tatty wizards in the forest, escapees from dinner parties traipsing across the fields, sitcoms stranded on islands and rock faces. Any sort of water seems to conjure up John Everett Millais's *Ophelia* and in the city there will be someone carrying significance in a suitcase. Students are not alone in this: I have watched able and well-known TV actors struggle to even 'appear' in a site. Trained and experienced in generating dramatic tension through their connection to other human actors, I have seen performers exhibit an almost jealous response to the 'magic' of their site; unnerved and trying to seize back their audience's full attention, they became almost boorish. Any success they had in deploying techniques created to draw attention, rather than share it, only served to detach their performance (and any hope for its effectiveness) from their site.

Yet there is no special reason why psychological, naturalistic or expressionist techniques cannot be adapted for use in site-specific performances. The key to adaptation seems to be in finding space (and a role) for the site in the technique and, complementarily, finding the spatial aspect of the technique itself. Access to the motivation of any action, to a material 'why' that is emotional and desirous more than intellectual, is hugely valuable to the site-specific performance maker. For example, there is a strong spatial element in the metaphorical matrix of Stanislavski's method. The ideas (and techniques) of 'objectives' and 'super-objectives' – that 'In a play the whole stream of individual, minor objectives ... should converge to carry out the super-objective of the plot' (Stanislavski, 1988, p. 271) – suggest a line of flight or trajectory, a route through some kind of territory that is mostly not explored. While this impulse to action might begin in some kind of inner life, the will to do or to have is mostly expressed as a journey from desire to whole or partial satisfaction in an outer world.

The spatial element can be literal; for example, the desire to escape a predator might be expressed outwardly by climbing through a window or breaking through a door. Obstacles to the characters realising their objectives may be literal obstacles. Or they might be expressed – as in the case of an over-arching 'super-objective' – in the form of a spatial metaphor: 'by the end of this day this is *where* I want to be with my life!' Even when the want is concerned solely with an inner change from one emotional or spiritual state to another, the dramatic journey is rarely wholly contemplative; even in the Gnostic narrative of De L'Isle-Adam's *Axël* the modulations through varieties of melancholy have architectural implications for the onstage castle representing the body's 'tomb of the soul'.

The challenge for the site-specific performance maker who is adapting a Stanislavski-based psychological acting technique to their work is the entangling of psychological and geographical objectives. In other words, making a psychogeographical performance expressive of 'the precise laws and specific effects of the geographical environment, whether consciously organised or not, on the emotions and behavior of individuals' (Debord, 1955, p. 8). Some interweaving of human objectives and super-objectives with their equivalents in the terrain is almost inevitable in a consideration of any performance; but what site-specific performance requires is that the objectives of the terrain are not accidental, but agentive without being conscious; an acknowledgement that sites act 'not only to impede or block the will and designs of humans but also act as quasi agents or forces with trajectories, propensities, or tendencies of their own' (Bennett, 2010, p. viii).

I once observed an unintended example of exactly this at the outdoor Minack Theatre in Cornwall (UK) when a play was upstaged by the sea beyond the cliff-sited stage. The performance was of Noel Coward's play *Blithe Spirit* (1941). The organisers seemingly assumed that the sea would serve as a neutral, but atmospheric backdrop to the action. I watched only parts of the theatrical action, its competent mimetic characters unable to match the power of the storm-tossed ocean heaving and breaking in giant 'white horses' behind them. The waters performed the starring role as 'collective unconscious' or 'world soul' transforming Coward's comedy of social manners and spiritualism into something far more poetic and unlikely.

Exercise

Turn Stanislavski on his head. Improvise a character whose objectives come not from within, but by accepting the affordances of the site. This might require a certain psychic sleight of hand; perhaps imagining a character who is hollow and chameleon-like, adapting to and sinking into her immediate social and physical terrain. Or a spy, an eavesdropper, a cartographer: a pair of human quotation marks to put around a site. Turn 'pathetic fallacy' – the idea that things, including landscapes, can embody human feelings – inside out: take your cue from that cliff-side production of *Blithe Spirit*, develop a character whose 'id' is the site.

Idea

In 2000 Simon Persighetti of site-specific artists Wrights & Sites proposed 'the actor as signpost' as a bridge between more overtly theatrical work, struggling for an acting practice appropriate both to site and to hybrid characterisation, and an impetus towards site itself as a performance yet to be discovered (Smith, 2009b). The idea retains a link to performance, but does not rest on psychological acting.

In 2006 Wrights & Sites organised their second festival. Where the first, *The Quay Thing*, had employed over 20 people and generated seven substantial productions, *Exeter Everyday* was widely, but inexpensively advertised as a week-long celebration of daily life with all of Exeter's citizens as its performers, and the city was then left to perform without further intervention. The members of Wrights & Sites signposted the week of the festival, carrying sandwich boards in the high street announcing each day's theme: Monday – feet and shoes, Tuesday – beaks and paws, Wednesday – waiting, and so on. A transition from psychological acting to exoteric gesture was completed.

Persighetti has described his 'actor as signpost' concept as 're-configuring the play or position of the artist as one of guide or mis-guide through real time and space rather than as narrator or interpreter of place … a *signpost* re-framing the geography of the city in rejection of the closure of historic interpretation' (2008, p. 68). The 'actor as signpost' points performer and audience directly to the immediate site and its material specificities; it starts as a localist gesture, a grounding of the performing body in its immediate environment, its senses as active feelers-out of information, not from a passive environment, but from an environment 'ready' to feel out for the sensory-feelers of its visitors (see Gibson, 1966). This gives equal priority to site and performer, the latter of which is most valued at the sensorial edge of their being; pointing away from themselves and the internal mystery narrative of the labyrinthine subconscious.

In place of objectives the 'actor as signpost' indicates routes, paths of perception, taking the journey rather than representing it, like Francis Alÿs's objectiveless 'desperado' in *Re-enactment* (2001) deploying a Fluxus-like instruction: 'Walk for as long as you can holding a 9mm Beretta in your right hand' (Francis Alÿs, cited in Hoffmann & Jonas, 2005, p. 108). The signpost is transparent in emptying functionality from the performing body, but camouflage-like in attention to detail; so for Alÿs his risky journey was not enough and he re-enacted the piece with the assistance of the police. The signpost always continues to point outwards. It never arrives; its gesture may be localised, but not by the need to stay in proximity to the Heideggerian 'thing to hand'.

Motion is one of the signpost's key elements: the encouragement to the spectator/participant to find their own trajectory. So, the Brazilian artist

Ducha drops a huge bag of oranges among pedestrians at a busy street crossing in Rio de Janeiro, creating trajectories of helpfulness and assistance in an existing chaos, for his video work *Laranja Public Disturbance* (2002). Or Chris Burden 'flies' a 100-ton steamroller in a 1996 work, the huge machine swung around on a central carousel of Burden's designing, the piece sublimating the immediate peril and injury of his earlier body work and handing the threat over to his audience. Acts of such *détournement*, 'insurrection at the level of representation' (White, 1993, p. 330), are bounded in how far they can subvert dominant processes before being co-opted back into them; but in their interactivity, they express the beginnings of more effective resistances: a road junction turned into a forum, a steamroller flown, and in Alÿs's *Re-enactment* a gun neutralised.

Where the focus on mobility and the here and now provokes a necessary disruption, there is also a complementary 'healing'; resisting the privileging of some sites over others. To defy such a hierarchical fetish, the extended organism of the actor (see Turner, 2002) operates as a signpost to the immediate site, wherever and whatever it may be, and, in this sense is a democratising activity, enacting a social as well as an organic interdependency. An example of such signposted interweaving is Stephen Hurrell's performative installation *Constellation* (2003): a set of large poles, painted in the colours of sea vessels, and sited on a new housing estate in Ayr, on the west coast of Scotland (Warwick, 2006, pp. 91–92). The poles contain model landscapes, viewable through peepholes, but only fully illuminated by torches stored in the foyer of each of the estate's housing units and available to visitors at the discretion of the residents. The work is partly visible to all, the poles are unmissable, but can only be fully realised by an act of collaboration, a navigation that is both social and physical.

This social interweaving is a 'connection' of the sort that Deleuze makes key to any strategy for change (see Rajchman, 2000, pp. 4–13). Visitor, resident and artist-installed pole act as signposts for each other; not simply pointing the way, but present with each other along a path of perception. The poles of Hurrell's *Constellation* thrust up into the estate, are softened by the interaction between residents and visitors that opens their interiors. And what is within? A return to landscape; a dispersal of the drama of conflict and interrogation, disassembled by social interaction and the dramaturgy of a performative journey.

Exercise

Create a persona without a history, without a past, through costume and movement rather than character or narrative, so that their presence is more symbolic (representative of something other than what we see) and unaccountable (without any 'character' depth to answer for their actions or to their motivation).

Exercise

Perform un-human. On the one hand you might follow the course of Charles Foster, stripping naked, digging his own set and eating earthworms, to get inside the body and mind of the badger: 'Wittgenstein said that if a lion could speak, we couldn't understand a word it was saying, since the form of a lion's world is so massively different from our own... I know he was wrong' (Foster, 2016, p. 21). Or like Oleg Kulik, the Moscow-based performance artist who so 'inhabits' the violent anger of a dog in his attempt to 'turn into a sort of a new Diogenes, a dog philosopher' (cited in Heathfield, 2004, p. 56) that his audience members have been bitten, or have to be constrained in protective clothing in order to view his performance. On the other hand, you might take a different route to the un-human; like Miranda Whall for her 'crawling project' (*Crossed Paths* [2017–2018] in which, dressed in a sheepskin and carrying multiple devices (numerous cameras, GPS, smartphone) and accompanied by a drone, she crawls for five and a half miles along sheep tracks on Welsh hills 'attempting to go deeply into a place by briefly being in it as something else, in this case a sheep' (Whall, 2017). Whall's embodiment as the something else of the sheep is far less imitative and far more fabricated (and perhaps far more honest) than the performances of Foster and Kulik. Can you create a performance that shifts between fabrication and imitation; that never allows its audience to know in which 'as if' you are or about to be, as when we are in the presence of non-domesticated and un-human animals?

Idea

It may be a mistake to think of character or personae as an exclusively human aesthetic production. Many people, some influenced by the more occult fringes of psychogeography and others by a simpler desire to explain the distinctive atmospheres of different places have used the phrase *genius loci* to describe the 'spirit of a place'. While today the phrase is mostly used to describe an ambience or, more rarely, a spiritual or supernatural presence at work, for the Romans who originated the term 'every grove, spring, cluster of rocks or other significant natural feature had its attendant spirit. Generally the locals gave such entities personal names... Especially awe-inspiring or beautiful spots possessed proportionately powerful *genii*' (Hutton, 1993, p. 202).

Illustration 7.3   Animating a found 'squid', 'Bonelines of the Lonely Well Project', Tony Whitehead & Phil Smith, 2018.

Photo: Phil Smith.

It is unnecessary to entertain a belief in the occult to imagine that spaces and places, individual buildings or vistas, even small objects have similar agency to that of a human psyche. The psychologist Christopher Bollas asks if there is 'an architectural unconscious ... a type of thinking that directs the projection of a building ... finding its own vision out of the constituent elements?' He describes this unconscious as subjective, recalling previous associations to a space – 'the energy of the ghost is of course my own, the ghost ... is of course me' (2000, pp. 28–29), but also as material so that the 'energy of the ghost' of a site's previous manifestation can continue, physically, in its present one, and he gives the example of the Tate Gallery in St Ives, UK, whose rounded shape mirrors that of the 'unsightly' gas cylinder that previously stood there.

This way of thinking is not simply nostalgic, channelling lost buildings or past lives. Many buildings are 'material testimonies to visions of the future' (Bollas, 2000, p. 30); though, when these are fairly recent modernist or postmodernist buildings there is now a tendency to see them as 'hauntological', expressing a sense of a former and now lost faith in utopianism that only remains in the form of 'nostalgia for a future that never came to pass' (Whitely & Rambarran, 2016, p. 412). There the ghost is not the energy of individual human memory, but of a collectively lost project of hope. As the materials of both hope and loss, looking forward and back, for Christopher Bollas a building 'is a form of prayer' that will 'outlive us' and 'nonetheless signify us in the future' (2000, p. 30); our everyday use of these spaces animating their 'play space for the living within a death zone ... the living animate the cold marble or mass of cement' (p. 31).

Understood rigorously (not as putting on existing plays in parks), site-specificity might almost be seen as a branch of architecture; not designing new buildings, but creating 'new space' from what exists in both the natural and built environments (which is, after all, what architects and builders do) through their re-animation by human presence, whether that is bodily, sonic, textual or whatever. If we then see the existing space, particularly its architecture, as a form of dramaturgy, a shape with intentions for human action, then a site-specific dramaturgy upends this primary architectural-dramaturgy by re-animating its shapes to give it a new kind of liveliness, a new kind of score, transforming its existing uses into new ones. Whether that site-specific dramaturgy involves a fictional plot with representational characters like in *Mephistomania* or a choreography of bodily installations like in *Bodies in Urban Spaces*, the space is no more passive in realising the new score than its human co-performers. Just as the human self is formed not given – 'we have thoughts and eventually thoughts demand the arrival of a thinker to think them' (Bollas, 2000, p. 40, paraphrasing Bion) – so a site-specific dramaturgy can (whether by a prescient repetition or by a parade of novelties) provide the thoughts that will 'demand the arrival' of a new or renewed space; the morphing of the site from backdrop to character/actor.

An imposition of a new place-character is likely to be no more effective than a cosmetic redecoration that leaves underlying problems unaddressed; so, while in certain cases a celebratory tone in an abject space (*The Last King of Devonport* was partly driven by this dynamic) may be enough to engage the real tensions, in others it will be necessary to animate the theatrical *agon* of protagonist and antagonist: 'cloning a mentality is not equivalent to working through the stages of human strife out of which a community grows its own true spirit' (Bollas, 2000, p. 41). In this sense, there is almost always something utopian, something creative of 'new space', in every site-specific intervention; but the dramaturgy that attends to the 'stages of ... strife' within the site is the most likely to be effective in allowing the site to arrive at a new 'self'; the dramaturgy that is most conscious of the spatial personae already at work in or emerging from the site is the one most likely to avoid 'cloning a mentality'.

Exercise

Identifying a site and a performance aesthetics, experiment with different performance-presences: costumed character, autobiographical, 'being yourself', ablative dislocation, symbolic presence and so on. Practise transitioning from one to another. In which do you feel the most comfortable? In which, the least? What is best for your performance and for your site? Could it be in a space between presences?

Exercise

When the Romans referred to the 'genius loci', the spirit of a place, they did not simply mean an atmosphere or ambience, but an identifiable genius, a vivid and independent personification of the place. Act that.

Exercise

Is there a river running through your site? Safe enough to swim? Feel the pull of its currents, the uneven ground of the riverbed, the warmer and colder parts. Swim both with and against the current, feel for how the water moves around you. Now transfer the same kind of feeling for currents and pulls, shifts of temperature, the same kind of sensitive adaptation to sand, then pebbles and rocks, to the persona you are performing there.

Exercise

Jane Collins, the director of a 'site-specific adaptation' of John Webster's *The Duchess of Malfi* (Brighton, UK, 2006, 2009) for Prodigal Theatre Company, describes how 'the heady fragrance of the Duchess's perfume – Chanel, of course – merged with the smell of cheap aftershave worn by the male chorus and the more subtle aromas worn by the Cardinal and Ferdinand' (2012, pp. 59–60). Can you construct characters starting with their aromas, their touch, their volume or pitch? Beginning with their environmentally mediated sonic and haptic identities, build from there towards their inner drives?

Exercise

The psychologist Christopher Bollas talks about how a 'monument is a kind of play space for the living within a death zone' (2000, p. 30). Flip this on its head and what kind of dramatic-necromancy do you require to bring the dead zone of your site back to life?

Exercise

Sleep in your site and record your dreams. Act who you are there; animate in the site the 'characters' in your dreams.

Readings

There is a section of Dee Heddon's *Autobiography and Performance*, specifically Chapter 3, 'Place: The Place of Self', in which she explores how the spatial metaphors in stage-based autobiographical performances – 'expanding horizontally (taking the self along for the ride) or delving vertically (to find the hidden self at the centre)' (2008, p. 88) – are transformed in performances about lives that 'happen somewhere' (p. 88). While these might be a space of home or belonging, and Heddon addresses the tendency to nostalgia in these performances, the complexity of located subjectivities are as likely to be sited in complex and labyrinthine spaces with recesses, secrets, hidden stores, as in comfortable or uncomfortable domestic spaces. Heddon's discussion of home is nuanced and sometimes paradoxical, citing David Morley's description of a performative living that includes 'doing things in which one makes one's home while in movement' (Morley, 2000, p. 47).

Heddon reviews in detail a number of the performances that are mentioned in this book such as *Bubbling Tom, The Travels* and *On The Scent*, addressing the research and performance presence of the creators of these works in terms of gender and sexuality. This is rarely confronted in discussions of site-specific performance, but the same or similar sites may have very different kinds of affordance for different people. Heddon describes in relation to how Carl Lavery 'can walk for 15 miles alone in "Mourning Walk", retracing the path his father used to take … if he were me he would continuously be looking over his shoulder and scanning the horizon ahead, rather than contemplating his father' (2008, p. 113) and, then, saluting Terry O'Connor's 'challenge – a risky one? – to cultural assumptions' (p. 115) for Forced Entertainment's *The Travels* (2003) when O'Connor ignores warnings about dangerous spaces, enters a deserted house in a dead end road and spends time with the workmen there: 'I am acutely aware of Terry's female body in these places (its seeming out-of-placeness) but I also get the impression that Terry is determined not to behave like prey' (p. 115).

Readings

A 'vampire squid from hell' might not be the first collaborator you would turn to when creating a site-specific performance. Vilém Flusser and Louis Bec's *Vampyroteuthis Infernalis* is an account of this creature, written to explore the space between a human being and an unhuman one.

Surprisingly, despite (or perhaps affirmed by) its propensity to commit suicide by eating its own tentacles if held in captivity, 'the vampyroteu-this is not entirely alien to us' (Flusser & Bec, 2012, p. 5); with it we share some common physical structures, an ancient life path, and mutual 'deeply ingrained memories' (p. 6). Flusser and Bec's monster is a means to re-thinking the human performer (See Illustration 7.3.) in the period of the Chthulucene (Haraway, 2016), with its odd relationship of brain to foot; swinging us through 'a ninety-degree shift in the symmetrical axis, so that what was once ahead is now below, and what was once behind is now above' (Flusser & Bec, 2012, p. 18). It challenges a reader to rethink their relationship to objects and spaces, to 'depart from both ... abstract poles ("organism" and "environment") to comprehend the reality of the vampyroteuthis' and its manner of being, rendering 'planet Earth ... scarcely recognisable' (p. 32). Rather than configuring specificity to human expectations, Flusser and Bec's *Vampyroteuthis Infernalis* challenges us to imagine, by displacing the arrangement of our senses and assumptions, how monsters and their spaces might intuit site-specificity. In the process they ask us to consider the nature of our own 'being in the world' (the *Dasein* of the phenomenologist Heidegger) as we 'begin to see with [the squid's] eyes and grasp with its tentacles', crossing metaphor-ically from our world of sites into the vampire squid's. Then we might begin to journey, now corporeally and theatrically, from space that is 'a lethargic and passive expanse' to 'a realm of coiled tension, laden with energy' (p. 42) – yet, all the time, aware that what we are swimming with is a monster, impossible to change without becoming changed by it, always needing to be 'wary of those who condemn surfaces in their pursuit of the depths' (p. 71).

Part III

Shaping a Production

8

Dramaturgy

When I was an undergraduate drama student in the mid-1970s, a professional playwright, David Illingworth (resident writer for Avon Touring
Theatre Company, Bristol, UK) came to teach us. When he told us that
his next play was about 'roads' we all laughed. Plays were surely about
personalities, melodramatic human events, heightened emotions, animated philosophy and visual poetry. Not roads.

There is an ambiguity that persists about the status of any playwright
who writes for, in, about or around non-theatre-designated sites. There
is a sense that, for writers at least, this writing is either novelty or 'hack'
work, a distraction from the real business of writing for 'the stage' which
is the generator/distributor of single texts to multiple venues.

So where does *Murder in the Cathedral* (1935) fit into this? It was
written by T.S. Eliot (how more literary and privileged does it get?) specifically for a first performance in Canterbury Cathedral, UK, in its
Chapter House, about events in 1170 that climax in the cathedral itself
with the killing there of the archbishop, Thomas à Becket. The play
explicitly recruits its site's ceremonial architecture into its performance.
With its literary reputation, as part of the canon of Eliot's poetical works
(and mostly known either as a literary text or through its subsequent
'transfer' to a West End theatre), *Murder in the Cathedral* disappears from
discussions of site-specific dramaturgy, as though site-specificity and high

literary or cultural value are either mutually exclusive or entirely separately located in critical discourse.

This separation is not just site-specificity's loss. For *Murder in the Cathedral* celebrates its site as didactic architecture and as a ritual space 'where the building itself and the various different places within the space (such as the altar, the pictures in the stained glass windows, the pulpit) became a symbol for the values it projected' (Govan, Nicholson & Normington, 2007, p. 117); this play, however, proposes not a 'recontextualisation' or a making of 'new space', but a renewal through self-sacrifice and martyrdom of an old space and its tradition of practice and meaning. Dramaturgically, it is structured around a linear and progressive narrative in which one action or choice drives the action on to the next. All this might suggest that the play and its performance are a conservative anomaly and sit outside the meaningful narrative of site-specific art. On the other hand: look at what we are missing out on.

Murder in the Cathedral amalgamates ritual forms (mashing High Anglican liturgy with classical Greek chorus), it incorporates aspects of the cathedral's performance architecture, it generates a theatrical 'ghost' (a pseudo-ceremony) in a ritual host (a church), its voices range from realistic dialogue to heightened declamation, its performance is configured as a memorial rather than an entertainment and it is accessible (its title parodies those of Agatha Christie's 'whodunnits'). The muffling of Eliot's specificity is a mark of how the genre of site-specific performance is often defined around changing criteria – originally radical and subversive breaks from cultural institutions and narrative drama, more recently around marketing ideas, novelty, intimacy, spontaneous sensuality and fashionableness – rather than technical forms. A 1930s verse drama about a powerful cleric performed in an Anglican church seems not to fit either; yet there are dramaturgical aspects of the text drawn from the material site that constitute a possible model: the use of banners and procession for the entrance of the Priests, the use of metaphorical space ('Come down Daniel to the lion's den' [Eliot, 1969/2004, p. 274]), the metaphorical use of actual architecture as when the doors to the roof and crypt represent moral escape routes that Becket refuses, and the overarching structure of loss and redemption: 'the church is stronger for this action, Triumphant in adversity' (p. 280).

Within the ritual themes and structure of T.S. Eliot's theoretical programme in *Murder in the Cathedral* – of individual sacrifice for institutional redemption (with ugly echoes, for all parties, of Brecht's teaching plays [*lehrstücke*], which pre-empted Schechner's aesthetic by abandoning any actor/audience separation) – there survives a dramaturgy of a more orthodox character: the setting of the narrative and ambient 'place' of the action rather than its site ('Here let us stand, close by the cathedral. Here let us wait' [Eliot, 1969/2004, p. 239]), the exposition of past events precipitating the present crisis of the drama (the doing), the entrance of a central figure and various antagonists (and undermining supporters), the challenging and changing of the central character within an unrelenting and unchangeable narrative (because it is fate, history, God's will, and 'in the script'), the climactic action and the invisible reaction to it (the Church is strengthened). Eliot matched his dramaturgy to the affordances of the site and its ongoing practices. When he later and similarly tried to wed classical Greek tragedy and myth (with its remnants of ritual practice) to a comedy of social manners in plays like *The Family Reunion* (1939) and *The Cocktail Party* (1949) he was far less successful; the stages of West End theatres might support the comedy, but offered little to the ritual and mythic sub-structures of the plays.

Eliot's general approach at Canterbury is re-applicable. Dramaturgical elements of character development, narrative autonomy, dialogue and declamation, symbolic psychology, crisis, back story, and so on are all deployable in site-specific performance *if* they take account of, and engage dynamically with, the existing architectural or landscape symbolisation of the site – 'the organisation of place and space … endowed with the impulse to make concrete representation of values and beliefs'

(Govan, Nicholson & Normington, 2007, p. 103) – and its existing everyday performance procedures (prosecution and defence, forensic examination, surgery, image production, team games and so on). Where orthodox dramaturgies struggle is if they ignore these factors: the re-enactment in a 'historic' site (where is not?) that tries to turn a blind eye to its heritage signage and tour guiding, the dance piece on an exposed hill that is oblivious to the flights of the birds or aeroplanes above it. Even where the site constitutes challenges to text-based dramaturgy – vast distances, fierce winds, environmental noise – there may be technological solutions. Kneehigh Theatre reported to Fiona Wilkie on how their 'Landscape Theatre uses text sparingly – words do not travel over distances or in strong winds' (2002, p. 155); yet there are solutions such as live broadcast to an audience in headphones, pre-recorded materials, and the kinds of 'site/non-site' structure used in Pearson/Brookes's 2004 performance *There's Someone in the House* (described in Chapter 11). Perhaps surprisingly, given its high literary form, Eliot's *Murder in the Cathedral* is exemplary of site-specific performance, because – in a rigour comparable with Pina Bausch's company's research into West Coast America's symbolic space and social dramaturgies at 'social gatherings, and in particular dance clubs, observing nuances of life before taking these back into the rehearsal room for further interrogation' for their 1996 production *Nur Du* (Govan, Nicholson & Normington, 2007, p. 113) – the poet put in the hard work of 'adaptation' to a site and synthesis with it.

Exercise

Redemption and transformation, in more orthodox stage dramaturgies, are often centred on the main protagonists of a drama. In site-specific work these qualities can be transferred sideways to the site and to its materials. In 2003, I attended a performance of *Sledgehammer Songs* by Lone Twin, at the conclusion of which the two performers carried water gathered that day from the local river to a cobbled space outside of the theatre. One performer, who had been energetically cavorting inside for some time under numerous layers of thick clothing, stripped to the waist, while the other threw the river water onto his body. As a result of the extreme body heat some of the river water rose from his reddened and exposed torso as steam. (See Illustration 7.2 above.) Though not quite by the martyring of a body, there

was an almost invisible and certainly misty renewal of a natural cycle of evap-
oration and precipitation, of clouds and rainfall and river, comparable to the
symbolic and wholly invisible renewal of the ecclesiastical institution through
what happens to Thomas à Becket's body. Choose a site and create a scenario
based on human characters and human narrative drama; then transfer any
elements of transformation or redemption to the materials of your site.

There is a temptation in site-specific art – given its usually recognised origins in modernism – to automatically embrace the fragmentary, the obscure, the conceptual and the reflexive. An archaeological approach to the deep or recent past of a place can be similarly inscribed: 'Archaeologists may dream of the past perfectly dessicated in the sands of time … But there are only ever fragments' (Pearson & Shanks, 2001, p. 56). Some site-practitioners arrive at these approaches by a more-or-less pragmatic engagement with specific sites; the incomplete and multiplicitous quali-ties of their sites have over-determined their aesthetic choices, and there is no necessary harm in that. For others, indeed, these approaches are part of an ideological or aesthetic-political 'break' in their work, a passionate rejection of a set of orthodoxies that include linear narrative, character, acting, and so on.

There is no obligation to write a play. Nor any version of storytelling or theatrical narrative. Equally, however, there is no absolute obligation to conform to postmodernism's urgent abandonment of an overriding, over-determining grand narrative and its replacement by a timeless and depthless immediacy that admits no unfolding of narratives at all. There are multiple alternatives – 'game-plan, plot, story-board, shooting-script … in place of script' (Pearson & Shanks, 2001, p. 26) – that need not conform to a linear structure. The best, though, might not exist as a prac-tice, or at least not be recognised as an aesthetic one outside of your site. The site may already have a dramaturgy all of its own that you can borrow or parasite upon. Indeed, the physical 'logics' and institutional polic-ing of certain spaces – such as the medieval underground passages for Simon Persighetti's *Passages* (Exeter, UK, 2001) or the Plus 15 Skywalk System for Melanie Kloetzel's *The Sanitastics* (Calgary, Canada, 2011; see Illustration 8.1) – may dictate the limits of what is possible dramaturgi-cally to what the material dimensions or the security forces of the sites

Illustration 8.1 *The Sanitastics*, a site-specific film by kloetzel&co, 2011. Choreography by Melanie Kloetzel. Performers: Deanna Witwer, Naomi Brand, Caileen Bennett and Kirsten Wiren.

Photo: kloetzel&co.

will allow; but they may also provide a dramaturgical structure or trajectory: 'The moment-to-moment "what happens next?" of conventional narratives is replaced by the "where is he going?" and "what's in the next room?"' (White, 2012, p. 227). While such constraints might be exploitable as a readymade structure for your performance, they can also be wearing, demoralising and intimidating.

Or you own up to the importing of patterns that you, maybe inevitably, will engage with. Embracing what a totality has to offer to a site-specific performance; the creation of an 'alternative world' (something that has become more common with the emergence of an 'immersive' tendency), which either accumulates layers until there is a qualitative change of site-identity, or uses fictions or other asymmetrical devices to change the totality of the site's identity. This is very different to using the landscape as a backdrop 'behind' a fictional narrative; it is about transforming a landscape by the sinking of an aesthetic work into it; a 'camouflage'.

Alternatively, rather than accumulate the layers in some kind of consistency, you can emphasise the quality of the layering, so that different elements of the site, in performance, retain their discreteness. As

Mike Pearson and Michael Shanks argue, 'Whilst we might expect performance to be a homogeneous mixture of elements created minute by minute over time, we might now imagine situations are run in parallel, with or against each other ... Or where from time to time performance exists variously as one, two, or three tracks only' (p. 25). Pearson has subsequently articulated this as a '*stratigraphic* model of dramaturgy' in which the layers are kept distinct: 'text, physical action, soundtrack and scenography, the latter to include all scenic installation, lighting, amplification, prerecorded media, technological and technical aspects' (2010, p. 167). Here there is a potential for a highly complex performance in which the different layers, running in parallel, starting and stopping according to their own logic, differently organised within themselves and in their own terms, and presenting quite different – indeed '*antithetical*' – things of and about their site. At the same time, Pearson proposes an organising strand, a kind of 'super layer' (though it may not always be the same one): 'Any one layer may from time to time bear responsibility for carrying the prime intended meaning. Such responsibility can be reassigned and shift rapidly ... Any one layer may provide the carrier frequency, the spine of consistent through-line upon which other layers are laid' (2010, p. 167).

Exercise

Identify different layers in a site – autobiographical, technological, occult, ironic, erotic – and make a layer of performance for each; then overlay them, one over another.

Exercise

As the exercise above, but then rub out sections of the performance from each of the layers so that the different layers show through each other – what does the audience see through the hole in the bottom layer? Then, repeat, but establish a 'super-layer' that defines the overarching meaning, allotting this role to different layers at different times.

Exercise

Find a place that reminds you of a painting. Decorate the place so it more nearly resembles the painting. Make a performance that animates the painting in the space, incorporating in some way a copy of its image into the performance.

With fragmentation, in any of these dramaturgies, and any consequent loss of narrative legibility – where narrative is relevant – there can be a temptation to anchor an audience in a single, fixed space in order to provide a substitute for the formal structure that is refused in, or failed by, the dramaturgy. Sometimes a formally innovative work can end up, becalmed, in conservative space. Equally, a mobile, agentive and inquisitive audience can quickly become an anxious and dissatisfied one if it feels that it is unable to find any meaningful structure, totalised *or* formally fragmented; or maybe just not find the action at all. The crucial criterion, then, is not whether the dramaturgy is linear or fragmentary, but how it aligns with the affordances (and, if you accept the argument for coevalness, the Other) of the site it is made for. Despite any talk of high political aesthetics, there is nothing to be ashamed about in seeking answers to the questions around dramaturgy in technical solutions.

For example, Punchdrunk responded to the frustration of audiences who enjoyed the freedom to explore the expanses and minutiae of carefully prepared sites, but often lost track of their performance narratives. In response they introduced a new structure to their performances: their narrative content, generally staged in multiple sites within a designated space, was condensed to about 30 minutes in duration and was repeated three times. The audience were, thus, still able to explore the space, while also likely to chance upon enough content to form a coherent experience of the overall piece, enabling the more insightful and experienced to assemble the narrative for themselves, chasing down the action they had missed the first or second time around.

In addressing these kinds of problems, it may be worth looking at performance structures that exist in your site and outside of theatre and studio work. For example, historical re-enactment – where we always know that under the armour is modern underwear, a mobile phone tucked in the folds of the toga – not only enacts educational, entertainment, archaeological and forensic narratives, but often aggressively presents itself in the 'now', with anachronistic jokes and popular cultural references. These are the kinds of multiplicitous and stratigraphically 'antithetical' discourses that a site-based performance can play with, disassemble and reassemble, making Time a key actor in the drama; in the doing of the place. The frames and structures of historical re-enactment – staging in numerous tents or spots across an open field, parades and dramas narrated and interpreted over a PA system, the presentation and celebration of performers and sponsors – are ones that lend themselves more to the needs of a mobile audience than those of building-based theatre. Other examples might be carnival, *son et lumière*, cookery demonstrations, street hawking, religious procession, beauty pageant and mumming/plough plays.

Looking at how different structures of performance-making can be adapted in site-specific performance – but also how the site can be its own generator of performance structure through journey, layer and unfolding – attention to the detailed interlocking and interweaving narrative threads are crucial. A narrative which only uses the site as backdrop is only satisfying or convincing to an audience who are already convinced of its provenance. Nothing changes in such performances. But a grasp of the fine details and a sound intuitive feel for broader sweeps and risk-taking, when informing a narrative, can produce powerful reciprocal effects from the terrain.

Narratives and connections to their site do not need to be rational. I still do not know why there were so many dead octopi in the kitchens of an old villa, why I was raced blindfold across a university plaza to be placed against an air-raid shelter wall and had bricks hurled at the wall beside me, why I was lined up with others in a wood as if for a firing squad and then kissed upon the lips, or confined in a small book-lined room to be shown pictures of shotgun suicides, and yet, although I probably have ethical and intellectual objections to them all, I not only remember these moments, but treasure them.

From all this it should be clear that just as there is no Stanislavski of site-specific theatre, there is no dominant (or even much-detailed) 'method' of site-dramaturgy. In 2004, the Vancouver-based dramaturg Heidi Taylor proposed five principles for a 'deep dramaturgy' of site-specific theatre: the significance of all signs in a site irrespective of the performance, the fundamental importance of accidents and coincidences, the management and reception of detail, intense audience interaction and a call for the transformation of 'Basic ideological, political, economic and technological structures' as necessary for the realisation of site-specificity (2004, p. 19). While each is a vivid principle or intention, they would not be evenly appropriate across different sites, and, together, constitute more an opening sketch for an exploration of approaches than a fully realised methodology.

When choosing or developing a site-dramaturgy, then, the task, appropriately perhaps, is more one of assembling from fragments rather than selecting a methodology 'off the peg'. There are numerous ideas that can be extracted from existing practices that hover somewhere between an abstraction and a technique and which may 'fit' your site or your ongoing and changing site practice. These might include packaging (*emballage*), wrapping and unwrapping your site (taking something from the massive textile drapings and wrappings of Christo and Jeanne-Claude); or dispersal in which a focused narrative 'infects' its site. An example of this is Charles Stankievech's *Loveland* (2011) which distils the 'dead planet' narrative of M.P. Shiel's 1901 novel *The Purple Cloud* – in which an intrusion at the North Pole releases a death-bringing cloud leaving a single survivor who travels the corpse strewn planet – to a release of purple cloud (created by using military smoke grenades) across a stretch of Arctic Ocean.

You might develop a narrative-geology. In the play *Partisans* (1977), created for the agit-prop theatre North West Spanner, touring factory gates, canteens and trade union halls in the north of England (see Dalton), a character 'emblematically named Mole, spends his time digging a tunnel, as if in some prisoner-of-war movie, to get him out of the factory, despite the everyday truth that he goes home through the gates every night' (Drain, 1979, p. 14). Consider how any stories or reflections gathered from a site might be realised in industrial and geological rather than narrative terms. If your site is less about stories and more about processes then you might consider whether a multi-form performance structure would better serve it. In Louise Ann Wilson Company's

Illustration 8.2 *The Gathering/Yr Helfa*, 2014. Creator, director and designer: Louise Ann Wilson. Writer: Gillian Clarke. Choreographer: Nigel Stewart. Performer: Ffion Dafis. Produced by National Theatre Wales.

Photo: Joel Fildes/National Theatre Wales.

The Gathering/Yr Helfa (2014), produced for National Theatre Wales, the performance drew on three years' observation of a sheep farm, Hafod y Lan, at the base of Mount Snowdon, studying the annual rhythms of farm work and landscape, and the reproductive cycle of the ewes (Illustration 8.2). The resulting performance drew upon different sources: a cycle of commissioned poems, a 'bespoke' choreography, research into regional songs, film and installation ('sheered fleeces pour down the hillside in a fluffy stream' [Gardner, 2014]), a silver band and a church choir. The four hour performance included participation by the farm's shepherds, their sheep dogs and a flock of around 200 sheep, while the audience accessed these different elements, weaving performance and intervention with everyday farm work, on a six kilometre walk. This kind of multiple dramaturgy, dispersing its effects across different aesthetic forms and terrain types increases the chances of recruiting multiple layers of space and natural process to the weave of the performance: 'it … makes you pay attention to what has always been there and will remain long after we are gone: the fall of water, the moss creeping across tumbled stones, the dark, secretive peaks against an endless sky' (Gardner, 2014).

In 2005 I was working with young teenage pupils from a local school on two 'after-school' projects. One was to physically model, through movement and dance, ideas and patterns from the students' physics lessons, the other was the devising of a site-specific performance for a nearby deconsecrated church and graveyard. The teachers had the idea of combining the two projects in a third: *Time and Light* put the physicalised physics-modelling into resonant sites on the city's high street for an audience of invited guests and passers-by. Rather than attempt to frame this performance through narrative, we provided the audiences with 'time maps', showing the places on the high street where and when (sometimes simultaneously) they might expect to find the performance. The audience were then left to find their way to the various micro-sites, to choose between scenes at moments when the performance bi-located. In this way the audience, as well as being challenged to question any assumption about a single, linear narrative, were drawn into the performance's modelling of concepts such as general relativity and the entanglement of quantum pairs (spooky action at a distance). The map served as the narrative of the performance, freeing the performers to enact concepts and images and to corporeally and materially realise invisible processes in pavement chalking, dances and optical demonstrations; turning the high street into a giant laboratory/planetarium.

Sometimes an object can *be* the dramaturgy. Standing on a river bank watching a tea party around a table set in the waters was engaging and amusing, but was only preamble to the arrival of a steam locomotive racing by along the tracks on the far bank. From the carriages, the passengers were hanging from the windows and waving handkerchiefs to the audience. The performance company (with the permission of train line managers) had recruited all of the passengers on a regular train service, transforming their performance from an evocation of a nostalgic *Winds in the Willows*-like children's fiction into a vivid few moments in which they precisely invoked a specific scene from E. Nesbit's *The Railway Children* (1906): 'they waved their handkerchiefs ... what was really remarkable was that from every window handkerchiefs fluttered ... The train swept by with a rustle and a roar.' As far as I am aware, the stretch of the river

Dart, Devon, UK, on which this was performed has no connection with Nesbit or her book (other than the coincidental proximity to the South Devon Railway's steam locomotives and this line's occasional use of the book for promotional purposes); none of the subsequent film and TV adaptations have been made there. However, what was startlingly precise was how the performers first evoked memories (see the comments of Van Eyck in Chapter 7) of a generalised literary ambience, and then, in a dazzling mobile tableau, crystallised those associations, both joyful and melancholic, in an ecstatic yet distressing display of an anachronistic object.

Beginning and ending a site-specific performance can present as many problems as opportunities, identifying when either actually occurs is not always simple. In 2003, after attending a performance I had made for beach huts (*The Crab Walks*, Dawlish and Teignmouth, UK), my colleague Simon Persighetti remarked that the performance had begun for him as he left his house to catch the train to the resort. Josephine Machon suggests that 'the immersive experience begins the moment you first hear about it' (2013, p. 23). Endings may be equally porous. The architecture of a theatre and the control of illumination in a performance studio assist in efficiently ending a performance; a climactic event or a subtle narrative turn followed by the fall of a curtain and/or the dimming of lights can round off the performance, allowing the performers to break, to leave, to return for applause or encore. This is sometimes subverted (for example, performers may refuse to leave until the audience does), but the variation is based on the understanding of what is possible and customary. In site-specific work only very occasionally does a building or a landscape offer a comparable facility; even then, but particularly when not, ending according to such conventions can impact negatively on a performance. I once watched a piece in a large field, at the end of which the performers moved away across the field holding a long banner for maybe four minutes until, just before they reached and disappeared into a line of trees, they stopped, dropped the banner and returned in full view to the audience for their applause. They denied the field, at least for a moment, the chance to be seen without them, and denied the audience the chance to savour how the field had been changed by the performance (a disappointment voiced by the audience as the performers returned). To the performers a four-minute exit felt absurd; for us observers it had felt powerful and beautiful. This was a cautionary learning experience for those involved not to import the assumptions of time and space from theatre buildings into their sites.

Exercise

The collapse of conventions offers its own opportunities. *Cancelled Menagerie* (Wrights & Sites satellite production, Royal Albert Memorial Museum, Exeter, UK, 2000), was set mostly in the museum's 'Natural History Room' packed with stuffed animals. After each performance, Simon Persighetti and I, dressed as 'big game hunters' stalked an audience member out of the museum and through the city streets, at close range, climbing through shop window displays and around ornamental plants, until spotted by the audience member – at which point we ran away. Create a performance, most of the action of which occurs after its ending.

Idea

Doreen Massey makes a powerful criticism of the addressing of a place as a series of layers or as a palimpsest (a text repeatedly overwritten but not yet obliterated by new texts) as 'too archaeological' and incapable of seeing or expressing what is being dismantled or disappeared in the present moment of the site. If the stratigraphic dramaturgy follows too archaeological a model and digs down, unpeeling layer after layer of its palimpsest, then 'the things that are missing (erased) from the map are somehow always things from "before"' and these gaps replace 'the discontinuities of the multiplicity in contemporaneous space' (2005, p. 110). Massey's approach is not to dismiss the layers or the palimpsest of a place, but to approach them coevally (as different elements operating within the same time zone, not as different times operating in the same space), drawing from the work of the cultural anthropologist Johannes Fabian to identity what is at work in, and making, the unevenness (from its injustices and inequalities to its varieties of velocity and acceleration for people, machines, information and objects) in multiplicitous contemporary space. Fabian points to an opposition between 'not the same societies at different stages of development, but different societies facing each other at the same Time' (2002, p. 155). In other words, what is waiting (as a protest right now, rather than a remnant of ancient potential) to be performed in a site is not evolving consistently from top to bottom, now to then, but is a clash of contemporary global structures and forces that eke out, eradicate and dissolve the missing things that would expose that 'consistently' for the illusion that it is.

What Cathy Turner sees as an abiding problem with the metaphor of the palimpsest is how it suggests that 'the subject (or artist) is outside space, inscribing it or deciphering the layers' (2004, p. 378). Doreen Massey addresses the problem by reconfiguring the identity of the subject. Her 'coevalness' is a political act (2005, pp. 68–70) that invokes the Other in the site by protesting its absence. So, for example, a performance might invoke the absence in any mark or symbol in an English 'stately home' of those whose enslaved labour generated the wealth to build it, not as the exposure of a historical crime, but as an indictment of the site's ongoing and living driver for continuing the exclusion of the Other (in this case the descendants of those colonised and enslaved) from spaces free from exploitation. Without the agency of people of that Other, a performance would struggle to escape from the force of 'consistency' implied in the time, text and building materials of the layers and palimpsest.

So, flip the argument. Because – at least in the way I am describing it – it, so far, assumes the agency of those in a 'site' where, even if not actually 'at home', they can feel reasonably secure in their relation to where and what it is. What if the agents of a site are constituted by its Other; is coevalness then possible for its performance? In *Way from Home* (2002–2008), for example, Misha Myers created a different kind of connection to a site by overlaying one place on another by inviting refugees and asylum seekers living in the UK to map a journey from 'home' to a 'special place' and then to walk that route, performing that journey, but in the place they are now, and in the company of walking partners (Myers herself, local public officials, and others): 'For some [this meant] initiating connections where there was estrangement, for generating an autobiographical map of a life journey, and for others … a painful reminder of differences and the desire to return' (Myers & Harris, 2004, p. 91).

Through coevalness, site-specific performance can look from the centre to the edges of its site, from the vertical, the digging down, to its horizon; looking for the arrival of the Other of the site from the margins. What that Other might be, and it is by definition a potential, always described within a future to which it does not have access yet, will still be specific to its site. However, it is no guarantor of a narrative or any other kind of coherency or consistency; to expect so is to de-Other it. Coevalness does not solve the technical issues, but adds one extra challenge to them.

Exercise

Create a performance made up entirely of exitings from a site.

Exercise

Create a scenario for your site that begins with its chaos and ends with its incarcerations.

Exercise

Bare-faced fakery can work as a dramaturgy. A ludicrous fabulation, if fully exposed to its 'dupes' along the way, can reveal something about a place, obliquely; in the same way that some stars are only visible to the naked eye if you look just to the side of, and not directly at, them. I recently devised a transferable trick for this: I prepare some empty beer cans, cut off the top quarters and insert squares of paper with identical images. Slipping the removed quarters back over the tops, I tape them shut, then tape over the ring-pull holes, and make a pinhole halfway down each can, adding a small piece of tape over each hole. During a performance, the cans are handed out with the explanation that they are pin-hole cameras with blank photographic paper inside. I encourage the audience to peel the tape from the pinholes, and hold the cans up to the site. After half a minute or so, I ask the audience to undo the cans and bring out the exposed photographic papers, which all contain identical images of the space, changed in some way, with something highlighted or superimposed on it (in a re-wilding site I added a wolf, in a site associated with the writing of *Dracula* I added an image of Sir Henry Irving, Bram Stoker's model for the vampire count). If the audience have not already guessed that this is all a nonsense, they do now. They laugh, the creaky deception parodying the re-presenting of the space. The performance becomes a little more questionable; but wolf and vampire are now part of the site. Choose a place and devise some fake devices to unpeel its meanings, hidden history, forgotten products...

Idea

In 1952 an untitled evening of performance took place at the Black Mountain College in North Carolina, USA. This event was to have a major influence on innovative performance-making in the USA and in Europe and was to spawn a new genre of performance: the happening. The event began with composer John Cage reading aloud: 'In Zen Buddhism nothing is either good or bad. Or ugly or beautiful ... Art should not be different (from) life but an action within life. Like all life, with its accidents and chances.' (cited in Goldberg, 1979, p.126) Cage, in black suit and tie, then played a sound piece by turning on and off a radio, according to time segments in the score. The artist Robert Rauschenberg played old records on a hand-wound gramophone, while a musician played a piano, its hammers treated to produce hampered notes. Water was poured from one bucket into another, while two poets spoke their work simultaneously. Dancers, led by their choreographer Merce Cunningham, danced through the aisle pursued by a playful dog. Coloured, non-figurative slides were projected onto the ceiling. Films of the college's cook and of a setting sun were projected. A baby screamed. Coffee was served by four boys dressed in white.

The dramaturgical preparation for this 'happening' was a mixture of precise structuring and a refusal to prepare, an insistence on improvisation and ordinariness. The nature of what the performers intended to do was kept private until the performance itself; there was no conscious link between one performer and another or one performance and another. There was a running order, chunks of time and indications to the performers to fill this time with action, inaction, silence; exactly how was up to them; the structure allowed the performer freedom and authority, but also conferred responsibility.

Happenings perpetuated – in less formulaic and manifesto-driven, and in more kinetic, ways – a shifting between exhibition and performance that characterised the work of the Surrealists (who inherited that tension from the Dadaists). The whole-environment installation for the 1938 International Surrealist Exhibition in Paris, for example, had greeted visitors with a drenched taxi, its shark-headed passenger covered in huge living snails and a passage of mannequins offering surreal-erotic 'services', while its main hall was like a precarious grotto, 1,200 sacks of coal (in fact, unknown to visitors, packed with screwed up newspaper) suspended from the ceiling; the only lighting came from a brazier and visitors stumbled around in the semi-darkness searching with supplied torches for paintings.

Like the Surrealists, the artists creating 'happenings' exploded their art beyond the picture frame, their sculpture stepping off the plinth and out of the vitrine. There was movement in the other direction too. When in 1911 the Futurist Umberto Bocconi had introduced a piece of a real window frame into a painting, the way was opened for the use of found materials, rather than placing objects within gallery rooms or setting ornaments in landscapes, artists began to create the rooms and shape the landscapes as extensions of their painting and sculpture. Allan Kaprow described the environments he made as 'spatial representations of a multileveled attitude to painting'. This painting was not only bursting out of its frame, but also out of its surface, out of its plane, becoming four dimensional, a space where things happened over time.

In popular memory a series of misunderstandings cluster around happenings; that they are improvised by the performers on the spot, they had no structure, and their defining element is the appearance of a naked young woman. None of this was true. Happenings were planned; as combinations of compartmentalised chunks of action. They had much in common with the Dadaist Kurt Schwitters's vision for a Merz Theatre with its 'fusing of all factors into a composite work … white wall, man, barbed wire entanglement … not to be used logically in their objective relationships, but only within the logic of the work of art' (cited in Steinitz, 1968, p. 60). Much of his call for performance to 'take buses and pleasure-cars, bicycles, tandems and their tires … Make locomotives crash into one another … make railroad mist' (p. 61) has been realised in site-specific theatre productions.

Happenings often cited elements of a popular mass production culture of movies, cars, rock 'n' roll, and so on, but they were also attempts to disrupt that culture; more about liveness than representation, just as Jackson Pollock's art was more about the act of painting than a splattered canvas. A mix of assemblage and separateness was key to the dramaturgy of happenings and their compartmentalised structures. Just as the Dadaists would compartmentalise poems by cutting them up into individual words or sounds, so in a happening the action was compartmentalised into space/time chunks and juxtaposed. These chunks of action were precisely arranged, but not to create a new single meaning. There was an allusive connection between the parts; an invitation to the audience to make their own meanings. There was no plot, no identifiable characters, no conventional story-structure based on tension, conflict, crisis, no information structure to guide an audience – even approximately – how to feel and what to understand.

Exercise

Collect some toys at random. Find a space and use the toys, and anything else that is to hand, to 'act out dramas of tin-soldiers, stories and musical structures' (Allan Kaprow, cited in Kirby, 1965, pp. 44–46). You might use a recording of John Cage's 'Suite for Toy Piano' (1948) as accompaniment.

Exercise

Find a space that is already divided into smaller spaces. Make a list of compartmentalised actions you are able to perform in these spaces, actions that have some meaning for you. Make sure there is some variety of actions. Organise a running order of actions in the different spaces, avoid any rational sequence. Keep the actions discrete, insulated from the others, let them (and an audience) make their own connections. Afterwards, ask the audience what meanings they read or forces they felt.

Exercise

Match a complex narrative, taken from a novel, short story, news story, or poem to a specific site, and work on that site with the story materials until the two are beginning to entangle with each other. In Paris you could try Hope Mirrlees's poem 'Paris', in London T. S. Eliot's 'The Love Song of J. Alfred Prufrock' or Paul Leppin's *Severin's Journey into the Dark* in Prague. Allow the terrain to influence the pace and development of the narrative, allow the fiction of the narrative to change the 'telling' of the terrain; how is it described, from where it is entered, viewed and touched, how is it defined by the relationship that different characters or performers have with it?

Exercise

Work with non-human but living 'performers' in a way that determines the spatial dramaturgy of your performance. Generate a flexible scenario that can be driven spatially by, say, the flight of birds across the sky above your site, or the passage of fish beneath it. Lie on your back and take your performance score from what you observe in the sky – clouds forming and dispersing, branches swaying, leaves falling, wasps swooping.

Exercise

Repetition can be as effective as variation. Make a piece based on duplication, reflection and repetition; create a momentum towards completion and then sabotage it. Perform 'not the goal of the drive, but rather the perpetuation of desire, which enables the drive to keep going' (Kartsaki, 2015, p. 126). Use large reflective surfaces (shop fronts, for example) in a busy space and create a performance which the audience watches in a reflective surface, in which they too may appear, only for its completion to be repeatedly avoided and for the performance to begin again. Perform until no one is watching anymore.

Idea

In 2017 at the Fourth World Congress of Psychogeography at Huddersfield, UK, I participated in a performance action of just under two hours' duration in a shopping street in the town's centre, led by Elia Rita entitled *I'm the City of Others Who Are The City: Participatory Urban Pilgrimage*'. The action was simple and complex, clear and ambiguous. Four of the participants, including Rita made their way slowly up the street, after each step prostrating themselves for about half a minute and then rising to take the next step (an action based on the Chinese *koutou* [kowtow]). Rita wore a white robe and the other three wore something white but did not appear to be ritually dressed. Accompanying these four were a further four (including myself) dressed in white socks over shoes or bare feet, who walked behind or to the side of those prostrating. There were also two organisers of the Congress who stood along the route, though not in any distinctive dress. The unannounced action generated intense interest from passers-by, many of whom stood for 20 minutes or more debating its meaning or quietly watching. The buzz of the street was mostly hushed. Repeatedly individuals or small groups would approach those of us who were accompanying those prostrating to ask 'what does it mean?' or 'is it religious?' The white robe, the repeated action and the focus of the four 'pilgrims' who did not respond to questions from the public was enough to mark this as a ritual, but not enough to allow it to be easily pigeon-holed or categorised. At the same time, the simple act of something like humiliation or giving exaggerated respect to the abject road (dirty and wet from a recent rain shower) created a striking tension with the brightness of the surrounding stores, their advertising images and the shoppers clutching their purchases.

The crowds that gathered were multi-ethnic and multi-cultural; as one of the junior participants I was concerned that some observers might take offence if they imagined this was a mockery of religious practice. In fact, there was occasional laughter from young teenagers, some misreading – 'Are they Jews?' – but no disruption, and an almost endless stream of curiosity and enquiry and discussion. Some passers-by did reference their own prayer practice, but saw the parallel with the street performance as a positive thing; a number located what they saw in terms of 'yoga' or were satisfied by the description 'pilgrimage'. One passer-by joined in passionately and briefly. Others seemed happy to contemplate the action without an explanation. As witness-participants, who were partly 'holding the ground' (with the two organisers) for the pilgrims, we could repeat to enquirers how the action was described to us by Elia Rita, but our own understanding (and the event's meaning itself) was also unfolding and changing all the time.

Informing the event's 'success', as well as its broader social conditions of cultural multiplicity, were the different layers and intensities of focus and heightened state among the various participants. Those of us participating more informally and more like witnesses or stewards could mediate between the passers-by and the intense and physically demanding action of the pilgrims. It felt as if this informality, rather than undermining the central ritual drew a clear but not aggressive line around its space (something similar to what I had seen operating within a Russian Orthodox church in Riga, Latvia, where intensely devout prayer and heightened mystical belief and observation operated loosely alongside begging, stray dogs, souvenir selling and chatter) which encouraged watchers to respect the integrity of the pilgrims while engaging in dialogue with those mediating the action.

Exercise

Through performance generate a fake site. But be careful what you wish for. The performance is as much what people believe and take forward from your changing of identity as what you do. In 1963 students at Carleton College, Northfield, Minnesota, disgruntled with compulsory church attendance, set up the Reformed Druids of North America in order to plead exemption on religious grounds. Today the Druids are going strong and have become a recognised religion with internal disputes over dogma. The campus is dotted with their ritual sites and their activities are poised between devotion and humour.

Exercise

In 1879 a postman, Ferdinand Cheval, tripped over a stone worn by water into an unusual shape; for the next 33 years Cheval used this shape to model a huge surreal palace – *Palais Idéal* – in Hautrives, France. Junji Ito's manga *Uzumaki* is about a town similarly taken over by spirals. In your site, choose a single action that somehow most closely performs the meaning of the site (maybe it is one you have observed someone in the site performing). Then repeat it; these repetitions of this single action are the building blocks of your performance.

Exercise

Make a publicly and randomly choreographed piece in a busy public place. Find a vantage point high above the site, from where you can observe and record the movements. Ask your performers to enter the site and discretely follow members of the public, subtly copying their progress (with discretion and respect). Once a performer fastens onto a member of the public the other performers should subtly follow and copy them. When the individual being followed leaves the site, find a new person to follow. Before you start, agree a strategy for explanation, should a member of the public (being followed, or not) challenge a performer. The aim, though, is for the copying to only be evident to those in the high observation point. This is not about making fun of the public, but giving up control. Record the patterns of movement and use them as a score for a performance. Try the exercise with a small group, then with many participants, then with participants in distinctive costume. Try the same exercise, but rather than following people choose a different action-generator: overheard conversations, the sounds of machines, gusts of wind.

Readings

Mike Pearson has played a formative role in making site-specific performance for a generation or more. His books *Theatre/Archaeology* (2001, with Michael Shanks), *'In Comes I': Performance, Memory and Landscape* (2006) and *Site-Specific Performance* (2010) are obvious starting points for anyone attempting their own site-based dramaturgy, but they are not straightforward manifestos or handbooks. They require a sympathetic understanding of Pearson's practice, his blending techniques and rigour from the 'holy theatre' tradition, his passionate orientation to certain localised communities and his resolutely anti-theatrical, modernist complexity. Consistent with the uniqueness of every site and the fragmentariness of his own modernism, Pearson eschews a unified praxis – he quotes with approval Gregory Ulmer's dictum 'do not choose between the different meanings of key terms, but compose by using all the meanings' (1994, p. 48) – assembling instead dozens of fecund ideas and techniques from diverse sources such as deep mapping and a technologically enhanced archaeology of the contemporary past. These are woven through accounts of his own, often collaborative, works. To extract them from their precisely given contexts and apply them to your own work will require an imaginative and sensitive transferral.

There are certainly practical techniques to draw upon, such as forensic crime scene analysis or the annexing 'of an existing institutional arrangement of watchers and watched ... pulpit and congregation ... beds and visitors in a hospital' (2001, p. 111); as well as critical ideas such as 'a material resistance to the ideologies of a homogeneous world' exuding from ruins and remains, recontextualisation, the agency of things, the erasing of the border between the academic and the artistic, and multiple others. Among these is a recurring idea of doubleness; something that applies to 'props' as much as performers (2010, p. 118). This idea appears in detail in the Afterword of *'In Comes I'*, where Pearson draws on Tim Ingold's suggestion that landscape would be better regarded as a taskscape in which 'inhabitants know their environs not as spectators but as participants' (2006, p. 219); through this prismatic idea, Pearson turns the archaeological performer into something that is both fixed and mobile. He challenges the duality of sitedness and nomadism, offering the alternative of doubleness – superseding even that of the useful concepts of 'host' (the site as it exists) and 'ghost' (the performance as you make it), even transcending their 'conflation of that which pre-exists the work and that which is of the work' (p. 201); Pearson conceptualises an ideal site-performer 'as both *dweller* and as *virtuoso* in *performance-as-taskscape* ... their activities bring[ing] the performance landscape into being and vice versa: there is no priority' (p. 220, emphasis in original).

In *Site-Specific Performance*, there are numerous transferable concepts (as throughout Pearson's work) and, particularly here, actions to glean, in the agricultural sense of scooping up the learning left behind by practice. There are long lists of statement/questions (provocations with the seeds of their own answers already working their way to the surface): on broad general concepts for different aspects of site-based work (p. 33), on using objects (pp. 118–119), strategies for devising (pp. 151–153), on the model for a '*stratigraphic* model of dramaturgy' (p. 167), on the dramaturgy 'of the site' and the dramaturgy 'brought to the site' (pp. 181–182), and on how the identity of the site is transformed by your choosing and working in it (pp. 182–183).

9

Scenographies and Enchanted Objects

The Sydney-based scenographer and dramaturg Benedict Anderson, in his 2013 essay 'Out of Space: The Rise of Vagrancy in Scenography', raised a, or perhaps the, key problematic for scenography in site-specific performance. First of all identifying how the theatre-designated building by its 'interior architecture … constructs a societal "self-fascination" or a constructed self-scenography: re-presenting and mirroring society in and as performance' he speculates on whether 'the experiencing of site-specific performance [is] a shift away from this outmoded historical "visuality" or just a repositioning of theatrical scenography into outer-theatre spaces?' (2013, p. 109)

For scenography this is an existential issue. Introducing recognisable scenic elements and props into a site implies that the site is, by that intervention, subjected to the same aesthetics as a building-based theatre production; that the privileging of the site has been replaced by the 'self-fascination' of the theatre. In his own practice, for example in *Forest* for the En Residencia festival in Gijón in 2009, where his upending of pews in an empty basilica evoked the woodland terrain of the title, a 'de-bunking of religious order' and the colonial harvesting of trees in an African colony (Anderson, 2003, p. 115), Anderson's scenographic utilising and rearranging of the resources from within the site was something quite distinct from the imposition of alien aesthetics. Instead, he argues, that *Forest* demonstrated both the scenographer and the scenography as a 'subject embedded in the performance rather than "representations" that inevitably vanish into the symbolic or imaginary realm of the theatre' (p. 116). Indeed, not only 'embedded' in the performance, but, he implies, accountable to the site; having to take responsibility for the use of the site's own resources and the subsequent 'disturbance' (see above) of the place and its meanings.

Anderson is aware that such an intervention 'can become the opposite of what [it] is supposed to be, that is, non-specific' (p. 116); for, even when deploying only the existing resources of the site, the results of an intervention may become detached from the meanings or social relations of the place. Anderson generalises out from this instability to recruit it for an approach to site that avoids the boundedness of specificity and instead privileges 'indeterminacy', particularly at 'the intersections of body and site' (2015, p. 1). He identifies this approach as reliant on an 'unconscious apprehension of space … giving opportunities for alternative performance and spectator programming of spatial exchange' (p. 11), particularly in unstable or toxic spaces where a necessity not to dwell too long in one place requires that spectators and performers are 'constantly on the move resulting in choreographical "writing" of themselves within [the] site and the performance through a continuance with time and occupation' (p. 10).

The importance of accidental and yet exemplary encounters (Anderson cites Jacques Derrida's 'blind writing' as his inspiration) and of keeping on the move suggests that Anderson's scenographic principle of 'indeterminacy' is close, in practical terms, to the ablative performance invoked by Mike Pearson. It also avoids the circular process whereby a strict adherence to the specificity of the textures and materials of the site ends up in homologies and naturalistic representations of appearances. The concept of indeterminacy has room, even, for the kind of scenographic absurdity I once witnessed at a 'Shakespeare in the park' production: a Roman city wall and medieval tower in the space behind the temporary stage was hidden by a set of flats onto which were painted representations of the wall and tower! Out-determining and out-homologising itself, the effect of this scenographic intervention was queasy and unstable, discomforting and making questionable the production's mechanics of pretence and imitation. Excessively conventional, the conventions themselves became contingent and open to challenge.

At the other end of some kind of continuum of spatial literacy, indeterminacy also applies to the assembled aesthetics of Tadeusz Kantor. Rather than found space, space found him; his (secret and illegal) production in 1944 of *The Return of Odysseus* by Stanisław Wyspiański, which began his interest in found performance spaces, was staged in a room in Nazi-occupied Kraków that had been damaged by the fighting: rather than going out to find his site, an exterior site had invaded his interior stage. Kantor described the experience for the audience as like being 'inside a work of art; surrounded by debris, different objects such as a broken wheel, decayed wooden boards, a stolen loudspeaker' (cited in Kobialka, 1986, p. 182). He would come to see his collection of certain objects he found in the streets, adopting and adapting them to his performances, as similar to Marcel Duchamp's appropriation (and often adaptation) of everyday objects as aesthetic *objects trouvés*. However, Kantor was as focused on the 'inner strength' of performance structure as on exterior material forces, advocating a formal purity which could 'blow up the structure of drama and ... reveal its pulsating and vibrant interior' (Kantor, 1993, p. 41).

Richard Schechner's description of how 'In orthodox theatre, scenery is segregated; it exists only in that part of the space where the performance is played', distinguishing this from the use of scenery installed in a site as part of an environmental theatre performance, where 'if scenery is used at all, it is used all the way, to the limits of its possibilities. There is no bifurcation of space, no segregation of scenery' (1994, p. 30 of the introduction), articulates the holistic approach of a site-specific scenography. It is the problem of 'preconception' (bringing to the site preconceived and site-unrelated ideas), rather than separation, that Schechner identifies as the 'first obstacle to environmental design', prescribing instead an intercultural borrowing or appropriation as his solution: 'Whether the environmentalist looks at American Indian, Asian, Oceanic, African, Siberian, or Eskimo societies, he finds many models that may stimulate his creativity' (1994, p. 25). This interculturalism, with its problematic issues of orientalism, colonialism and appropriation, is something that site-specific performers have largely skirted (with some exceptions like Anna Halprin and Red Earth) in favour of narrower, homogenising cultural fixations, the particular problematics of which are less often questioned.

In common with Schechner's writings on environmental theatre, the approach of scenographer Kathleen Irwin is to generate a sensibility that crosses between conventional stage space and what she calls 'found space'; the site is not necessarily primary, but provides 'a text among other texts, such as the script or musical score'. Although the found space, of course, pre-exists its being chosen as a site, once it has been it is one layer among others to be mapped 'through myth, memory, personal narrative, and material detail'. In 'The Weyburn Project' (2002), in the disused buildings of a former psychiatric hospital in Weyburn, Saskatchewan, Irwin worked to recruit what she calls the 'social energies' hidden in the materials of the site as prompts to recover the memories and stories of those who had lived and worked there; in tune with her general approach to working with a site's materials to create an allusive other; to recover what it is or has been. For Irwin, rather than fixing the performance to the site, the performance releases the site 'in a kind of performance in which narratives form and fragment … revealing the interpenetration of people, place, culture, and history'; the 'site' of performance shifts from the geographical place to 'the space of the glance between artist and spectator' (2012, p. 94), a space that Benedict Anderson also privileges. Rather than agents in their own right, the things of Irwin's and Anderson's sites are ambassadors, or mediators, between human agents or between human agents and themselves (Illustration 9.1).

Illustration 9.1 'The Weyburn Project', Knowhere Productions, Weyburn Mental Hospital, Weyburn, Saskatchewan, 2002. Director: Andy Houston. Producer/scenographer: Kathleen Irwin.

Photo: Kathleen Irwin.

Exercise

For her sculpture *House* (London, 1993/4), the artist Rachel Whiteread made a hollow cast of the interior of a house due shortly to be demolished. When the house was knocked down the concrete artwork remained. Consider how you could make a performance about the gaps, the voids, the emptiness around or inside things. How can you perform the absences of your site? That may not mean simply what is not there, but as in the case of *House* what was being or had been removed; in Whiteread's case, a highly controversial clearing of homes for the development of a financial district.

Exercise

In 1972, performance company Welfare State ended a four-week-long pseudo-Arthurian pilgrimage-performance from Glastonbury to Cornwall (UK), *The Trials of Lancelot Quail*, with the entire company embarking by rowing boat from Land's End and being picked up (by prior arrangement with the Royal Navy) by a submarine, HMS *Andrew*, which then proceeded to take them beneath the waves. Transforming themselves into a collective Excalibur, they engaged 'with the socio-economic and geopolitical reality of our time ... by entering one of its most dominant icons, the *Leviathan* of the military industrial complex' (Welfare State International, 2017). Two of the submariners subsequently 'defected' to the arts. How big or sophisticated an object can you recruit to a performance?

Idea

Phenomenology has been highly influential among site-specific performance makers and writers on the practice. Flicking through the bibliographies of a number of the books mentioned here, it is rare not find at least one major phenomenologist cited, usually either Martin Heidegger or Maurice Merleau-Ponty. A whole branch of philosophy given over to learning through direct and immediate feelings and experiences rather than by remote reflective interpretation was always likely to appeal to, if not deeply influence, the practice of site-specificity.

There is an intellectual modesty and flexibility in the basic ideas of phenomenology that add to its attraction for artists; less a philosophical system and more a set of approaches to life through experiences and varieties of consciousness. Phenomenology addresses things as they appear in consciousness, as phenomena of human experience rather than as distant, discrete objects out there in the world. In simple terms, phenomenology buttresses site-specificity's immersion in the material of the everyday world, rebuking those artistic practices that make separate representations of that world. It empowers direct experience over the construction of fictions, and repeatedly drives the artist and performance maker back through their feelings to the things themselves in and of their sites.

It is not difficult to see the importance of phenomenological ideas like Heidegger's 'being-in-the-world' (*Dasein*) (1962, pp. 78–82) and his emphasis on being as a dwelling, 'a staying with things' (1971, p. 151) for a performance maker such as Mike Pearson, for instance, who – in works like *Bubbling Tom* (2000), performed in and about the village where he grew up as a young child, or his 'mediated manifestations of site-specific performance' *Carrlands* (2007) about the same county – is addressing 'Landscape not [as] something to be looked at but something to be lived in, a unity of people and environment' (2006, p. 11). The theoretical depiction of space as 'neither an external object nor an inner experience' (p. 11) but as a place of unity and community is a challenge, an indictment even, to any site-practice that models itself on a rapid appropriation of a place, intense immersion and smooth exit; instead (despite, or maybe even because of, phenomenology's problematic ethical nature, mentioned above) it privileges 'staying' and suggests that the artist's responsibilities to a site and its dwellers are long-standing.

It is one of the ironies of site-based performance that it is only a minority of companies and artists – people such as Amara Tabor-Smith in the Market and Mission areas of San Francisco and Beatrice Jarvis with her extended workshops and processional performances in Derry, or companies like Welfare State International in Cumbria (UK), Tracing The Pathway in Milton Keynes (UK) and Carol Brown Dances in Auckland (New Zealand) – who return repeatedly or work over extended periods with particular sites. The model described by Melanie Kloetzel for dance festivals of 'Site-adaptive dance … created to tour and adapt to a series of unconventional (i.e. non-theatre) sites … that tends towards the spectacular' (2017, p. 112) or one-off 'smash and grab' productions (and I confess to a number of these) are far more likely than an extended commitment. The reasons may be largely circumstantial, and wholly understandable – the commercial non-viability of returning to the same local audience, the short term or one-off nature of funding awards, commission practices and so on – and performance makers are not unique in having to travel in order to find work; nevertheless, these accommodations and circumstances have coalesced (as with the distance between autobiographical performances and autobiographical spaces) into a divorce of practices from the ideas about them.

Phenomenology, like any kind of philosophy, is always in danger of becoming the subject of itself; the idea of experiences standing in for experiences themselves. Site-specificity is equally vulnerable to performing an idea of itself, generating, demonstrating and commodifying the thrill of immersion rather than inviting others into the immersion itself, selling the sizzle not the sausage. Ideas like those of 'reversibility' (the affect of being experienced reciprocated by the original experiencer) or 'intersubjectivity' (where two people experience perceptions of each other, while aware of their own experiencing) are attempts to steer wide of solipsism (in which the self is the only knowable thing), but they can rebound if the entanglements themselves become separated and marketable things that are out there in the world rather than being the phenomena of the performance experience.

A recent development in phenomenology, Object-Oriented Ontology (OOO), emerging around the millennium, has significance for site-specificity. In the anxiety to avoid solipsism, phenomenology has previously emphasised the human affect and undervalued the object. OOO, however, challenges the idea of such a human-centred cosmos, denying that things are ever drained of their presence or significance just because humans have stopped thinking about them. Instead, OOO asserts the independence of things from human perception and from each other. It grants some discreteness to objects; the thingness of things includes their resistance to being swept up and immersed in human-centred ideas about 'full sensorium', about the flows and currents of all things or, indeed, any advocacy for a taxonomy of spaces. OOO rejects the idea, designated as 'correlationism' by philosopher Quentin Meillassoux, that 'we never grasp an object "in itself", in isolation from its relation to the subject' (p. 5), and it rejects any thinking that 'subordinate[s] *what is known* to our *way of knowing*' (Shaviro, 2014, p. 3, emphasis in original) or that leaves things 'pacified, retreating to an exterior, silent and uniform world of "Nature"' (Henare, Holbraad & Wastell, 2007, p. 9).

There does seem to be some object-oriented autonomy at work in the regularity in which certain objects, or categories of objects, appear in site-specific performances. Just as certain categories of site have repeatedly attracted performance makers, so there is also a taxonomy of objects that are similarly attractive: flags, water, salt, boats, and even the sun: for example, the recruiting of the predictable changes in sunlight for Pentabus's *Shot Through the Heart* at Ludlow Castle to accompany changes of mood in the action. A similarly profound scenographic transformation, in this case of the abject into the nostalgic (a former Eurostar terminal at King's Cross into a 'working' Edwardian railway station), was achieved by the deployment of another repeatedly attractive object – a working steam locomotive – for an adaptation of *The Railway Children* by designer Joanna Scotcher. In most cases such objects are used as part of a 'pyramid of supporting elements [that] may lift the performers to the apex'. However, there are times 'when the performers are at the base of the pyramid' (Schechner, 1994, p. xl) and the performers and the dramaturgy are preparations for the presence of the unhuman thing.

OOO is also not restricted to small things, but embraces sites themselves. Its emergence has coincided with several new publications from different disciplines proposing a similar agency of objects and a move away from the belief that 'Spaces and things passively await manipulation' (Beauregard, 2012, p. 2). These include Daniel Miller's popular *The Comfort of Things* (2008); Joshua Sofer's *The Stage Life of Props* (2003) in which properties used in performances are characterised as 'tak[ing] on a life of their own as they weave in and out of the stage action' (p. vi); Performance Research's special edition *On Objects* (2008); and Leanne Shapton's novel masquerading as an auction catalogue: *Important Artifacts and Personal Property from the Collections of Lenore Doolan and Harold Morris, Including Books, Street Fashion and Jewelry* (2009).

At times these ideas and their promulgators have steered close to animism (the belief that things have souls, that all things are alive). The political theorist Jane Bennett has instead, though, proposed a 'vital materialism' attributing something close to agency to things without granting them personalities; objects have 'thing-power', 'the capacity ... not only to impede or block the will and designs of humans but also act as quasi agents or forces with trajectories, propensities, or tendencies of their own', 'an active, earthy, not-quite-human capaciousness' (2010, pp. viii, 3). Among some performance makers this respect for the vibrancy of things extends beyond a simple regard for their energy to a working through its multifaceted qualities: 'inherently unstable, serving representational, decorative, functional, fictive or cognitive purposes, moment by moment. Their identity and meaning may be only partly controllable' (Pearson, 2010, p. 119).

In more general terms, this vibrant materialism, even when it equally acknowledges both the active and the obstructive power of objects (Bennett, 2010, pp. 1–2), works as a torque placed upon the (mostly human) trajectories idealised in some conceptions of space. Against that fluidity, the recalcitrance of things can be revelatory and illuminating, bringing things to a halt for closer examination (rather like Brecht's revealing interruption of processes), or exposing everyday motions that are generally taken for granted by changing their direction. There are precedents for such an approach to 'things' in the work of theatre makers like Tadeusz Kantor whose props – such as the 'waltzing bike' and the 'thudding cradle' in his *Umarła Klasa* ('Dead Class', 1975), or the cross mounted like a cannon in *Wielopole, Wielopole* (1981) – manifest the discreteness of the things of OOO and 'carry enough inner tension and meaning to be considered autonomous works of art' (Legierska, 2015), or the machines of Sharmanka Kinetic Theatre (scary enough to send young members of the audience running for the exits during a Sharmanka performance I saw in St Petersburg, then Leningrad, in 1990), or the broken chair in Théâtre de Complicité's *Mnemonic* (1999) that is first characterised as a family heirloom of the performer Simon McBurney, then as a 'fake', then something used in numerous previous productions, including Ionesco's *The Chairs*, until it finally 'opens up to reveal arms and legs that are jointed like human limbs. The performers move the limbs and give the chair breath and intention … the chair had become a "performing object"' (Margolies, 2016, p. 8).

Performance makers, given the initial thrill of a vista, or the overwhelming ambience of a building as a container of mysteries or treasures, may miss the vibrancy or vitality of those things in their site that are already 'performing objects'. The crane by the dockside is not mere set dressing but can still work, the ferry is not simply transportation with seating that stands in for an auditorium but is a traveller in itself, the annoying ventilation unit may be the drone around which you build your soundscape if you can resist the temptation to turn it off. The site is not your shell.

Eleanor Margolies's account of the broken chair in *Mnemonic* becoming an active thing includes a description of revelations about the chair, some accurate and some not; a tension between authenticity and fabulation that is something that animates the museums and conserved spaces of the heritage industry (spaces that are often favoured by makers of site-based performance). Where objects or artefacts within heritage sites are granted agency, the tendency is to legitimate that agency through a human interpretation. So, for example, Robert Pahre describes how objects acknowledged as 'inauthentic' (modern or inaccurate substitute artefacts bought in stores or second-hand shops) are often used in the historic forts under the management of the US National Park Service to '*define* the site, locking in certain stories of the buildings', explaining that this locking in of meaning turns buildings into 'props for telling stories' (2015, p. 67, emphasis in original).

However, in a complementary but contradictory reaction, in the process of telling the stories of heritage, the authentic objects – let alone their agency – can start to disappear. The artefacts are still there in the collection, but they fade from its iteration. So, Jeff Camhi, director of the Nature Park and Galleries at the Life Sciences Institute, Hebrew University, Jerusalem, collated 58 'different types of communicative acts' (2008, p. 275) for guides to perform with artefacts in local museums; and yet only five of the 58 are communications from object to guides or object to visitors, the other 53 communicate at the object (pp. 288–289), and four of the five exceptions involve the guide manipulating the object as a puppet. The only truly agentive exception in Camhi's list is where an artefact, hidden from view by the guide, 'reveals itself only by its sound or smell or touch' (p. 289).

A performance maker should ask themselves: Am I doing any better than these museums? Am I subjugating the things of my site as mere decor, or as illustrative examples serving my narratives, themes and dominance? The anthropologists Henare, Holbraad and Wastell have called for a deferral of this kind of interpretation of things by human stories, advocating 'the absolute productivity of non-definition' and the setting loose of things against theory, proposing 'a methodology where the "things" themselves may dictate a *plurality* of ontologies' (2007, p. 7). In other words, your site does not need to be explained, but can be allowed to tell itself; possessed of many ways of being that do not require a human narration or synthesis in order to be understood. This may be hard for any performance maker to take from a pile of old rocks, or a room of moth-eaten dresses or a supermarket shelf of brightly packaged processed food. It suggests that site-work that is an interpretation, even if it is a daring act of critical subversion of homogenised spaces, is no more, in these terms, than a progressive form of anthropomorphism. There is a hint of what an Object-Oriented dramaturgy might look like in the proposal by Henare, Holbraad and Wastell that 'meanings are not "carried" by things but just *are identical* to them' (2007, pp. 3–4).

Exercise

The nineteenth-century utopian philosopher Charles Fourier, committed to the transformation of lives of work into lives of pleasure, proposed that humans might evolve new senses and the requisite organs for them. He proposed an *archibras*, a tail with fingers and an eye (Wark, 2013, p. 78). Take some modelling clay – this can be done by one person or a performance group, maybe even something for an audience – each person then moulds a new head for themselves so they look at the site from more than one perspective. Or moulds the shape that expresses the feeling the site gives them; then put the different shapes together to model its ambience. Or mould the new sensory organs that the site requires to be fully understood; put these together into a new 'character', a bundle of senses specific to the site, or upscale them on a computer and 3D print full-size proboscises for your performers.

Exercise

Use land artist Robert Smithson's ideas about 'site and non-site' to map and collect objects from a site; and then choose a 'non-site' where you can show these objects and perform with them. Smithson listed the qualities of sites as 'open limits, a series of points, outer coordinates, subtraction, indeterminate certainty, scattered information, reflection, edge, some place (physical)' and 'many', while for non-sites he wrote of 'closed limits, an array of matter, inner coordinates, addition, determinate uncertainty, contained information, mirror, center, no place (abstract)' and 'one' (1972, pp. 152–153). Adapt Smithson's approach of choosing appropriate means for displaying his objects (for example, dividing his displays into boxed sections that mirrored the physical aspects of the original site) to a way of performing the objects in the non-site (for example, if the objects have been taken from a river bed, use the flow and currents of the original site to animate the objects in the non-site). In 1997 a work of Smithson's was recreated in a Brooklyn (New York) gallery: *Dead Tree* (1969) had involved the installation of a fallen tree in the Kunsthalle Düsseldorf (Germany). The 1997 version barely fitted its location, leaving walls scraped and damaged and boughs broken. Can you imagine a performance created in a natural space that, if transferred to a theatre, would damage both venue and action?

Exercise

Take the example of Lygia Clark's *Pedr e ar* (Paris, 1966) – a stone balanced on a bag of air held by a participant – an artwork that is a kind of sculpture and yet relies upon human action to sustain it, and, at the same time, obliges the human participant into an ethical relationship, sustaining their agency or destroying the artwork and returning it to its constitutive materials. Look for and experiment with different objects and materials until you find something that 'obliges' the human performer and determines the action, both human and non-living.

Exercise

Use models and maps to make small interventions which have meaning for large sites. Consider how Cluster Bomb's *Marooned Miniatures* at the Victoria & Albert Museum (London) recreated in matchboxes the assembly line of the Lesney Matchbox Toy Factory, playing with the ambiguities of display and production at work in a museum. Use as inspiration the work of the remarkable criminologist Frances Glessner Lee and her *Nutshell Studies of Unexplained Death* (tiny models of crime scenes used to train police officers in the art of detection); create a piece that employs models, simulations and different scales to explore how you might express and unveil a site through the performance of analysis, hypothesis and detection.

Exercise

When a student at Dartington College of Arts, Sarah Williams devised a performance where an audience clustered around an installation of small silvery objects. Depending on how the audience arrived and then shifted around, the performers inside the installation moved the parts of the shiny installation to mirror the audience's movements. When this happened, the audience then moved again in order to see the new positions and, in response, the performers moved the pieces. And so on. Can you invent a performance process where the audience, unknowingly, are the authors and directors of the action, the final arbiters of the design?

10

Communities, Audiences and Immersion

A dramaturgy is only ever likely to make sense if it is informed by an approximate idea or intuition of how it will be received by its audience; an attitude that is sure to establish some tension (creative or otherwise) with an art form that prioritises the existing site rather than a forthcoming reception. For the performance maker, the audience may already be 'present' in the site, part of its meaning, the moment that they decide or are asked to make work in a particular place. The thinker of these hybrid thoughts may be a playwright, or a social science-based adviser; inscribed into their pondering may be existing ideas about an ideal entanglement of literary texts and interpreting audiences or of the potential receptions of, say, a piece of activist or educational theatre. It is coming to a consideration of this moment, when the audience are let into the production of performance, that the virtues of what might have seemed like an invasive craft of site-based work now appears more pronounced in the face of a potential flood of assumptions irrespective of any specific qualities of a place.

From quite another perspective, the audience may not be arriving, but have been present for a very long time. Given the attractions of conceptualising abstract space or investigating textures and the unhuman agencies of vibrant things, it might be easy to forget that many, maybe most, sites of performance are places of belonging, home or neighbourhood. Even where legal ownership is held by an individual or single organisation, with whom you have negotiated over access, you may still find that for many other people there is a sense of common proprietorship over the space, or loyalty to it, or there may be temporary occupation of it. Close attention from the start will help you avoid actions like those of the company mentioned in Chapter 4 who cut off the route used by homeless people in their site. Official permissions may only be the start of your negotiation with a community. Working with Nicola Singh in the allotments of a small Devon village in 2008 (see Chapter 5) although we had official permission from the legal owners and managers of the land (a local government authority) we quickly learned that it was still necessary for us to negotiate, as best we could (not everyone was welcoming), with each individual allotment user about working on their particular plot of land within the allotments.

In site-specific performance, and with the collapse in many cases of traditional conventions of spatial separation and active/passive roles, you will always need to be thinking, even in the simplest of practical terms, about the role of audience as key players in your dramaturgy. If you leave no room for them and for their engagement, participation, or agency, then they may seek that room by leaving, withdrawing their interest or intervening in destructive or explosively creative ways that challenge the integrity of performance. In the conventional theatre space the audience participates by close attention, interpretation, empathy, identification and (usually) by small acts of physical engagement (laughter, applause), but if you bring that audience to a place that has no fixed point for spectatorship, mingling performers and audience, then you are creating expectations of agency and entanglement that you should disappoint (or relieve) only if you intend to.

The affordance of certain sites and of certain unfolding performance practices offer you the possibility of characterising your audience, of giving them functions, of recruiting them into the site and the action or fiction, of engaging their bodies as shapes, supports, backdrops, of engaging their imagination and creativity in improvised actions, world-making, of involving them as citizens and decision-makers in relational performances.

No matter how they may be characterised or invited by you, however, they are unlikely to wholly abandon their role as audience members or, often, as customers. Not only will they be watching the directed action, but watching and being watched by the other members of the audience; and in those rare occasions where spectators become wholly incorporated, sometimes ecstatically, into the action and prepared to dispense with self-consciousness and inhibitions, they are still likely to retain some awareness of, and even play up to, their being gazed upon. Breaking the potential intensity (and distraction from a text-based narrative) of that secondary loop in these events was directly addressed by Punchdrunk director Felix Barrett when he introduced masks to be worn by all audience members. For him, the mask 'is the key thing that removes the other audience members … the mask solves the problem of the audience' (Barrett, 2008); this might dilute the *demos*-like, collective response and responsibility of audiences, mediated by their surveillance of each other, but it also deflects from the autonomous impetus of an event towards displays of social presence and identity, and facilitates a more subjective relationship of audience to the performance content and context.

This constraining and hiding, to retain a more personal and individual spectatorship within mobile and sometimes clustering groups of audience, contrasts with other performance practices that have emphasised the collective presence of the audience as responsible co-creators and co-checkers (or co-witnesses) of a joint action. Site-specific theatre and performance (although it may not always be called that) is sometimes a way for communities to engage in a collective event to memorialise historical events, public identities, or trauma and loss; if repeated, the origins of these rituals and ceremonies may be lost, but something continues to power their repetitions as performative actions that not only protest, but even inspire a change in the contexts or circumstances (a 'recontextualisation') of their production. *In the Mountain/On the Mountain* (Mount Tamalpais, California, USA, 1981) is an example – even a model – for how a public 'atmosphere' (a collective feeling that is tied to a specific place), aesthetic discipline, an open dramaturgy and a series of transformations for participants *within* the dramaturgical structure, can generate an event that creates, but also leaves a residue of 'new space' (see Worth & Poynor, 2004, pp. 97–102).

In the Mountain/On the Mountain was a two-day event that arose as a response to the murders of several women walkers between 1979 and 1981 on the trails of Mount Tamalpais, just outside of San Francisco. At the time a series of workshops for the project 'A Search for Living Myths and Rituals through Dance and the Environment' were being run nearby by Anna and Lawrence Halprin; their intention was to find myths through ritual performance in the environment that could reflect back the concerns of the local community to that community as an audience. *In the Mountain/On the Mountain* was an extension out from the workshops, a generative performance based on intercultural traditional sources 'for the purpose of having an effect on the world' (Halprin, 1984/1997).

The 1981 event consisted of three parts: the first was an evening of ritual dance in a designated performance space; various natural elements were imitated and honoured and when fire was invoked in dance the violence of the killings was referenced and then dispersed by the taking on of both murder and victim roles by all the dancers. After this, all the participants (dancers and audience) feasted together and then slept in 'dream wheels' (lying like the spokes of a wheel with their heads together at the hub), awaking and sharing their dreams at sunrise. This liminal section of the performance was designed to allow the audience to hold on to the experience of the evening's ritual dance and begin to move from spectating into performing. On the second day, for the third part of the event, all participants processed to the peak of the mountain. Large bamboo poles were carried and swung; these 'connector' objects (whatever their literal role or function) are suggestive of a drawing down of an energy or inspiration from an 'elsewhere', an environmental source, as with the conductor's baton or the magician's wand; in this case they were 'invested with the energy of the evening's performance', connecting the first and final parts of the ritual. The participants then walked back down the sides of the mountain, singing and chanting and 'challenging the killer directly' (Halprin, 1984/1997, n.p.), strolling along the mountain's various trails (many of them officially closed due to the killings), pausing at times for the reading of poems, visiting the murder sites and offering tributes to the lives of those murdered; at one point Anna Halprin danced with a group of small children.

Although the preparations for *In the Mountain/On the Mountain* and the three-part structure were geared to creating the maximum solidarity and security for those participating, the highly charged nature of the event (and a sense of what was at stake) can be read in the account of journalist Ira Kamin who participated in the performance and reflected at the time that 'There are those in this Halprin party who don't know each other and certainly the thought must occur to them: Which one of you is the killer?' (cited in Halprin, 1984/1997, n.p.).

Shortly after the performance of *In The Mountain/On The Mountain*, a man was arrested, charged, convicted and imprisoned for murders on the mountain and elsewhere. Although Anna Halprin does not directly answer her own question 'to what extent did this ritual play a role in [the killer's] apprehension?' she implies that such rituals, if engaging directly with the 'living myths' of a specific location (in this case, the life and death struggle for safe access to the mountain), do have the power and connectivity to 'hav[e] an effect on the world'. Significantly, perhaps – particularly given that so many of the performances described in this book did not initiate regular events, at least not in their original sites, nor become part of an ongoing performance practice in their original sites – *In the Mountain/On the Mountain* did continue in a five-yearly 'Return to the Mountain' at the 'mother-site' of Mount Tamalpais, and also beyond, morphing into workshops and dances as 'Circle the Earth', 'Circle the Mountain' and 'Planetary Dance'; a version of which, authorised by Anna Halprin, opened the Venice Biennale in 2017.

A far subtler attempt to effect change through performance was present in Jooyoung Lee's *Fantasy Real Estate Agency* (Seoul, 2013) which engaged its audiences as participants on quite different terms to *In the Mountain/On the Mountain*, yet still addressed issues of trauma and threat in leisure, heritage and (formerly) residential spaces (Illustration 10.1). It took the form of a 'fake' estate agents where 'customers' could view details and images of neglected heritage sites and former sacred spaces as if they were properties available on the market, and then travel on 'mis-guided tours' to view them. Similarly, Jooyoung Lee conducted visits (interweaving and gently subverting official tours) to the blighted buildings around the notorious DMZ or 'demilitarised zone' that has separated North and South Korea since the end of the Korean War in 1953, secreted within an official tour but departing from its conventions. Jooyoung Lee's work draws on the comic subversions of 'counter-tourism' (Smith, 2013); her work is a protest against contemporary circumstances, leading its participants into direct contact with difficult and abject spaces, but unlike the explicit and resourced attempt to affect a change in the world in *In the Mountain/On the Mountain*, *Fantasy Real Estate* parades the helplessness of its ostensible resources (property retailing

Illustration 10.1 *Fantasy Real Estate Agency Temporary Office#1*, installation view, Work on Work Studio, Seoul, 2013. Jooyoung Lee.

Photo: Jooyoung Lee.

and tourism) to bring change; as much a critique of them as of the abject conditions they operate in.

The multiplicity of events that make up Halprin's ritual and Lee's office visits and site tours, may have something of an exemplary quality in delivering community-based site-specificity; offering a portmanteau of experiences for engaging a wide range of participants (not simply an 'arts crowd'), rather than a single product. Examples of this promiscuous form could also include *Signs and Wonders* (2012, a satellite Wrights & Sites production) in Lancaster (UK), marking the 400th anniversary of the Lancashire Witch Trials, which included a 'decanting' (declaiming) at the Williamson Folly overlooking the town on the first day, 'visitations' to the key trial and execution sites in Lancaster (with further decantations) on the second, a trading of objects (wax objects that passers-by were persuaded to secrete in their homes), pamphlets and conversations at Lancaster Market on the third, and, on the final day, performance walks around Newchurch-in-Pendle, a key location for the 1612 events. Another example would be *Le Centre de Fribourg* (2008) performed by

Blaise Roulin and Yoann Chassot in Fribourg (Switzerland) in which audiences contributed to identifying the centre of the city according to a variety of criteria (this was performed on a number of occasions; each time a different centre was identified) and then participated in an opening ceremony for the new 'centre', to which local and festival 'celebrities' were invited to officiate.

Jooyoung Lee's work shares the intimacy (despite sometimes working in epic spaces) of the 'performances for life' to be found at the home of the late Dennis Severs at '18 Folgate Street' in London, where the artist had transformed his eighteenth-century home into a living public manifesto of pre-Romantic aesthetics (Severs, during his lifetime, made himself available in the house to intervene in the public's visits; now the house is invigilated by volunteers), or at James Turrell's *Roden Crater* (Arizona, USA) where the artist is turning the inner cone of a crater into an auditorium for which the stars, moon and sun will perform. In each case, and in common with the Halprins' project at Mount Tamalpais, there is a direct engagement with loaded, overshadowed and even grand landscapes; yet in the case of Lee and Severs (and even of Turrell, in some aspects of his architecture) there is an intimacy and subjectivity for the visitor that is every bit as intense as for a masked and immersed Punchdrunk spectator.

Perhaps informed by the intensity (and fashionableness) of the experiences of, and the vivid visuals often necessitated by, site-specific performance, the genre is now increasingly seen by powerful companies and institutions as a means to mark a space with spectacle and ritual. A recent example of this was the director Volker Hesse's spectacular opening of the Gotthard base tunnel (Switzerland) in 2016, the longest railway tunnel in the world, with a cast of 600 including orange-overall-wearing dancers representing the nine construction workers who died during the making of the tunnel, hovered over by a half-naked woman in a bird/baby costume. The imagery developed for this event – of horned god, giant scintillating beetles, clusters of eyes and mass obeisance before a clock whose hands whirred erratically in different directions (not to mention the participation of yet another train as racing object) – was ostensibly esoteric (and occasionally erotic) in thematic nature. Despite the efforts of conspiracy and fundamentalist Christian websites there appeared to be no particular structural, political or religious meaning to the event. The folk tale – the tricking of the devil into building a bridge for locals at no cost – from which the imagery was partly appropriated, was largely indecipherable from the performance; instead, there was a pervasive sense of opportunistic 'otherness': bodies jerked by unseen forces, grotesque costumes that borrowed from familiar phantasmagorias, the coordinated and soulless gestures and marches of mass workers' celebrations.

While Hesse's ceremony might have shared some superficial similarity with *In the Mountain/On the Mountain* – its mass cast, intercultural borrowings, emblematic costumes and elements of ritual – the role of the audience in the two events was utterly different. It was passive and privileged and unengaged in the Gotthard event, increasingly engaged and active on Mount Tamalpais. While both Hesse and the Halprins mobilise (very different) communities and their collective lexicons of symbolism, and Lee, Severs and Turrell offer welcome and hospitality to their publics, some performances generate a quite different, sometimes conflictual and critical, relationship with their communities. Indeed, in some cases, performances have set out to directly disrupt a community; like the anti-consumerist actions in retail stores, banks and corporations by the Reverend Billy and the Church of Stop Shopping (1998 and ongoing), conducting exorcisms of bad loans and toxic assets, and by The Vacuum Cleaner's 'Church of Immaculate Consumption' (2003–2005) whose 50-strong praying to commodities led to the Selfridges store on London's Oxford Street temporarily closing its doors. In other performances, the disruption may be more oblique and ambiguous; in Delia Brown's 'Guerrilla Lounging' project of 2002, she and female friends gained access without permission to some mansions of the rich in Beverly Hills, held their own parties inside them, and from these Brown painted 'flamboyant' portraits of her friends in their newly 'acquired' lavish surroundings (Hoffmann & Jonas, 2005, pp. 122–23). Brown and her friends' furtive performances are fuelled by a militant nihilism, a resignation to the belief that all art, no matter how radical or elusive, will eventually 'be appropriated by the mainstream', and so choosing figurative oil painting as the medium of documentation as the one most 'ready to be consumed by the market' (p. 122).

Exercise

---topia. Ask residents of a particular area or community to separately make a model of a new feature that they would like to see in their ideal future version of their town or city. Ask everyone to bring their models to a space where there is a large table erected, plus quantities of cardboard, paper, paint, scissors, paintbrushes and so on. Together make a provisional construction of a new town or city using the elements that have been brought in by the individual residents. Then together create connections between the different elements or make new buildings in the gaps from the materials provided. Friends can be invited along to add what they wish, or to move the elements about. Eventually, gather all the participants at the end of the day to observe and discuss the 'utopia' that has emerged.

Exercise

Research and identify a place where a building has fallen down or been demolished and a safe 'empty' space now remains; create a simple performance by performing some of the actions that would have been done in the original building in the space that remains. At first try one, then add others. If the building stood for some time add time layers – perhaps costumes or objects that identify particular time periods or roles. Invite former residents or users of the site; ask them to participate in the performance with you. Research how 'real people' become performers in sites like 'Big Pit' in Wales where former miners are the tour guides, or those former Republican activists who give tours of the Falls Road in Belfast.

Idea

While the substance (the liveness) of a performance might be said to disappear, clearly a site does not; though it may change to varying degrees (differently for different participants) once the performance has passed through it. Here there is a profound distinction between those members of an audience who may only ever be present in a site for the duration of a single performance and members of the communities for whom that site will continue to constitute a home, landmark, threat, haunt or identity-marker long after the performance is, formally, ended. Unlike a designated theatre space, most sites for site-specific theatre are unlikely to be addressed by any formal performance again. So, perhaps a new kind of 'acid test' is necessary; one that takes into account the ecology of both

> performance and environment and the contradictions between the two (Kershaw, 2009, pp. 315–318). Unlike theatre buildings and studios which are designed to 'blank' themselves during and between different perfor-mances and to expedite performance's tendency to disappear, other sites may facilitate another tendency in performance: for it to run on, as conse-quence and echoes and in unexpected ways.

In 2010, I made an ambulatory performance with Simon Persighetti called *Water Walk* (Exeter, UK) during which we invaded the trashed and long-unused communal drying area behind some homes, hanging a piece of wet cloth there. A few months later and the area was repaired and in use again. Likewise, a performance by a student of mine around the rem-nants of a stone gate at the entrance to her university's campus prompted the authorities to gather up the stones, where they had laid for more than 50 years, overgrown with brambles, ready for re-assemblage. As in Victoria Hunter's schematic model of 'influence' in site-specific perfor-mance (2015a, pp. 36–38) what drops down from the linear trajectory of these projects from 'site' to 'product', is 'New space created'.

Some performances attempt to directly address the future development of their site. In Opéra Pagaï's *Enterprise de Détournement: Chaniter#5: L'Île de Carhaix-Bretagne* in Carhaix-Plouguer (France, 2007), the company staged the (not entirely serious) hopes expressed by some residents that climate change might flood the surrounding countryside and turn the city into a beach resort. The street performances – practising Chinese to welcome new visitors and migrants, visiting an amphibian vegetable patch – and their accompanying exhibition 'insert a "hijacked reality" intervention into the environmental debate' (Haedicke, 2012, p. 111), not in order to develop an intellectual discussion (the scientific explana-tions were purposely unlikely), but to encourage the imagining (and the beginning of the making) of a new space, a new city, in a new terrain.

When the site becomes an aspiration to a new space – when that newness is realised in the material present or immediate aftermath of the performance (as with the washing area or the university gate) – then there is a reversal of the 'host' and 'ghost' roles described by Cliff McLucas (2000). The performance, now, hosts the future of a site which becomes 'ghostly', a premonition of what it can become.

All this suggests that – just as academics and critics might consider devoting a greater proportion of their reviews and documentations of site-based performances to their spaces, following Mike Pearson's suggestion that 'Any full description of a site-specific production surely requires as much said about the site – its architecture, its atmospheres, its climate, its history – and the emplaced scenography – its surface, substances, objects, locales – as about the themes and dramaturgy, to fully account for what happened' (2018, p. 310) – as a practitioner, you might shift more of the focus of your performance making to the conscious production of 'new space'. Just as one test of a studio-based performance's success is the transforming effect it has upon its audience, so at least part of the success of a site-specific performance is the transformation, enduring or fleeting, of the site itself. Hunter herself interprets this changed space as 'the "place" of performance, transforming the accepted and conventional properties ascribed to a particular space, while simultaneously creating a temporary place of performance' (2015a, p. 38). Beyond the formal end of the performance, the transformation can run on in the space, potentially far more enduring, given the possibility for a more intense entanglement than is likely in the 'blanked' space of a studio: in the way, for example, that Brith Gof's *Gododdin* (1988) – based on an early medieval manuscript (possibly based on a much earlier oral composition) by a Welsh poet concerning the defeat of an outnumbered tribe, the Gododdin of the title – staged in a disused Rover car factory in Cardiff, constituted an attempt to remake such post-industrial spaces, to win them back from models of appropriation, resource-stripping and invasion by performing an act of resistance against the odds, in the face of defeat (see Hodge & Turner, 2012, pp. 99–101).

Exercise

In Fiona Templeton's *YOU – The City* (1988, New York and other cities) there was a moment when a participant audience member, who has just passed someone they assume to be a performer, is directed to double back on their route and is then seen by a third audience member who looks at them and clearly assumes *they* are the performer (in the London version the equivalent moment occurred on the phone). Create a participant performance in which the performance loops the participants back on themselves so that they can re-understand and embrace their role as performers.

Exercise

Visit the building of a large mainstream theatre, explore it as a geography; how are its spaces working to create a temporary community (an audience) from disparate individuals and groups: cloakroom, socialising space, information, ticketing and ushering. Now choose a non-theatrical site and devise a means of using the space and generating 'rituals' to create a similar temporary community for your performance. (This may *be* your performance.)

Exercise

Richard Schechner advocated that in a performance site 'there ought to be *jumping-off places* where spectators can physically enter the performance ... *vantage points ... pinnacles, dens and hutches*: extreme places far up, far back, and deep down where spectators can dangle or burrow or vanish' (1994, p. 30, emphasis in original). Choose a site and work to discover or open up such spaces, or their equivalents, for your audience.

Idea

In the early years after the millennium, site-specific theatre and performance began to catch the interest of the mainstream media; certain qualities, more present in some performances than others, drew particular attention. These were 'immersive' qualities that offered not only striking and often vividly experienced events for spectators, but also something amenable to the media, whose journalists and critics, putting themselves 'at the mercy' of these intense and sometimes intimate experiences, generated copy that was both personal and engaging. Such was the impact of both the performances and their coverage, that 'immersive' was, and is still, regularly 'assigned, often inappropriately, as a defining term for all kinds of theatres that occur in non-traditional venues' (Machon, 2013, p. 66), suffering a similar conceptual-blurring as 'site-specific' had for many years before.

It is important to understand that there was nothing new in absolute terms about these performances; they have often replicated, assembled and developed existing elements from installation art, participatory theatre-in-education programmes, and physical theatre event-workshops in the Grotowski tradition. This happened not necessarily through direct borrowing, but through the unfolding and sharing of practices that were available across performance communities and educations. What was new, however, was the way that this assemblage was noticed and celebrated.

The breadth of performances that are now characterised as 'immersive' by curators, producers, critics and performers is so extensive – from intimate one-to-one performances like Adrian Howells's *Foot Washing for the Sole* (2010) to the grandeur of hyper-detailed fictions like Punchdrunk's *The Masque of the Red Death* (2007) – that it sometimes obscures their precise qualities, such as audience agency and participation and audience–performer interaction. This difficulty arises partly because these qualities, and others identified as characteristic of 'immersion', are not always compatible or easily reconciled with each other.

So, for example, the hyper-detailing of sets and the sensual excitement of the invitation into alien and unfamiliar spaces have undoubtedly generated feelings of adventuring into 'worlds' for audiences. With no designated 'audience spaces' or seating, and with prompts to interact, audiences are often encouraged to discover a sense of their own agency, to go looking for the action and to mingle among the performers: 'Immersion implies access to the inside of the performance in some way' (White, 2012, p. 221). Something is taken here from the enterprise of urban explorers and ravers, occupying derelict or disused spaces, from the collectivism and co-operation of 'happenings' and from group-improvised performances; the results are not unique, but recognisable in Richard Schechner's description originally written in the early 1970s of spectators who 'experience great extremes – of deep, perhaps active involvement and participation ... Sometimes a spectator will freak out, go so far into the experience that he is lost inside it' (1994, p. 19). However, these encouragements of the audience's agency are not unproblematic; sometimes limited by what aspects of a performance a spectator can get to see, which may be dictated more by chance (or 'theatre-literacy') than choice, as Maxime Doyle, Punchdrunk's choreographer, has acknowledged, 'if you're not responding on a physical level you lose out ... you see audiences who are not aware of their physical body, who aren't aware, and then you see audiences who are really on it' (cited in Machon, 2007, n.p.). Equally, the invitation to

interact with performers is sometimes at odds with the equally powerful offer of a 'full-sensorium' immersion in the performance experience
that Josephine Machon suggests can be like a bodily immersion in water
(2013, pp. xiv–xv).

Machon's analogy is instructive: in critical discourse, a fluid environment certainly fits with the conceptual liquefaction of 'place' into
'space'. In terms of reception, what is gained for the spectator is a tactile
intensity and proximity, if sometimes at the expense of certain senses
and an intimidating feeling of being overwhelmed. As much as a 'full-
sensorium' experience, the watery metaphor also suggests something like
a selectively heightened, altered state of consciousness. Captivated audiences are inspired 'to feel *feelingly* – to undergo' experiences in which 'the
human body is addressed "polysensually", where "full-body" inclusion
demands that the observer "relinquish distant and reserved experience" and embrace "mind expanding" or "mind assailing" perception'
(Machon, 2013, pp. 22, 36). This kind of characterisation falls comfortably within a behaviourist view of perception, the spectator being
stimulated by outer agencies in order to respond through their existing
conditioning. This passivity is very different to the agency of the senses
in, say, the gestalt or ecological approaches to perception (see Gibson,
1966, 1979; Gilchrist, 2006) – adopted by numerous site-specific artists
(see, e.g., Hunter, 2015, pp. 30–32) – which emphasise the senses as
active, reaching out into the world to gather information, rather than
passively soaking it up.

Given the sometimes febrile debate around these performances –
ranging from condemnations of the exploitation of unpaid or poorly
paid theatre makers to eulogies for exciting transgressions of traditional theatre practice – it may be hard to hold on to the possibility
that many of the qualities particular to immersiveness in site-based
performances are contradictory, sustaining positive and negative,
passive and active elements simultaneously (and not simply for technical reasons; how well or badly they are delivered), but as parts of a
complex shifting of meaning and meshwork within the practice of site-
based performances.

So, the similarity between a body–mind immersion into a performance of an 'aware' spectator, and a hyper-sensitised presence of an

exploring/visiting site-artist is certainly real, but there is no equivalence, and Machon makes this very clear in her theoretical characterisation of what makes immersiveness in site-based performance special. This specialness is, perhaps surprisingly, not particularly connected to place or site. For, despite the performance makers' often very close attention to the details of their site and to its special ambience, the descriptions and focus of 'immersive' performances often edit out the context or reduce it to a mere prelude to the main business of the affects of the performance's sensual reception. This is a shift in the understanding of what is happening in site-performance itself, conceptualised by Josephine Machon as its 'live(d)ness' (2013, p. 43) rather than its liveness, a distinction forced by immersiveness's 'lasting ephemerality' (p. 44).

In contrast to Peggy Phelan's idea that live performance 'becomes itself through disappearance' (1993, p. 146), Machon seems to suggest that in 'immersive' theatre there is little that is live to disappear. Given its relative indifference to context, its ephemerality (the tendency to disappearance that makes performance precious for Phelan) is spatially evacuated and temporally extended, describing the latter as 'the receiver's embodied memory of the event' (Machon, 2013, p. 44), emphasising a characterisation of the immersive theatre audience as consumers rather than co-producers. The 'live(d)' of immersive performance is a liveness that is somehow frozen in the moment, that is, as it is experienced, already an affect of something passed; to be savoured in the moment as a what-will-be-savoured-in-the-future. In other words, rather than directly and presently experiencing by a 'full sensorium' engagement, the immersive theatre spectator is encouraged, by the event-ness and popularity, to 'feel *feelingly* – to undergo', to self-consciously save up the 'in the moment' for later consumption and exchange. What is usually fleeting ('ephemerality') is objectified and commodified (made 'lasting') by being 'charged by the sensual aesthetic and the specific energies of the piece' (2013, p. 44), providing grounds, repeatable and reproducible, for the popular and commercial success of 'immersiveness'. Modernism's dematerialisation of the art object (see Lippard, 1973) is put into reverse and in its place 'immersiveness' realises a materialisation of the performance experience.

Nothing absolute or unchangeable has happened here; but a tendency has developed in a strain of site-based performance for a popular objectification of the intense and intimate through the immersive. On the one hand it holds out the prospect of securing and sustaining a transitory and passing art, while on the other it risks squandering the vulnerability that made it different. Site-specific performance is not alone in navigating such quandaries; from them comes new forms.

11

Technology

Prior to the general availability of GPS and smartphones, there were two dominant ways in which technology informed site-specific performances. The first was predominantly visual and, at the time, involved cumbersome machines that were not always easy to operate in the wet. Mostly, this concerned the use of conventional theatre lighting (although other light sources such as searchlights were deployed) to illuminate scenes or change colouring. The effects, where conditions permitted, were not always very different from the dynamics of a theatre-based design. The use of film and video, however, particularly when imaginatively deployed in relation to the terrain or architecture of a site, produced visual effects and enabled narrative forms that were profoundly innovative.

An example of the transformative results possible was Station House Opera's *Snakes and Ladders* (1998) which deployed numerous screens to the facade and within the window frames of a five-storey 'arts and crafts' building, a former fire station in Bow, London. Six live characters were repeatedly doubled up in video projections, pursuing and being pursued by their virtual doppelgangers; at first the video representations mirrored the live performers, then seemed to become separate from and independent of them. There was no clear narrative offered, but the escalating and farce-like confusions suggested a world of existential crisis in which material reality and its virtual representation were becoming dislocated and inverted; live performers meticulously recreated the appearance of the video only to conclude episodes (such as a leap from an elevated walkway) with physical objects, dragging on a 'body', arranging its limbs according to the virtual image. Chasing their own ghosts, the live characters – under apparent threat of a fall, challenged by the vertiginous setting – seemed always in peril of surrendering their agency to that of the recordings of themselves.

The second of the two most influential kinds of older 'new technology' used in site-based performance were sound-playing devices – small tape or cassette players, then Walkmans and eventually MP3 players. These facilitated the phenomenon of 'audio-walks' and other (generally more static) performances where the action was enhanced for the audience by (usually recorded) soundtrack. The technology could also be used to bring dialogue and other sound, otherwise likely to be drowned out by environmental noise or dissipated by distance, to an audience. This sometimes had the effect of creating a privileged space for the audience; privy to a commentary, drama or soundtrack of which passers-by were unaware or incapable of accessing.

There is an interesting relationship here with 'soundwalks', a term first used by the Canadian-based World Soundscape Project in the 1970s to describe unenhanced listening walks that were a part of the group's actions against noise pollution and 'for an ecologically balanced soundscape where the relationship between the human community and its sonic environment is in harmony' (Canadian Encyclopedia). A useful reminder to any maker of audio walks is that they rarely start from a silent environment; more generally there is already a rich soundscape, and unless very powerful earphones are worn, an artist is likely to be adding layers of sound to existing ones that creep in through earpieces rather than wholly composing their own.

Perhaps the most inspirational figure in the early days of audio walks, Janet Cardiff, used this layering to powerful effect, most famously in *The Missing Voice (Case Study B)* (1999) for the Whitechapel Library (now a gallery) in London, when participants were often at a loss to distinguish recorded footsteps from the footsteps of actual library users, adding to the uneasy feel of a narrative about crime and detection. This recruited the library and its users and, later on in the walk, the buildings and passers-by in the streets nearby as performers, so that the listener-walker was often unsure how much of what they heard was accidental and how much adapted for Cardiff's narrative. At the same time, doubling the duality, Cardiff's fragmentary texts challenged the listener-walker to work to make a meaningful assemblage: 'The recorded voices begin to overlap and interconnect. (DETECTIVE – As far as I can tell, she is mapping different paths through the city. I can't seem to find a reason for the things she notices and records.) Fragments of a love story emerge' (Cardiff, 2005, p. 19).

The facility to seemingly generate voices inside a user's or audience member's head, coupled with the inflexibility of pre-recorded tracks, often informed a subjective, psychological or poetic quality in these audio walks. As more sophisticated technology became generally available, versatility and flexibility increased. So, for example, Circumstance's *A Hollow Body* (2014, ongoing), created for the Museum of London, is designed for two walkers, who at times part and then rejoin, are sometimes in view and at a distance, opening up the suspicion of more than one narrative, of different intimacies. The walk poses its mysteries (it was commissioned as part of the museum's Sherlock Holmes programme), but does not ask the walkers to solve them; instead, a (once again) fragmentary soundtrack allows the audience space to make their own associations and connections, encouraged by the cinematic effects of the soundtrack, reinforced by the location-like artificial lighting of some of the spaces, to entangle with, rather than resolve the meaning of the terrain. Unlike Fiona Templeton's text, in *A Hollow Body* the emphasis is on 'we are the city'; the audio recruits the walker into the identity and architecture of London.

In 2017 I experienced Circumstance's audio walk *It Must Have Been Dark by Then* in Bristol (UK). From the beginning there is dislocation in its reception; there is printed matter to travel with and read as well as the MP3 player to operate and listen to; in addition, there is the awareness that this is a site-promiscuous piece: it can be pretty much reprogrammed for whatever space the makers choose, and the listener-walker partly determines the route by completing certain open tasks. Then there are the precisely located but far distant recordings, the sounds and accounts from Latvian villages, Louisiana swamplands and the fringes of the Sahara, first-hand witnessing of places that are disappearing, inundated or desiccated, touchstones of climate change. The overlaying of recorded and live sound that one gets on these walks, as before with *The Missing Voice*, is particularly poignant. As I was directed around the restaurant quarter on the former Bristol Docks, overhearing waiters chatter in various languages, I wondered if there was any overlap of their experiences and those of the recorded speakers. Voices from a here and an elsewhere are jumbled. I have been precisely directed by the handheld device to my 'here', but I am not transported; instead it is the connections between my temporary here and the many elsewheres in crisis that are impressed upon me.

Audio technology is useful not only for a listening spectator, but for an active one too. For example, Rotozaza's site-generic *Etiquette* (2004 and ongoing) is very similar to FrenchMottershead's *My Word Is My Bond*; except that its two audience members play the parts, unbeknown to the bar or café clients around them, receiving their lines, prompts and 'stage instructions' through earpieces. The script allows space for some improvisation. Technology does not necessarily inhibit spontaneity; for example, in Oliver Hangl's *Guided by Accident* (Vienna, 2007) and his subsequent *Guerrillawalks* (Wroclaw 2008; Taipei 2011; Pilsen 2015; Graz 2017 and ongoing) the performances are open to chance prompts (lost gloves, poodles and so on); coincidence is director. The audience listens to a live commentary, part precise and part fanciful, on radio headsets, for which Hangl draws upon fragments of materials he has pre-recorded, while all the time responding to whatever the site throws at him in the moment.

Exercise

Sophia Lycouris's *City Glimpses* (Edinburgh, 2013) consisted of three dances performed simultaneously in different sites around the city; each one viewed by passers-by and Edinburgh Fringe Festival audiences through either large windows or glass surfaces and, thanks to live streaming, available to be viewed juxtaposed on a single screen online. Technology shrinks space. So, does site, as somewhere to be specific to, disappear? Use technology (broadcast, streaming, Skype) to make a performance in multiple sites, a performance that begins by asking the question: What is all this specific to?

Idea

There is a willing audience, good arguments and powerful circumstantial foundations (including the arrival of the colonially exploited in the lands of the exploiters) for the idea that globalisation, information technology with digital representation and the hyper-acceleration of communications (along with air travel) have constituted a new kind of space. This space is somehow everywhere and nowhere at the same time. When the rhetoric of 'space' threatened to overwhelm the idea of 'place', when the influence of 'flow' grew as part of a popular neo-vitalism, and when with Doreen Massey's concept of 'coevalness', the characterisation of those arriving at global 'centre stage' was not just of people of the margins, but of 'people from *the past*. Distance was suddenly eradicated both spatially *and* temporally' (Massey, 2005, p. 70).

'In comes I, Virtual Space or Cyberspace!'

Miwon Kwon's expansion of the remit of 'space' to include 'cultural debates, a theoretical concept, a social issue, a political problem ... a neighbourhood or seasonal event, a historical condition' (2002, pp. 28–89) excludes very little. Democracy's gain by inclusivity, though, was meaning's loss. Despite its footprints in 'meatworld' – those giant cooled servers, which outside an episode of *Mr Robot* rarely appear in popular culture – the understanding of cyberspace is more magical than mechanical, close to what Edmund Leach called 'Techno-magic in the home' (1976, p. 32): the assumption that a light switch on the wall is enough to signify that an electrical circuit is present. We know how to use it, but not what it is or how it works. An ethereal geography of 'clouds' and floating 'platforms' has been conjured, a new and unreal layer of the cosmos (rather than super-sophisticated and real connections) to be accessed through a PC or handheld device, like the narrow entrance to a secret *souterrain*.

The kind of critical scepticism that would baulk at the idea that at a performance of *As You Like It* the audience enters a 'Forest of Arden', has been largely waived for virtual space. An optimistic futurism (which feels strangely retro and hauntological and at odds with the dominant discourse of critical theory) overlooks the clunkiness of much of the technology in order to idealise the almost-Gnostic state of the outcome (see

Davis, 1998), just as enthusiasts for 1960s and 1970s small-scale theatre might once have ignored and forgiven errant analogue lighting states and jerky tape-recorded sound cues.

In the worst instances of site-based digitally enhanced performance, the novelty of the technology has been called upon to redeem or disguise games of hide and seek, aggressive electronic-stewarding or the reception of disappointingly banal messages at random locations. At its profound best, we can experience precise displacements and multi-placements in defamiliarised everyday spaces, entangling materiality and presence with daunting and revelatory networks of information. We confront power-meshworks in all their slippery complexity and (as best we can) our ambiguous existential presence in a world that is, now, mostly not 'there', let alone 'here'; while at the same time reiterating the hedonistic virtues of Fatboy Slim's 'right here, right now'.

Makers of site-specific performances, eager to exploit the possibilities of digital technology and communications, have done best when rigorously addressing the materiality, vulnerability and presence of the technology itself as a site (stealing a trick from Miwon Kwon). So, some of the audience/participants in Blast Theory's exemplary *Uncle Roy All Around You* (London, Beijing, Atlanta, Tokyo, 2003 and ongoing) are operators/directors of the technology, partnered with others who are street players, combining to find Uncle Roy's 'office'; the online manipulation hidden in many such programmes is made explicit, forefronted and patched into the fabric of this performance, and ends with the possibility of conviviality: the operator/player pair are offered the chance to commit to a 'meat-world' obligation to each other for 12 months.

In Gob Squad's *Room Service (Help Me Make It Through the Night)* (Hamburg and elsewhere, 2003–2010) four performers, each in one bedroom of a (fully operational) InterCity hotel, wait through a long and isolated night (10 p.m. till 4 a.m.), under the gaze of surveillance cameras (Illustration 11.1). Feeds from the cameras provide viewing for an audience draped around the lobby of the hotel. During the night, performers ring down to the lobby in attempts to lure audience members up to the rooms (always under camera and audience surveillance) to help them pass the time. The audience are free to choose whether to watch throughout, come and go, or enter the rooms as a 'guest-performer'; while there

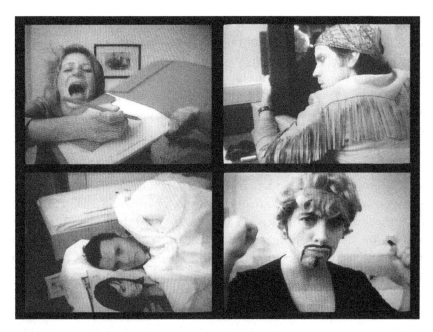

Illustration 11.1 *Room Service (Help Me Make It Through the Night)*, A durational performance in a hotel, Gob Squad, 2003.

Photo: Gob Squad.

might seem to be a rather banal, salacious, erotic charge to these offers and possible outcomes, Gob Squad's careful use of the technology of communication and surveillance creates a loaded dynamic to the audience's agency; trading added power to influence the performance against their falling under the gazes of their fellow audience members.

There is an anomaly in virtuality (though it could equally be characterised as an apotheosis) that seems to challenge the limitations, bounded spaces and striated textures of site-specificity. In the almost Gnostic realm of 'virtual world' platforms, particularly that of Linden Lab's *Second Life*, there is the impression, at least for the player/observer (the 'resident' in *Second Life* terminology), of a free-floating digital world shorn of real consequences, but of expanded possibilities, in which 'meatworld' propositions and desires can be realised in a frictionless state. Mel Slater, an academic researcher of virtual environments, has sought to describe and explain the intensity of

feelings for these players/observers, portraying two kinds of duality operating together through the 'smooth' experience of virtual reality. The first
duality is that experienced by players as of a 'being there' even while they are
well aware that they are not. This 'place illusion' sits within a second duality
between the experience and its content that Slater calls 'plausibility illusion':
the sense that not only does the experience feel real, but that 'what is apparently happening is really happening' (2009, p. 3554).

According to Slater, the level of immersion in a system is a key driver for
these mutually supporting dualities, generating a sense, which powerfully
feeds the 'plausibility illusion' that 'events in the virtual environment over
which you have no direct control directly refer to you' (p. 3554). Slater
defines the level of this immersion as the degree to which the system supports 'sensorimotor contingencies ... actions that we know to carry out
in order to perceive, for example, moving your head and eyes in order to
change gaze direction, or bending down and shifting head and gaze direction in order to look underneath something' (p. 3551). In other words,
the same kind of hyper-attentiveness that you might use on an exploratory visit to a real-world site (as described in Chapter 5 above), in order
to break through and beyond a generic understanding, is in virtual reality
used to generate all the actions and experiences of presence, but within
an illusion of a world that is 'there' and in which all things 'refer to you'.

While the utopian quality of *Second Life* is somewhat clouded by its
'meatworld' trade in 'land' and 'artefacts', through the Linden Dollar and
its exchanges with real-world currencies, there remains the thrill of entering an alternative world, a virtual 'Forest of Arden', by agentive operation rather than imaginative observation. Players, through their avatars,
wed, collect art, wander and debate. They stage performances, produce
theatre with enhanced virtual stage architecture that can hark back to
the Constructivists or the early days of Renaissance perspective-illusions,
they give speeches, and they improvise interactive dance duets (like Niki
McCretton's *Viral Duets* [2008]).

What is not in the 'there' of the online world is consciousness – unlike
an actor, an avatar has no qualia – an absence that may partly explain the
gentle decline in participation in *Second Life* as the possibilities of virtual
reality and augmented reality technology begin to be realised. For the time
being, however, *Second Life* is a revealing anomaly: a site of representation

equated by its users to the site it represents (a real world with added simulacra), sufficiently flexible to generate imaginary spaces for online performance. However, it remains a mostly specialist and specialised space. Its general ordinariness and vast expanses, in which little happens, had seemed to hold out, for consciously postmodern users, the prospect of smooth and universal space; an accessible, anti-representational, Fluxus-styled rolling reality. In practice, against the ambiguity of a real-world theatrical 'Forest' which is obviously fake while 'as if' real and always, through a performance, 'right here, right now', the liveness and place illusion of *Second Life* is mediated by a somewhere else, a distance between operator and space, between everywhere and nowhere.

This may all change with new virtual reality and augmented reality technology. The recent (2017) sight of snooker champion Ronnie O'Sullivan, wearing a VR headset, falling on his face attempting to lean on a virtual snooker table perhaps presages the kinds of real/unreal, here/not here, encounters that could profoundly influence understandings and practices of both site and performance, presence and agency. Given its preoccupations, site-specific performance need not wait. A provisional and inadequate technology may be useful, both for its particular affordances and for the possibilities of hyper-accelerations and augmentations of representation that it may prefigure.

In 1792 the Celtic-revivalist and fantasist Iolo Morgannwg (Edward Williams) convened (in his mind, 'revived') a druidical 'Order of Bards' for a *gorsedd* or assembly on London's Primrose Hill; no stone circle remaining there, Williams brought along his own: some stones he carried in his pocket which he proceeded to lay out in a circle (Hutton, 1993, p. 140). He carried a theatre in his pocket, amplifying what, at least in his mind was the original architecture of a sacred site. Today, a handheld device can fulfil the same function as the stones, if the ritual-maker considers the new and developing technologies as tools rather than portals; as very sophisticated flints rather than caves (at least until they can be hard-wired to the mechanism of consciousness).

Avoiding the Gnostic aura of 'cyberspace', site-specific performance makers can utilise these mechanisms and systems as those most apt for site in a globalised society of networks and meshworks (see Cassells 1996; Ingold 2011) to reconfigure site as a node or knot, as much about arrivals and departures as dwelling, a queasy 'place' to which history comes, coevally, both from elsewhere and from the past. In such a mesh, ties of responsibility are as present as vectors of escape, transcendence or representative substitution. This is equally true of enhanced performances, like Blast Theory's *Kidnap* (1998), rooted in concerns around agency, consent and violence raised by the imprisoning of individuals participating in consensual sadomasochistic acts, where a violent incarcerating act is performed with the consent of a participant 'fed and cared for by the kidnappers' (Blast Theory, 2017), who for 48 hours is exposed online and addressed by online audience members.

Guardian theatre reviewer Lyn Gardner (2010) flagged up a potential hazard for all enhanced performances when she complained of Suzanne Kertsen, Clair Korobacz, Paul Moir and Julian Rickett's *En Route* (Edinburgh, 2010), another piece for headphones, during which 'I was so busy multi-tasking, I probably noticed less about the city than I would on a normal stroll'. Emily Puthoff (2006) has articulated concerns that digital connections amplify the expanding 'non-places' in the real world identified by Marc Augé (1995) – homogenised spaces, often related to travel, colonising public space globally – through the 'non-place' of cyberspace. However, just as there is a question of scale around real-world 'non-places' (a close attention to these 'non-places' often reveals that at a textural level there are unique artefacts, patterns and histories that do not conform to global uniformity) similarly, an augmented performance can draw upon multiplicitous informations precisely related to location. Not A Theatre Company provides an audience with an MP3 file (for $1.99, the low price encouraging a diverse audience) to play layers of dialogue, recorded sound and commentary, all related to the Staten Island Ferry (New York) on which the performance *Ferry* (2015 and ongoing) takes place (two acts, one for each crossing).

Openness and affordant vacancy works for Back to Back's site-generic *Small Metal Objects* (Melbourne, Adelaide, Dublin, Singapore and so on, 2005–2012, 2016), for which its audience is placed on a raised seating bank in a busy urban space and listen to the relayed dialogue of performers who are often lost among the crowds. Given the anonymity of the performers, the prominence of the audience often attracts the 'performances' of passers-by and buskers; yet the openness of the dramaturgy and the acoustic resilience of the technology mean that the performance can accommodate interventions by drunken crowds, streakers and breakdancers. The performance's director, Bruce Gladwin, commented in an interview that he was 'surprised at how much space there is in our show for that' (Logan, 2007).

Used as a tool, rather than as a distraction, handheld devices can help unpeel layers of a site and animate its silenced voices, and identify its covert or ambiguous agencies, while all the time (and this is where the 'tool' analogy falters) the mechanism is mapping you, recording and analysing the voices you animate, and assembling your questions and searches as the data of your predilections. This is the sinister and real side of the rhetoric about 'sharing qualia' and dissolving the limits of public and private space: the actions of invasive algorithms seeking out our subjective choices and desires. The danger of making 'the visitor's sensing, moving body in the artwork ... the critical factor in its specificity as a site' (Popat, 2015, p. 168) is that it lays across the geography of the performance site, the consumer-producer 'target' of social media's and others' digital algorithms. By connecting the real-world footprint to the machines of virtual space, the main players are no longer the site, the things and the organisms in it, but those digital programmes that are 'exploring' for the patterns of a consumer-audience's behaviour in order to enhance them and echo them back in loops threaded with affirmative commercial, political, cultural or retail propositions. The site enhanced becomes a performance displaced to a programme; the 'web' becomes the actor.

Since 1996 (the company themselves acknowledge antecedents in Australia), the Surveillance Camera Players in New York – along with their sister companies in large cities worldwide, including Vilnius (Lithuania) and Istanbul (Turkey) – have been staging captioned and condensed versions of surveillance or alienation-themed plays plus adaptations of Samuel Beckett's *Waiting for Godot* and George Orwell's *Nineteen Eighty-Four* to CCTV cameras for small audiences of security guards. Artists Robin Hewlett and Ben Kingsley have similarly 'hijacked' an existing system, staging an elaborate street scene (including, somewhat anomalously, a sword fight) for the benefit of Google Street View's camera van as it passed through (Pittsburgh, USA, and online, 2008). Activists have sought to 'occupy' the space of surveillance by dressing up as CCTV cameras or carrying cardboard models of surveillance equipment. As with the Surveillance Camera Players, there are often elements of both protest and pranking combined in these actions; attempts to draw attention to the extent and invasive nature of surveillance, while acknowledging the absurdity of playing to its tiny (or accidental) audiences.

Though they used only analogue technology, Pearson/Brookes's *There's Someone in the House* (Exeter, UK, 2004) vividly demonstrated how such loops of information can be deployed in self-reflective ways. While the audience were assembled in a central room, around a gridded table supplied with various texts and other artefacts, the action took place and was videoed in short sequences and photographed on Polaroid cameras in nearby spaces; the documentation was then rushed to the central space where it was rapidly projected or displayed. The 'almost live' quality of the images, often depicting intense or violent content which one knew had been perpetrated a few metres away, a few moments before, strangely implicated the audience in actions in which it had not participated and which it had not witnessed, while forefronting the very mechanics of that implication.

Exercise

Experiment with how your body can negotiate mixed realities. Take a busy, multi-use urban space; somewhere (perhaps a tourist area) where there is plenty of messaging going on. Relentlessly photobomb. Send messages through CCTV. Generate patterns of micro-information to draw attention to yourself; repeatedly withdrawing tiny sums of money from an account via cash machines and cashback facilities in a concentrated area. How many levels of digital communication can you piggyback?

Exercise

Devise a digital dramaturgy. Step 1: Consider 4 or 5 'layers' of a site; how can each be navigated digitally? Perhaps, by a locational app that allows the user to relate to otherwise unidentified 'players' in the site? Or a 'Pokemon Go'-style augmented reality adding mythic figures or scenarios from local folk and foaf tales? Or create a live stream from a local 'hotspot' (bus terminal, auction house, sports stadium)? Or ... and so on. At the same time as devising Step 1, for Step 2 create a live, 'meatworld' framework – a narrative to follow, a persona to play, a report to compile and deliver ... a structure that can align, slide and direct your multiple digital layers.

Exercise

Contact three or four global partners in contrasting situations. This is probably best done through some kind of institutional mediator: university
departments, arts organisations, local government, global retail chains.
Identify comparable generic spaces in each of your communities and devise
actions or scores which are practically (technically) feasible for all of you.
Put in some kind of 'feedback' loop (Skype, live streaming, texting), so
that when you simultaneously perform the scores the way the different
sites and their other 'residents' (including the weather) respond is fed back
into all the scores, so that the performers are, in their turn, responding to
both a live and local response and a displaced one. Use this as a means to
explore cultural specificities and commonalities that then develop across
your multi-place 'platform' of performance.

Reading

Published back in 1998, Erik Davis's *TechGnosis: Myth, Magic and Mysticism
in the Age of Information* remains a useful reminder that changes in technology are not simply a process of accumulated technical developments,
but a transformation of ways of thinking and orders of imagination. They
may be changing and improving efficiency, rapidity and reach, but in doing
so they are changing the shape and feel of almost everything. The arrival
of the digital age and the expansion of the virtual world have delivered to
performance making a new set of tools and lines of communication, but
just as significantly they have transformed the world's understandings of
what performances are. *TechGnosis* recognises and predicts just how deep
and profound the changes in thinking and imagining would be as analogue
technologies are replaced and we contemplate what the consequences will
be of virtual reality, augmented reality and hardwiring directly into the
brain.

Davis's argument is that there is nothing particularly modern about
the theorising and lauding of these changes; instead, they are giving fresh
impetus to older ideas about the inferiority of the material world, the
renouncing and denouncing of things of flesh and matter, and the ecstatic
and transcendent possibilities of an abstraction from human bodies and
the natural world. Davis suggests that older traditions with these values –
early Christian Gnosticism, Neo-Platonism and the Hermetic tradition (based on the writings of the 'thoroughly fabricated' [1998, p. 17]

Hermes Trismegistus) – are returning in digital form, helping to provide ideological foundations or cover for technological acceleration and the transcendence and replacement of industries of manufacture and agriculture. He echoes Marshall McLuhan's suspicion that what is new about new technology is that rather than extending parts of the natural human body 'electricity may be said to have outered the central nervous system' and externalised dreams and desires into binary code. Logic, linearity and causality will be replaced by a new era of oral rather than textual culture, 'a resonating world akin to the old tribal echo chamber where magic will live again' (McLuhan cited in Davis, 1998, pp. 59, 175).

Pre-empting these changes, the 'look' of the world has already transformed with a fusion, particularly in the USA, of 'marketplace and imaginal space' with its 'Golden arches, Trump towers, Gotham cities, and Las Vegas pyramids now tower[ing] over the landscape of imaginative desire ... collective symbols ... forged in the multiplex, our archetypes trade-marked, licensed and sold' (Davis, 1998, p. 177). While much in Davis's vision has already been swamped if not replaced by technical developments, the value of *TechGnosis* is in the way that Davis has put down a description of the direction in which things, space and the body in particular, are changing in and through representations of them; how 'the bright grid of [William] Gibson's cyberspace' is always accompanied by 'a Tolkienesque world of swamps' and how new levels of brain–machine connectivity are creating equal feelings of immersion and separation in 'a profoundly unsettling and frequently nauseating disjunction between the body's kinaesthetic self-awareness and the nervous system's perceptual reorientation toward a concocted otherworld' (p. 238).

While a site-specific performance maker may well wish to take advantage of new performance possibilities facilitated by digital technologies, they can use Davis's book to consider for themselves what will eventually be left of anything recognisable as a site, let alone anything specific to it, and whether performance as a 'thoroughly fabricated' behaviour will be so pervasive as to be invisible and unrecognisable.

12

Site Etiquette

In a book about specificity to places loaded with history and recalcitrant meanings and the importance of paying attention to how the idiosyncratic details of the 'right here' connect to the bigger picture 'over there', it should come as no surprise that what you might find most helpful is not a checklist of universal principles, but an ugly agglomeration of disparate tips, tactics and tellings-off. So in this chapter I will address some of disparate issues that may arise for you in making site-based performance.

Access

This is probably the primary concern of any site-based arts. It is not a late consideration, although the likelihood is that many companies and individuals are caught out at the back end of their process trying to improvise a means to enable access to their space for people with different kinds of mobility. This is a misunderstanding of the meaning of access, as much as it is a travesty of welcome and conviviality. Access is crucial to the aesthetics of meaning-making in a site; it is not some bureaucratic bolt-on or afterthought tick box. The interface of different bodies and precisely understood textures is a primary feature of any site-specific project; consider the effect of a mechanical wheelchair on different suspended floors and surfaces; ask the question. The ethical and aesthetic aspects are indivisible; performance is all about the relativity of relationships between bodies and space. The ethics are not there to restrict anything, but to reveal and demand more.

Backstage

There is no 'offstage' or backstage in site-specific performance. Unlike a studio, where the audience is strictly controlled, there is no clear performance/non-performance demarcation. Leaving bags behind trees will be quickly noticed (unless you mean to puncture the ambiguous spectacle, then you probably don't want the adventurous or quick-witted spectator spotting these).

Health and safety

These are political things. Rather than simply putting up with the bureaucratic obligation to make a risk assessment and submit your proposals to manage any risks, consider this process as part of your performance making. Not only do you have an obligation to look after the safety of your audience and passers-by, you have a political responsibility and opportunity to manage certain risks: risks of offence, risks of challenge to accepted ideas, generating risks to identity and allegiance. Your work is not just about de-fanging risk, but inviting the right risk. Health and safety is not simply about avoiding physical hurt to your audience and passers-by but about considering your obligation to not ignoring them, to not leaving them alone and isolated, to challenging corrosive relations in the street.

Duration

Sometimes sites move at a slower rate than a human playwright; so by creating durational performance over, say, 12 or 24 hours, you allow the site to perform; the sun rises and sets, the sun warms and then burns, snow gathers into huge drifts, a few passers-by becomes a rush-hour crowd, the night silence becomes a dawn chorus.

Scale

Directing (or performing with) actors who are a quarter of a mile away is very different from working with actors in a studio while sitting in the front row of the stalls or standing a few centimetres apart. Not only is there the challenge to create work that can have an effect across considerable distances, 'elements of individual and group choreography articulated in ways that allow them to have resonance when viewed from afar' (Pearson, 2006, p. 212), but it is also necessary to know how to perform without an accustomed feedback loop of response and attention from an audience, when due to expansive terrain or environmental noise it is 'largely impossible for the performers to monitor the response of the audience and to adjust their work accordingly' (p. 213).

Weather

In some places they 'have a lot of weather'; the climate is varied and unpredictable. Even in more stable climates there are variations; and we are subject now to the muddled effects of long rhythms of climate change and more recent ones for which humans are responsible. Meteorological forecasts are only ever reliable up to three or four days in advance of any event, and even these are subject to unpredictable local changes of wind speed or direction that alter everything. Complex outdoor site-based performance projects have to be planned when only the most general idea of likely weather patterns and temperatures is available. So, you can risk your performance, by hoping for the best, or you can make it resilient and porous, so that it not only survives, but entangles beneficially with various possible weather conditions. Working as a teacher on the 'Site Projects' module at Dartington (UK) I went, one wet morning, with a colleague to ask a group of students to postpone their performance in the middle of the river Dart. There had been heavy rain overnight and water levels in the river were rising. We arrived to find both the river and the performance in full flow: both had been transformed. A rather slight and 'site-inappropriate' performance – a comic sketch performed on a table in the river – had become a real and epic struggle against the river, the jokes were now dark and strangled, the situations were spectral, barely sustainable: we watched an incapable culture being swept away by forces it neither understood nor could speak to.

Clearing up

What you leave behind in your site may be the most profound result of your performance. During a folk panic in the UK in the 1980s, the remnants of burned candles left behind by a women's theatre group were mistakenly declared to be evidence of 'Satanic Ritual Abuse'. Today, non-biodegradable objects left behind may speak of your performance as insensitive and dim of thought and that may be its abiding meaning. On the other hand, you may actively wish to leave some trace; a fading, changing mark of presence that disappears more slowly than you do. The consequences of occupation and performance are important to consider. The 'urban explo' or 'place hacker' movement (Garrett, 2013) considerably altered their behaviour, including the uploading online of images and locations, after it became clear that their 'pioneering' explorations of tunnels, bunkers and derelict sites was quickly followed by 'raves' and other events, many of whose organisers and participants had little interest in the curating or conservation of the sites, sometimes leaving them trashed. Performance makers might want to consider whether a similar review of the aftermath of site-specific events is in order.

Idea

One way of getting an active understanding of a place is to map it, but, for the purposes of performance, fancifully. There may, of course, be something to be gained by a serious cartographical study of your site – certain abstract patterns, lines of motion or connections that are not evident on the ground may be revealed – but, as has been said famously, by numerous folk from numerologist Eric Temple Bell to situationist Ralph Rumney, 'the map is not the territory' (Korzybski, 1936, p. 58). Direct and literal representations sometimes reveal little more than a direct observation of the space, as available to you as to a map-maker (though certain kinds of technologically enhanced mappings, such as geophysical surveys, may reveal invisible features).

A more fruitful way of mapping for the performance maker may be found at the crowded crossroads of mapping and art. Here we can more easily enjoy the map's double-layering by 'inhabiting the mind of its maker, considering that particular terrain of imagination overlaid with those unique contours of experience' (Harmon, 2004, p. 11). What is mapped, then, is a third thing: the experience of the terrain as much as the terrain itself. In Katharine Harmon's two most wide-ranging collections of cartography-based art – *You Are Here* (2004) and *The Map as Art* (2009) – terrains include the sitings of Halloween pumpkins and the route to Paradise. There are fear-filled political mappings of stereotypes, maps of pleasure and experience resonant with Christian Nold's emotion-mapping (see Chapter 5), maps drawn or printed on mattresses and folded towels, maps distorted by subjectivity and viewpoint. Frank Jacobs's collection *Strange Maps* (2009) contains edible maps, charts of word usage, hauntological-political maps (portraying unfulfilled imperial ambitions) and the mapping of variations in social etiquette.

All these maps have a triple use for a site-specific performance maker; not only do they map the ground and serve as a possible score for a performance, but they also provide a response to the challenge made by theatre scholar Peggy Phelan for documentation: 'Performance's only life is in the present. Performance cannot be saved, recorded, documented, or otherwise participate in the circulation of representations of representations: once it does so, it becomes something other than performance' (1993, p. 146). Working with Phelan's formulation, not against it, mapping can develop a difference, a 'something other than performance' that does not force performance into anything that 'betrays and lessens the promise of its own ontology', but allows it to 'be' once more as something else. In the case of site-specific performance, documentation can become a mapping of the 'new space' product of performance, something more than a residue and more like an ongoing 'site' (with all the potential for future performing which that word implies).

A fanciful map, radically dislocated from the representation of a surface and imbued with utopian or idealist messages and symbolisms, is itself performative; a parting of the relation of the map from the object of that relation. Terrain and map float about each other; rather than one lain over the other. Sometimes the destabilising force may be that of the very site itself, sufficient to upset the usual representational order of mapping. At other times it may be some play upon the tradition of fanciful cartographic relations, drawing upon hoax maps, mistaken maps (like those of a Hollow Earth), dream maps, pseudo-scientific maps (sightings of the never-aging Count St Germain), maps accompanying novels, novelty maps (like the 1937 *Whimsical Map of Hollywood* where the stars' homes, the studios and the scenery on the lots all appear equally flimsy) or activist maps (like The Institute For Infinitely Small Things' map of Cambridge, Massachusetts, USA – *The City Known Formerly as Cambridge* [2006–2008] – on which familiar public places have been renamed by local people for new heroes or for ironically quotidian functions or to mark personal and even private associations). 'Fanciful' might also include maps of procedural unreliability, such as Emma Kay's maps of the world drawn from memory – *The World from Memory I, II & III* (1998–1999). All of these, as much as the metaphorical and allegorical maps of religious evangelists and authoritarian political groups, are desperate to squeeze meaning from their symbols, generating such an excess of referential ambition and such a decay of representational validity that they call out for misuse and inappropriate juxtaposition. Their 'failures', and their floating free from the intended meaning of their signs, complement that trope of performance art that 'resist[s] the metaphorical reduction of the two into the one' (Phelan, 1993, p. 152).

At the end of Forced Entertainment's playful guided coach-tour through Sheffield (UK), *Nights in This City* (1995), local audience members were able to search for their own addresses on a huge A–Z street-map index that had been chalked across the immense concrete floor of an empty warehouse. Resisting any obvious cartographic representation, the absurdity of the a-geographical alphabet served to prise the trip free from its simpler ironies and juxtapositions, challenging the audience to site themselves unsatisfactorily: immediately, on the index in the warehouse, and yet abstractly displaced from their home in the city.

Mike Pearson's *Bubbling Tom* (Hibaldstow, UK, 2000) was an iconic journey of recitation around the village where Pearson grew up; its widespread influence has been disproportionate to its tiny audiences. Given its intensely personal content, the generative properties of an ambulatory autobiographical performance, accompanied by small groups of family, friends and invited guests, might seem to be very limited. However, the performance's documentation in *Small Acts: Performance, the Millennium and the Marking of Time* (Heathfield, 2002), and its subsequent referencing by various scholars such as Cathy Turner (2004) and Fiona Wilkie (2004) and in Pearson's own *In Comes I: Performance, Memory and Landscape* (2006), generously invited re-exploration. In *Small Acts*, the Ordnance Survey grid reference for each section of the performance was given, enabling its quick location by a visitor to Hibaldstow. In 2002, theatre scholar and performance maker Dee Heddon re-enacted Pearson's walk 'for those who, like me, were not there' (Heddon, 2002, p. 175). Heddon was responding in tune with a growing resistance to an archive that turns performance into 'something other than performance' and to make 'some other performance'. Heddon's documentation repeats the grid references and juxtaposes photos of her own recitation with elements from the original documentation. Like the increasingly diluted mapping of Hy Brazil – an island that was accidentally charted twice, its simulacrum-twin hopelessly pursued by sailors and map-makers until it floated further and further away into the Atlantic – there is a draining away of authenticity from *Bubbling Tom*, freeing the site for 'creative interpretation' (p. 174). These two performances, Pearson's and Heddon's, have been subsequently cited, and Heddon's re-enactment has, itself, been re-enacted. It is not so much that 'Performance's being ... becomes itself through disappearance' (Phelan, 1993, p. 146) but that it re-becomes as 'some – *other* – performance', not an 'it', but a fluidity, a course like that of a river, a concourse, a *dérive* in the sense of a diversion of flow.

Exercise

Create a performance on and for a particular site that invites repetition: How can you leave voids or invitations in your performance to draw in further performances? After your performance, distribute documentation that provides sufficient information to inform a repetition of, or variation upon, your original piece.

Exercise

Can you devise a performance that works by being blown away? Or a porous show that is best when it is drowned out? Or just drowned? Recruit those climatic elements in a site that you might usually regard as menaces (sudden gusts of wind, blinding reflections from large windows) and make them the lead characters.

Arriving again: A contentious kind of conclusion

In 2001, Stephen Hodge drew up a simple graphic for defining varieties of site-based theatre and performance along a continuum, with 'outside theatre' (Shakespeare in the park) at one end and a rigorous site-specificity at the other. Almost immediately, Fiona Wilkie (2002) shared this in her much-read article 'Mapping the Terrain', and for a while it served for many practitioners as a critical marker for understanding different relations of production to site. I happened to be present at the moment of this graphic's provocation, and the circumstances are instructive.

It all kicked off at the 2001 'Out of Place' conference in Birmingham (UK) during a chaired dialogue and discussion with the director of Grid Iron Theatre Company, Ben Harrison, about their first production of *Decky Does a Bronco* (2000–2002). The chair of the discussion persisted in using the term 'site-specific' despite the explicit discussion of the production as having been devised for playgrounds in general, rather than any one in particular. This prompted Hodge to draw up his continuum. However, the form of the conference discussion, with arguments rehearsed and then ignored, is what has prevailed rather than the terms of the continuum that resulted from it (though Harrison did switch from using 'site-specific' to 'site-sensitive' for describing Grid Iron's work [cited, in Govan, Nicholson & Normington, 2007, p. 118]). For, while Fiona Wilkie suggests that 'practitioners are now [2014] far less concerned with labelling the work and with issues of the 'purity' of site-specific performance than they were a decade ago' (p. 41, 2015), a certain lack of concern around 'terminological exactitude' has been evident all along.

Despite Miwon Kwon's powerful 2002 critique, the term 'site-specific' continues to attract artists, performers and critics. Once the term had become a popular novelty among journalists (at least in the UK) in the mid to late 2000s, as a sure mark of original theatre making, companies and individuals were less than keen to trade it in for a less 'sexy' but more accurate 'site-generic' or 'site-sympathetic'. This opportunistic and lazy flexibility reached some kind of nadir in 2007 when the *Guardian* newspaper published a blog comment (partly about Grid Iron Theatre's 'Roam' [Edinburgh International Airport, 2006]) that read: 'I'm a bit of a sucker for site-specific theatre: sling some fairy lights in a tree and stage a play in it, and chances are I'm yours' (Szalwinska, 2007). What had begun (and been sustained by many practitioners) as a serious, politicised shift from culturally bounded galleries, theatres and studios to everyday spaces, incorporating architectural, ecological and property issues into performance, was increasingly and explicitly being deployed as commercial currency and (cheap) cultural capital.

Fiona Wilkie's comments above hint at a problem for anyone seeking to redress this; 'specific' is more easily articulated as 'pure' than 'generic' or 'adaptive', with their connotations of compromise; although there is nothing (except for the imbalance of descriptive notes) on Hodge's continuum to valorise one term more than another. Indeed, something is lost by its even-handedness: the radicalism of the break from theatre space and the entanglement with the everyday. That something is the recontextualisation that is possible through performance's specificity to a place and its relations: 'the latest occupation of a location at which other occupations – their material traces and histories – are still apparent' (Pearson & Shanks, 2001, p. 23).

An easy-going approach to terms skirts a certain kind of critical opprobrium (I do remember feeling that we were the embarrassing 'zealots' in the room at Birmingham for insisting on a debate around definitions), but it can also throw up exaggerated assertions – for example, that a performance site might be constituted by 'the affective experience of the visitor, sharing the qualia that the artists felt' (Popat, 2015, p. 167) – and it can obscure real differences in practice; one such difference being that between work that successfully (in reception terms) transfers theatrical performance to non-theatre spaces, but leaves the spaces largely untouched, disengaged, and that which 'transform[s] the accepted and conventional properties' of its site. On the other hand, Wilkie adroitly and perceptively contextualises earlier concerns about categories and definitions around a desire among practitioners and academics (she does not spare herself) in the years immediately after the millennium, to 'stak[e] a claim to some kind of territory' for site-based work (2015a, p. 41); the dim echo of old colonial habits.

The distinctive upside of the conceptual dissolution around site-specificity is a turn to mobility in performance, to nomadism and mobilities in theory and to 'mobile methodologies' in research (see Urry, 2007; Wilkie, 2015b). In performances, this ranged from Punchdrunk's letting loose its audiences in hotels in New York, Boston, London and Shanghai (*Sleep No More*, 2011–2016) to the train journey and 20 miles of carefully guided processional trekking of Louise Wilson's *Fissure* (Yorkshire Dales, UK, 2011). While consistent with contemporary ideas about a 'mobility paradigm', this shift also echoed the works of an earlier generation of site-specific practitioners in postmodern dance and live art, like Lucinda Childs's *Street Dance* (New York, 1964) where spectators stood in a high window to watch dancers move through the passers-by in the streets below, Meredith Monk's *Juice* (New York, 1969) that moved from venue to venue over a period of a month or X6's *By River and Wharf* (London, 1976) performed 'down alleys, on old bomb-sites, suspended from Victorian girders, deep in Thames mud' (Early, 1987, p. 12).

However, while mobility suggested that there might be some relativistic bridge between the immediacy (or few hours passing) of the human cultural occasion of performance and the unhuman aeons of matter, there remained a discrepancy that Melanie Kloetzel (2017) has discovered within the process of site-adaptation with significance for site-based performance in general. What might seem like a mutual resilience shared between its sites and a performance moving between them and adapting itself to them, obscures a 'more disturbing' rationale of 'expendability'. Kloetzel describes how resilience often comes at the expense of the less privileged parts of a site; adaptation is applied to the site as much as to the performance. Less convenient parts – parts of the site less specific to the performance (specificity turned on its head!) – are regularly dispensed with, excluded or ignored. Kloetzel points out how this 'adaptation' rather precisely echoes the institutionalised 'management' of climate change that, by editing out the inconvenient in favour of the resilient, claims to 'allow us to move calmly forward and make the changes necessary with little real alteration of the status quo' (2017, pp. 114, 122). Configuring this as part of a 'globalist "we can manage" fantasy' (p. 123), Kloetzel, drawing on Bruno Latour's work, argues that site-adaptive performance's hubris – just like institutionalised climate politics – rests on 'deanimating the Earth, by robbing it of its agency … reducing the planet to an object' (p. 121). Site-adaptive performance – and here is the wake-up call for performance makers, if Kloetzel is right – re-establishes (and spreads) the conventions of the building-based institution, the 'empty space' of the blank theatre-designated building that returns to 'zero' at the end of each production's run; now operating (through 'site-specific perfor-mance') way beyond the theatre walls! Instead of the 'recontextualisation' and 'new space' promised by Pearson and Shanks and by Hunter, Kloetzel suggests that the site-adaptation at work in much so-called 'site-specific' performance and theatre refines its sites, adds 'value' (in redevelopment and gentrification terms), while leaving its 'status quo' untouched and sustained. The fantasy of 'managing' stands in for performance, fairy lights stand in for a planet.

There are at least two ways for a performance maker to respond to Melanie Kloetzel's radical critique of the practices that I have spent this book advocating: one is to accept that it brings to a stasis and sad con-clusion a series of bold experiments and disastrous compromises; another is that it represents an opportunity, an edifice just waiting to be hauled down, a poisoned playing field to be navigated, a stable reading to be cleaned out with performance fire. To me, Kloetzel's critique changes the game. I have often felt out of kilter with those predominating tendencies to take a more *laissez-faire* or tolerant approach to categories and practices. Now, I want to ask again: What if the qualities that have been described as the reactionary limitations of place specificity, as giving oppressive location-meaning to a site, as nailing it to its past, obsessing on its materi-als, disrupting its everyday life by too aggressively addressing it, are what continue to be useful about performance? While, on the other hand, the-orists who sought to mobilise and accelerate the categories around 'place' and 'site' and thus escape specificity's limitations have risked thinning their meanings as they expanded them and adding unintentionally to a broader ideological belief that technology and globalisation have transcended borders and expunged any meaningful remnants of colonialism and genocidal nation-building, consistent with site-adaptation's illusion that it 'allows us to ... make the changes necessary with little real alteration of the status quo'.

As I wrote the first draft of this chapter, in late 2017, the USA was teetering towards civil unrest over the statues of historic white supremacists. Yet site-specific performance now rarely addresses such things. Did site-specific performance's mobilities-turn de-politicise it? Was that part of its adaptation at a general level to neo-liberalism and its entering into the business of selling thrills: not immersion itself, but the thrill of immersion? Would this go some way to explaining site-specific performance's 'dirty little secret': just how few of its manifestations – particularly those informed by nostalgic, historic or futurist aesthetics – include any explicit engagement with race (gender histories fare very slightly better).

Kloetzel warns against the dangers of terminological opportunism: 'we know meanings are slippery, but sprinkling these terms [*space* and *place*] about haphazardly can too often undermine our attempts to examine the goals, actions, feats and foibles of site-specific performance' (2015, p. 240). There are attempts to define and resist the nexus of terminological/creative opportunism, particularly a critical questioning around the idealisation of immersion – like Royona Mitra's attempt to 'decolonialise' the Anglophonic theorisation of immersion characterised solely by the participative and interactive roles of audiences who are offered a '"full-sensorium" experience' and proposing instead an alternative model – from Indian performance traditions – of a 'psycho-physical state that transpires interstitially between any audience, artist and any art that is primarily premised on gestural dimensions of communications, and regardless of interactivity' (2016, p. 89) – but for both the performance maker and the early career researcher, the contradictions, tensions, inequalities and obfuscations experienced in any chosen site are likely to be echoed in their critical apparatus. If it were not simply adding one more relativism to the flood, I might suggest that the 'site' of site-specific theory is in serious need of critical re-performance.

Instead, I can only suggest that performers and researchers attend to the developments in vital materialism, OOO theory, in the more cosmic reaches of geophilosophy and eco-criticism as a torque upon the impetus to dissolving specificity in technologically enhanced acceleration and the commodification of thrills and 'experiences'. Pearson and Shanks' definition of site-specific performance as 'inseparable from their sites' and something that 'recontextualises such sites' (2001, p. 23) may seem clunky and excessively grounded for a digital age, but its assertion of the importance of location, with all the layers of the palimpsest, is one of the torques by which a recontextualisation, a change in the limits and orders of a space, can begin – another being the arrival in the site of those historically made absent from it, the Other of the site, coming as new agents arriving from what, for much site-specific performance, has been the margins. This may have less to do with a formalistic finessing of actor–audience relations through the use of unfamiliar sites of performance, and more a re-making of behaviour in the particular space of performance by a radical re-gesturing and re-agenting, the doing of what is not allowed, what is 'not done', by those who are not admitted (in more than one sense).

Here are torques (like Kloetzel's objections to the 'site-adaptive', like the rise of the 'thing' and like the entrance of the unhuman into human spaces) that can do more than place a critical thoughtfulness around site-specific performance's popular immersiveness and intimate spectacles; they can shift the focus back to the site, in the context of thinking about the matter of the cosmos, and add some modesty to strategic thinking about how such sites are changed by being expertly performed.

Gregory Bateson once advocated as the exemplary critical practice 'a combination of loose and strict thinking … the most precious tool of science' (p. 75). In terms of site and place, this is the passage that was navigated by Doreen Massey between 'a long history of understanding space as "the dead, the fixed" … and, in total contrast … a veritable extravaganza of non-Euclidean, black-holey, Riemannian … and a variety of other previously topologically improbable evocations' (2005, p. 13). Similarly, you, as performance maker, student or researcher, can similarly navigate. There are exemplary practices to be inspired by and make your own departures from: whether Melanie Kloetzel's combination of close attention to the agency (and needs) of site and her critical use of the adaptive as a 'tool in the adaptation debate' (2017, p. 124), at a scale far beyond that of theatre and performance, or Punchdrunk's repeated-narrative structures facilitating a content 'totality' as well as the wandering of audiences. A 'loose and strict' thinking, rigorously specific while mean-deringly mobile, can be efficacious; but it can be opportunistic. To that unevenness the solutions may not be critical or aesthetic ones, but won in hard practice.

Given the difficulties, would it be more creative if 'specificity' – even in its 'purist' form – was understood more as the rigour of its attention, of its 'attending to' and 'tending of'? In other words, that while the meaning of 'site' can speak mostly for itself (if, hopefully, in more tongues than it did when you started this book), 'specificity' needs to be re-thought, re-defined and re-spoken; this time much less as a geographical-research term and more as an ethical one. Incorporating the utopian aspirations of Hunter's 'new space' and Pearson and Shanks's 'recontextualisation', an ethical site-specificity would reject site-adaptive's expending of site and embrace an obligation to add to its multiplicity, to 'its scene of plenitude' (Pearson, 2010, p. 1), extending the way it imagines its relationship in time with a site. This means a more careful consideration of the choice of sites, not simply as the best containers for performance, but as actors-in-themselves (sites that are making their own demands for attention such as re-wilding spaces or spaces of abuse), and a more careful intention in leaving; not simply discarding the site after a performance is over, but recognising that as performance disappears – indeed, intentionally thin-ning out the thickness and impact of performance – its space contin-ues on, leaving in charge neither critical experts nor eager developers, but 'locally based spectators', who were always already ahead of the per-formance makers with 'an enhanced kind of creative agency in … their knowledge of the place and its history … continu[ing] to frequent the place' (Irwin, 2012, p. 37).

Bibliography

Anderson, Benedict. (2013) 'Out of Space: The Rise of Vagrancy in Scenography'. *Performance Research* 18 (3), pp. 109–118.

Anderson, Benedict. (2015) 'Indeterminacy in Site-Specific Performance'. In *Contemporising the Past: Envisaging the Future* (Refereed proceedings of the 2014 World Dance Alliance Global Summit).

Anderson, Mary Elizabeth & Richard Haley. (2014) 'Art and Civic Engagement in Mike Kelley's Mobile Homestead'. *8 Mile, A Journal of Art and Culture(s) in Detroit*, 7 June. http://www.infinitemiledetroit.com/Response_and_Responsibility.html, Retrieved: 17 September 2017.

Anon. (2013) 'Drop in the Ocean'. [video], 29 October. https://www.youtube.com/watch?v=LIyiIbDKZKM. Retrieved: 13 July 2017.

Antony, Rachael & Joel Henry. (2005) *Lonely Planet Guide to Experimental Travel*. London: Lonely Planet.

Armitage, Simon. (2012) *Walking Home: Travels with a Troubadour on the Pennine Way*. London: Faber & Faber.

Arnold, Bram Thomas. (2015) 'Walking Home (Again)'. Talk at Walk 21, Vienna. http://walk21vienna.com/?dg_voting_submission=walking-home-again. Retrieved: 1 March 2017.

Ashley, Tamara & Simone Kenyon. (2007) *The Pennine Way: The Legs That Make Us*. Oxford: Brief Magnetics.

Aspinwall, Rachel & Ruth Mitchell. (2010) *The Hidden City Festival Handbook*. Plymouth: University of Plymouth Press.

Augé, Marc. (1995) *Non-places: Introduction to an Anthropology of Supermodernity*. Trans. by John Howe. London: Verso.

Bachelard, Gaston. (1958/1969) *The Poetics of Space*. Trans. by Maria Jolas. Boston: Beacon Press.

Barba, Eugenio. (1985) *The Dilated Body*. Rome: Zeami Libri.

Barrero, Marcus Garcia. (2017) 'Se Traspasa: Site-Specific Theatre in the Heart of Madrid'. *Theatre Times*, 30 March. https://thetheatretimes.com/se-traspasa-site-specific-theatre-heart-madrid-interview-sandrajimenez/. Retrieved: 1 November 2017.

Barrett, Felix. (2008) 'Performance with a Punch'. *The Cambridge Student*, 31 January. Retrieved: 16 August 2017.

Bateson, Gregory. (1972) *Steps to an Ecology of Mind*. Chicago: University of Chicago Press.

Beauregard, Robert A. (2012) 'Planning with Things'. *Journal of Planning Education and Research*. 32 (2), pp. 182–190.

Benjamin, Walter. (1973) *Understanding Brecht*. Trans. by Stanley Mitchell. London: NLB.

Bennett, Jane. (2010) *Vibrant Matter: A Political Ecology of Things*. Durham, NC & London: Duke University Press.

Bennett, Melanie. (2012) 'Mapping the Non-Aristocratic in Lawrence Park'. *Canadian Theatre Review*, 151, pp. 44–49 (University of Toronto Press).

Bennett, Melanie. (2013) 'Domestic Train Wreck: A Radical Utopia'. *Performance Research*, 18 (2), pp. 46–55 (London & New York: Routledge).

Bennett, Melanie. (2014) 'Performance Theatre and the Poetics of Failure'. *Performance Research*, 18 (6), pp. 126–129 (London & New York: Routledge).

Best, Anna. (2003) *Occasional Sites*. London: Photographers' Gallery.

Bianchi, Victoria. (2015) 'The Path to *CauseWay*: Developing a Feminist Site-Specific Performance Practice at the Robert Burns Birthplace Museum'. *Platform*, 9 (2), Performance, Place and Geography (Autumn 2015).

Bion, Wilfred Ruprecht. (1967) *Second Thoughts*. New York: Jason Aronson.

Bissell, Laura. (2016) 'Water Matters: TUG Onboard and TUG Footpath'. *Studies in Theatre and Performance*, 36 (2), pp. 177–190.

Blast Theory. (2017) 'Kidnap'. Blast Theory (*website*). http://www.blasttheory.co.uk/projects/kidnap Retrieved: 10 August 2017.

Bollas, Christopher. (1987) *The Shadow of the Object: Psychoanalysis of the Unthought Known*. New York: Columbia University Press.

Bollas, Christopher. (2000) 'Architecture and the Unconscious'. *International Forum of Psychoanalysis*, 9 (1–2), pp. 28–42 (London & New York: Routledge).

Bonta, Mark & John Protevi. (2004) *Deleuze and Geophilosophy: A Guide and Glossary*. Edinburgh: Edinburgh University Press.

Bourriard, Nicolas. (2002) *Relational Aesthetics*. Paris: Presses du reel.

Boym, Svetlana. (2017) 'Nostalgia and Its Discontents'. Essays. http://www.uib. no/sites/w3.uib.no/files/attachments/boym_nostalgia_and_its_discontents. pdf Retrieved: 18 September 2017.

Brecht, Bertolt. (1964) 'The Street Scene'. In John Willett (ed.), *Brecht on Theatre*. London: Methuen.

Brook, Peter. (1968) *The Empty Space*. New York: Atheneum.

Butler, Judith. (1990) *Gender Trouble: Feminism and Subversion of Identity*. London & New York: Routledge.

Camhi, Jeff. (2008) 'Pathways for Communicating about Objects on Guided Tours'. *Curator: The Museum Journal*, 50 (3), pp. 275–295.

Canadian Encyclopedia. (2006) 'World Soundscape Project', 2 July. http:// www.thecandianencyclopedia.com/en/article/world-soundscape-project/. Retrieved: 10 August 2017.

Cardiff, Janet. (2005) *The Walk Book*. Vienna: Thyssen-Bornemisza Art Contemporary.

Case, Sue-Ellen. (1989) 'From Split Subject to Split Britches'. In Enoch Brater (ed.), *Feminine Focus: The New Women Playwrights*. New York & Oxford: Oxford University Press.

Casey, Edward. (1996) 'How to Get from Space to Place in a Fairly Short Stretch of Time'. In Steven Field & Keith H. Basso (eds.), *Senses of Place*. Santa Fé: School of American Research, pp. 14–51.

Castells, Manuel. (1989) *The Informational City: Information Technology, Economic Restructuring, and the Urban-regional Process*. Oxford: Basil Blackwell.

Castells, Manuel. (1996) *The Rise of the Network Society*. Oxford: Basil Blackwell.

Chandrasekera, Vajra. (2016) 'The Great Mongoose'. In Reppion, John (ed.), *Spirits of Place*. Brisbane: Daily Grail Publishing.

Chang, He Yun. (2006) 'The Rock Touring Around Great Britain'. Asia Art Archive. http://www.aaa.org.hk/Collection/Details/21369 Retrieved: 2 March 2017.

Chaudhuri, Una. (1995) *Staging Place: The Geography of Modern Drama* (Ann Arbor: University of Michigan Press).

Chaudhuri, Una. (2001) 'Introduction: Instant Rachel' in Rachel Rosenthal, *Rachel's Brain and Other Storms*. London & New York: Continuum, pp. 1–14.

Cohen, Josh. (2013) *The Private Life: Why We Remain in the Dark*. London: Granta.

Chryssides, George D. & Benjamin E. Zeller. (2014) *The Bloomsbury Companion to New Religious Movements*. London & New York: Bloomsbury.

Collins, Jane. (2012) 'Embodied Presence and Dislocated Spaces: Playing the Audience in *Ten Thousand Several Doors* in a Promenade, Site-Specific Performance of John Webster's *The Duchess of Malfi*'. In Anna Birch & Joanne Tompkins (eds.), *Performing Site-Specific Theatre: Politics, Place, Practice.* Basingstoke: Palgrave Macmillan.

Crabman & Signpost. (2012) *A Sardine Street Box of Tricks.* Axminster: Triarchy Press.

Crang, Mike & Nigel Thrift. (2000) *Thinking Space.* London & New York: Routledge.

Crawford, Stephanie. (2016) 'A (Re) (Re) Retelling of the Narrative of 'Womanhouse', Or in the Beginning There Was a Woman with a Hammer'. 16 February, http://www.womanhouse.net/related-content/. Retrieved: 17 September 2017.

Cresswell, Tim. (2001a) 'Mobilities – An Introduction'. *New Formations, A Journal of Culture/Theory/Politics*, 43 (Spring 2001), pp. 9–10.

Cresswell, Tim. (2001b) 'The Production of Mobilities'. *New Formations, A Journal of Culture/Theory/Politics*, 43 (Spring 2001), pp. 11–25.

Cresswell, Tim. (2006) *On the Move.* New York & London: Routledge.

Dalton, Ernest. (2010) *The Spanner Experiment.* Bridport: Just Press.

D'Andrea, Anthony. (2006) 'Neo-Nomadism: A Theory of Post-Identitarian Mobility in the Global Age'. *Mobilities*, 1 (1), pp. 95–120.

Daniels, Stephen. (1993) *Fields of Vision: Landscape Imagery and National Identity in England and the United States.* Princeton: Princeton University Press.

Davis, Erik. (1998) *TechGnosis: Myth, Magic, and Mysticism in the Age of Information.* New York: Harmony Books.

De Certeau, Michel. (1984) *The Practice of Everyday Life.* Trans. by Steven Rendall. Berkeley, Los Angeles & London: University of California Press.

De L'Isle-Adam, Villiers. (1986) *Axël.* Trans. by M. Gaddis Rose. London: Soho Book Company.

De Palma, Brian, Robert Fiore & Bruce Rubin (directors). (1970) *Dionysus In '69* (movie). https://www.youtube.com/watch?v=K9MFd3Tgins. Retrieved: 1 November 2017.

Debord, Guy. (1955) 'Introduction to a Critique of Urban Geography'. In Ken Knabb (ed.), (1981) *Situationist International Anthology.* Berkeley: Bureau of Public Secrets.

Deleuze, Gilles & Felix Guattari. (1987) *A Thousand Plateaus.* Trans. by Brian Massumi. London & New York: Continuum.

Diamond, Elin. (1997) *Unmaking Mimesis.* London & New York: Routledge.

Diener, Richard & Steve Wolfson (directors). (2004) *Weyburn: Archaeology of Madness.* [90 mins].

Doherty, Claire. (2004) 'The New Situationists'. In: Claire Doherty, *Contemporary Art from Studio to Situation*. London: Black Dog.

Dorner, Willi (2017). 'bodies in urban spaces'. https://www.ciewdorner.at/index.php?page=work&wid=26. Retrieved: 23 August 2017.

Drain, Richard. (1979) 'Spanner at Work 2: Some Notes on Style'. *Platform* (Winter 1979), pp. 13–15.

Easterby, Caitlin. (2011) 'Being There'. *Total Theatre Magazine*, 23 (4), pp. 26–27.

Early, Fergus. (1987) 'Liberation Notes, Etc'. *New Dance* 40 (April–June 1987), pp. 10–12.

Edensor, Tim. (2005) *Industrial Ruins: Space, Aesthetics and Materiality*. Oxford & New York: Berg.

Eliot, T.S. (1969/2004) *The Complete Poems & Plays*. London: Faber & Faber.

Elkin, Lauren. (2016) *Flâneuse: Women Walk the City in Paris, New York, Tokyo and London*. London: Chatto & Windus.

Ellis, Carolyn, Tony Adams & Arthur P. Bochner. (2010) 'Autoethnography: An Overview'. *Forum: Qualitative Social Research*, 12 (1), 273–290.

Fabian, Johannes. (2002) *Time and the Other: How Anthropology Makes Its Object*. New York: Columbia University Press.

Ferdman, Bertie. (2013) 'A New Journey Through Other Spaces: Contemporary Performance Beyond Site-Specific'. *Theater*, 43 (2), pp. 5–25.

Ferrer, Esther. (1991) 'Esther Ferrer's Letter to John Cage'. http://www.anarchicharmony.org/AnarConomy/ferrer.html. Retrieved: 13 July 2017.

Fiennes, Sophie. (2006) *The Pervert's Guide to the Cinema*. Mischief Films/Amoeba Film.

Flusser, Vilém & Louis Bec. (2012) *Vampyroteuthis Infernalis*. Trans. by Valentine A. Pakis. Minneapolis: University of Minnesota Press.

Foster, Charles. (2016) *Becoming A Beast*. London: Profile Books.

Friedman, Ken, Lauren Sawchyn & Owen F. Smith (eds.). (2002) *The Fluxus Performance Workbook*. e-Publications.

Fuchs, Elinor. (1996) *The Death of Character: Perspectives on Theater After Modernism*. Bloomington and Indianapolis: Indiana University Press.

Gardner, Lyn. (2010) 'Walking theatre must look where it's going'. *The Guardian*. 20 September. https://www.guardian.com/stage/theatreblog/2010/sep/20/walking-theatre-accomplice-enroute. Retrieved: 1 March 2017.

Gardner, Lyn. (2014) 'The Gathering review'. *The Guardian*, 15 September. https://www.theguardian.com/stage/2014/sep/15/the-gathering-review-national-theatre-wales-hafod-y-llan-snowdonia?CMP=twt_gu&utm_source=Sign-Up.to&utm_medium=email&utm_campaign=10773-326240-News. Retrieved: 4 November 2017.

Garrett, Bradley L. (2013) *Explore Everything: Place-Hacking the City*. London & New York: Verso.

Gerhard, Jane H. (2013) *The Dinner Party: Judy Chicago and the Power of Popular Feminism (1970–2007)*. Athens & London: University of Georgia Press.

Gershwin, Lisa-ann. (2013) *Stung! On Jellyfish Blooms and the Future of the Ocean*. Chicago: The University of Chicago Press.

Gibson, James J. (1966) *The Senses Considered As Perceptual Systems*. Boston: Houghton Mifflin.

Gibson, James J. (1979) *The Ecological Approach to Visual Perception*. Boston: Houghton Mifflin.

Gilchrist, Alan. (2006) *Seeing Black and White*. Oxford: Oxford University Press.

Goffman, Erving. (1971) *The Presentation of Self in Everyday Life*. Harmondsworth: Penguin.

Goldberg, RoseLee. (1979) *Performance Art From Futurism To The Present*. London: Thames and Hudson.

Govan, Emma, Helen Nicholson & Katie Normington. (2007) *Making a Performance: Devising Histories and Contemporary Practices*. London & New York: Routledge.

Graves-Brown, Paul, Rodney Harrison & Angela Piccini (eds.). (2013) *The Oxford Handbook of the Archaeology of the Contemporary World*. Oxford: Oxford University Press.

Grills, Scott. (1998) 'An Invitation to the Field: Fieldwork and the Pragmatists' Lesson'. In Scott Grills (ed.), *Doing Ethnographic Research: Fieldwork Settings*. London: Sage, pp. 3–18.

Grosz, Elizabeth. (1995) 'Women, *chora*, Dwelling'. In: Sophie Watson & Katherine Gibson (eds.), *Postmodern Cities and Spaces*. Oxford & Cambridge: Blackwell.

Haden, David. (2011) *Walking with Cthulhu*. Self-Published.

Haedicke, Susan. (2012) 'Beyond Site-Specificity: Environmental Heterocosms on the Street'. In Anna Birch & Joanne Tompkins (eds.), *Performing Site-Specific Theatre: Politics, Place, Practice*. Basingstoke: Palgrave Macmillan.

Halprin, Anna. (1984/1997) 'Healing the Mountain'. Context Institute. http'//www.context.org/iclib/ic05/halprin/. Retrieved: 30 October 2017.

Hammersley, Martyn & Paul Atkinson. (2007) *Ethnography: Principles in Practice*. London & New York: Routledge.

Hannam, Kevin. (2009) 'The End of Tourism? Nomadology and the Mobilities Paradigm'. In John Tribe (ed.), *Philosophical Issues in Tourism*. Bristol/Buffalo/Toronto: Channel View Publications.

Haraway, Donna. (2016) 'Tentacular Thinking: Anthropocene, Capitalocene, Chthulucene'. *e-flux*, 75 (September), n.p. http://www.e-flux.com/journal/75/67125/tentacular-thinking-anthropocene-capitalocene-chthulucene. Retrieved: 21 August 2017.

Harmon, Katharine. (2004) *You Are Here: Personal Geographies and Other Maps of the Imagination*. New York: Princeton Architectural Press.

Harmon, Katharine. (2009) *The Map As Art: Contemporary Artists Explore Cartography*. New York: Princeton Architectural Press.

Heathfield, Adrian. (2002) *Small Acts: Performance, the Millennium and the Marking of Time*. London: Black Dog Publishing.

Heathfield, Adrian (ed.). (2004) *Live Art and Performance*. London: Tate Publishing.

Heddon, Deirdre. (2002) 'Performing the Archive'. *Performance Research*, 7 (4), 64–77.

Heddon, Deidre. (2008) *Autobiography and Performance*. Basingstoke: Palgrave Macmillan.

Heidegger, Martin. (1962) *Being and Time*. Trans. by John Macquarrie & Edward Robinson. Oxford & Cambridge: Blackwell.

Heidegger, Martin. (1971) *Poetry, Language, Thought*. Trans. by Alfred Hofstadter. New York: Harper & Row.

Henare, Amiria, Martin Holbraad M. & Sari Wastell. (2007) *Thinking Through Things: Theorising Artefacts Ethnographically*. London & New York: Routledge.

Herzog, Werner. (2015) *On Walking in Ice*. Minneapolis: The University of Minnesota Press.

Hind, Claire & Clare Qualmann (eds.). (2015) *Ways to Wander*. Axminster: Triarchy Press.

Hodge, Stephen & Cathy Turner. (2012) 'Site: Between Ground and Groundlessness'. In Deirdre Heddon & Jennie Klein (eds.), *Histories and Practices of Live Art*. Basingstoke: Palgrave Macmillan. pp. 90–120.

Hoffmann, Jens & Joan Jonas. (2005) *Perform*. London: Thames & Hudson.

hooks, bell. (1991) *Yearning: Race, Gender, and Cultural Politics*. Boston: South End Press.

Hulton, Dorinda. (2008) 'Sites of Micro-Political Theatre', *PAJ: A Journal of Performance and Art*, XC, pp. 94–103.

Hunter, Victoria. (2015a) 'Experiencing Space: The Implications for Site-Specific Dance Performances'. In Victoria Hunter (ed.), *Moving Sites: Investigating Site-Specific Dance Performance*. Abingdon & New York: Routledge, pp. 25–39.

Hunter, Victoria. (2015b) 'Spatial Translation, Embodiment and the Site-Specific Event'. In Victoria Hunter (ed.), *Moving Sites: Investigating Site-Specific Dance Performance*. Abingdon & New York: Routledge, pp. 178–196.

Hunter, Victoria. (2015c) 'Introduction'. In Victoria Hunter (ed.), *Moving Sites: Investigating Site-Specific Dance Performance*. Abingdon & New York: Routledge, pp. 1–24.

Hutton, Ronald. (1993) *The Pagan Religions of the Ancient British Isles: Their Nature and Legacy*. Malden, Oxford & Victoria: Blackwell.

Ingold, Tim. (1993) 'Globes and Spheres: The Topology of Environmentalism'. In Kay Milton (ed.), *Environmentalism: The View from Anthropology*. London & New York: Routledge.

Ingold, Tim. (2007) *Lines: A Brief History*. New York & London: Routledge.

Ingold, Tim. (2011) *Being Alive*. London & New York: Routledge.

Irwin, Kathleen. (2007) *The Ambit of Performativity: How Site Makes Meaning in Site-Specific Performance*. Helsinki: University of Arts and Design.

Irwin, Kathleen. (2012) 'Toiling, Tolling, and Telling: Performing Dissensus'. In Anna Birch & Joanne Tompkins (eds.), *Performing Site-Specific Theatre: Politics, Place, Practice*. Basingstoke: Palgrave Macmillan, pp. 84–102.

Jones, Kathy. (1996) *On Finding Treasure: Mystery Plays of the Goddess*. Glastonbury: Ariadne Publications.

Jones, Jonathan. (2002) 'The myth-maker'. *The Guardian.*, 16 October. https://www.theguardian.com/film/2002/oct/16/artfeatures. Retrieved: 30 August 2017.

Kantor, Tadeusz. (1993) *A Journey Through Other Spaces: Essays and Manifestoes, 1944–1990*. Berkeley & Los Angeles: University of California Press.

Kaprow, Allan. (1965) *Happenings: An Illustrated Anthology*. New York: E. P. Dutton.

Kaprow, Allan. (2003) *Essays on the Blurring of Art and Life*. Berkeley & Los Angeles: University of California Press.

Kartsaki, Eirini. (2015) 'Circular Paths of Pleasure in Marco Berrettini's *iFeel2*'. *Performance Research*, 20 (5), pp. 125–131 ('On Repetition').

Kashmiri Cabbage Walker. 2016. 'Here's Why This Kashmiri Artist Is Walking A Cabbage'. https://www.scoopwhoop.com/Heres-Why-This-Kashmiri-Artist-Is-Walking-Cabbage-On-A-Leash-On-The-Streets-Of-Srinagar/. Retrieved: 12 July 2017.

Keith, Michael & Steve Pile. (1993) *Place and the Politics of Identity*. London: Routledge.

Kennedy, Christina. (2017) 'A Chant for the Forgotten'. Financial Mail, 23 February. https://www.businesslive.co.za/fm/life/2017-02-23-a-chant-for-the-forgotten/. Retrieved: 1 November 2017.

Kershaw, Baz. (2009) *Theatre Ecology: Environments and Performance Events*. Cambridge: Cambridge University Press.

Kimball, Lucy. (2002) 'My Word Is My Bond'. http://www.frenchmottershead. com/aboutus/writings/pdfs/an_wimb.pdf. Retrieved: 29 August 2017.

Kirby, Michael. (1965) *Happenings*. London: Sidgewick & Jackson.

Kirby, Michael. (1972/1995) 'On Acting and Not Acting'. In Zarrilli, Phillip (ed.), *Acting (Re) Considered: A Theoretical and Practical Guide*. London & New York: Routledge, pp. 40–52.

Kloetzel, Melanie. (2015) 'Site-Specific Dance in a Corporate Landscape: Space, Place and Non-place'. In Victoria Hunter (ed.), *Moving Sites: Investigating Site-Specific Dance Performance*. Abingdon & New York: Routledge, pp. 239–254.

Kloetzel, Melanie. (2017) 'Site, Adapt, Perform: A Practice-as-Research Confrontation with Climate Change'. *Dance Research*, 35 (1), pp. 111–129 (Edinburgh: Edinburgh University Press).

Kloetzel, Melanie & Carolyn Pavlik. (2010) *Site Dance: Choreographers and the Lure of Alternative Spaces*. Gainsville: University Press of Florida.

Kobialka, Michael. (1986) 'Let the Artists Die? An Interview with Tadeusz Kantor'. *The Drama Review*, 30 (3), pp. 177–183.

Koplowitz, Stephan (quoted). (1997) 'DANCE; Shaping a Marathon of Dance That Was Inspired by the Web'. William Harris. *New York Times*, 14.9.97.

Korzybski, Eric. (1936) *Science and Sanity: An Introduction to Non-Aristotelian Systems and General Semantics*. Lancaster: The Science Press Printing Company.

Kristoffersen, Erik Exe. (1993) *The Actor's Way*. Trans. by Richard Fowler. New York & London: Routledge.

Kwon, Miwon. (2002) *One Place After Another: Site-Specific Art and Locational Identity*. Cambridge & London: MIT Press.

Lavery, Carl. (2009) 'Mourning Walk'. In Roberta Mock (ed.), *Walking, Writing and Performance*. Bristol: Intellect, pp. 25–40.

Lawrence, Kate. (2015) 'Stop. Look. Listen. What's Going On?'. In Victoria Hunter (ed.), *Moving Sites: Investigating Site-Specific Dance Performance*. Abingdon & New York: Routledge, pp. 255–273.

Leach, Edmund. (1976) *Culture and Communication: The Logic by Which Symbols are Connected*. Cambridge: Cambridge University Press.

Legierska, Anna. (2015) '10 Stage Props by Kantor'. *Culture.pl*, 3 February. http:// culture.pl/en/article/10-stage-props-by-kantor. Retrieved: 30 August 2017.

Lehmann, Hans-Thies. (2006) *Postdramatic Theatre*. Trans. by Karen Jürs-Mundy. London & New York: Routledge.

Lippard, Lucy R. (1973) *Six Years: The Dematerialisation of the Art Object from 1966 to 1972*. New York: Praeger.

Logan, Brian. (2007) 'Streets Ahead'. *Guardian*, 7 November. https://www.theguardian.com/stage/2007/nov/07/theatre4. Retrieved: 10 August 2017.

Long, Declan. (2017) *Ghost-Haunted Land: Contemporary Art and Post-Troubles Northern Ireland*. Manchester: Manchester University Press.

Lovelock, James & Sidney Epton. (1975) 'The Quest for Gaia'. *New Scientist*, 65 (923), pp. 304–306.

Machon, Josephine. (2007) 'Space and the Senses: The (Syn)aesthetics of Punchdrunk's Site-Sympathetic Work'. *Body, Space & Technology*. Vol. 8. London: Brunel University Centre for Contemporary and Digital Performance.

Machon, Josephine. (2013) *Immersive Theatres: Intimacy and Immediacy in Contemporary Performance*. Basingstoke: Palgrave Macmillan.

Mackay, Robin (ed.). (2015) *When Site Lost the Plot*. Falmouth: Urbanomic.

Manderscheid, Katharina. (2009) 'Unequal Mobilities'. In Timo Ohnmacht, Hanja Maksim & Manfred Max Bergman (eds.), *Mobilities and Inequality*. Aldershot: Ashgate, pp. 27–50.

Margolies, Eleanor. (2016) *Props*. Basingstoke: Palgrave Macmillan.

Massey, Doreen. (1994). *Space, Place and Gender*. Minneapolis: University of Minnesota.

Massey, Doreen. (2005) *For Space*. London: Sage Publications.

Matless, David. (2016) *Landscape and Englishness*. London: Reaktion Books.

McKinnie, Michael. (2012) 'Rethinking Site-Specificity: Monopoly, Urban Space, and the Cultural Economics of Site-Specific Performance'. In Anna Birch & Joanne Tompkins (eds.), *Performing Site-Specific Theatre: Politics, Place, Practice*. Basingstoke: Palgrave Macmillan.

McLucas, Cliff. (2000) 'Ten Feet and Three Quarters of an Inch of Theatre'. In Nick Kaye (ed.), *Site-Specific Art*. London: Routledge, pp. 125–138.

Meillassoux, Quentin. (2008) *After Finitude*. Trans. \by Ray Brassier. New York: Continuum.

Mentz, Steve. (2015) *Shipwreck Modernity: Ecologies of Globalisation, 1550–1719*. Minneapolis: University of Minnesota Press.

Miller, M. H. (2017) 'Mike Kelley's Underground Afterlife'. *New York Times Style Magazine*, 8 March. https://www.nytimes.com/2017/03/08/t-magazine/art/mike-kelley-mobile-homestead.html. Retrieved: 17 September 2017.

Mitchell Jnr, Richard, G. & Kathy Charmaz. (1998) 'Telling Tales and Writing Stories: Postmodernist Visions and Realist Images in Ethnographic Writing'. In Scott Grills (ed.), *Doing Ethnographic Research: Fieldwork Settings*. London: Sage, pp. 228–248.

Mitra, Royona. (2016) 'Decolonizing Immersion: Translation, spectatorship, *rasa* Theory and Contemporary British Dance'. *Performance Research*, 21 (5), pp. 89–100.

Mock, Roberta. (2009) '*Tohu-bohu*: Rachel Rosenthal's Performances of Diasporic Cultural Memory'. In Colin Counsell & Roberta Mock (eds.), *Performance, Embodiment and Cultural Memory*. Newcastle-upon-Tyne: Cambridge Scholars Publishing, pp. 59–79.

Morley, David. (2000) *Home Territories: Media, Mobility and Identity*. London: Routledge.

Müller, Volkhardt & Dawn Scarfe. (2017) 'Broadcasts from the Edge of the Horizon: The Beacon'. *Uniformagazine* (10, Summer). Axminster: Uniform Books.

Myers, Misha & Dan Harris. (2004) 'Way from Home'. *Performance Research*, 9 (2), pp. 90–91.

Nesbit, E. (1906/1998) *The Railway Children*. Ware: Wordsworth Editions.

Newman, Hayley. (2008) *MKVH: The Screenplay*. Milton Keynes: Milton Keynes Gallery.

Ninjalicious. (2005) *Access All Areas: A User's Guide to the Art of Urban Exploration*. Toronto: Infilpress.

Nold, Christian. (2014) *Emotional Cartography: Technologies of the Self*. Mountain View: Creative Commons (self-published).

Olimpias, The. (2013) 'Salamander Project Description'. http://www-personal. umich.edu/-petra/salamnder/html. Retrieved: 10 August 2017.

Ono, Yoko. (1964) *Grapefruit*. Tokyo: Wunternaum Press.

Pahre, Robert. (2015) 'Material Falsehood: Living a Lie at This Old Fort'. In Mike Robinson & Helaine Silverman (eds.), *Encounters with Popular Pasts*. New York: Springer, pp. 61–80.

Parker-Starbuck, Jennifer and Roberta Mock. (2011) "Researching the Body in/as Performance". In Helen Nicholson & Baz Kershaw (eds.), *Research Methods In Theatre and Performance*. Edinburgh: Edinburgh University Press.

Pearson, Mike & Michael Shanks. (2001) *Theatre/Archaeology*. London & New York: Routledge.

Mike Pearson & Lyn Levett. (2001) 'Devices and Desires'. *Contemporary Theatre Review*, 11 (3/4), pp. 81–92.

Pearson, Mike. (2006) '*In Comes I*': *Performance, Memory and Landscape*. Exeter: University of Exeter Press.

Pearson, Mike. (2010) *Site-Specific Performance*. Basingstoke: Palgrave Macmillan.

Pearson, Mike. (2012) 'Haunted House: Staging the Persians with the British Army'. In Anna Birch & Joanne Tompkins (eds.), *Performing Site-Specific Theatre: Politics, Place, Practice*. Basingstoke: Palgrave Macmillan.

Pearson, Mike. (2018) 'Site-Specific Theatre'. In Arnold Aronson(ed.), *The Routledge Companion to Scenography*. London & New York: Routledge, pp. 295–301.

Persighetti, Simon. (2008) 'Mis-Guided Exploration of Cities: An Ambulant Investigation of Participative Politics of Place', PhD thesis, University of Plymouth. https://pearl.plymouth.ac.uk/bitstream/handle/10026.1/2724/SIMON%20BERNARD%20PERSIGHETTI.PDF;sequence=1

Phelan, Peggy. (1993) *Unmarked: The Politics of Performance*. London & New York: Routledge.

Poole, Matthew. (2015) 'Specificities of Sitedness: A Speculative Sketch'. In Robin Mackay (ed.), *When Site Lost the Plot*. Falmouth: Urbanomic.

Popat, Sita. (2015) 'Placing the Body in Mixed Reality'. In Victoria Hunter (ed.), *Moving Sites: Investigating Site-Specific Dance Performance*. Abingdon & New York: Routledge.

Prior, Dorothy Max. (2011) 'Being There'. *Total Theatre Magazine*, 23 (4), pp. 26–27.

Puthoff, Emily. (2006) 'The Patina of Placelessness'. In Leslie Hill & Helen Paris (eds.), *Performance and Place*. Basingstoke: Palgrave Macmillan.

Quick, Andrew. (2004) 'Taking Place: Encountering the Live'. In Adrian Heathfield (ed.), *Live: Art and Performance*. London: Tate Publishing.

Rajchman, John. (2000) *The Deleuze Connections*. Cambridge & London: The MIT Press.

Rendell, Jane. (2009) 'Constellations (or the Reassertion of Time into Critical Spatial Practice)'. In Claire Doherty & David Cross (eds.), *One Day Sculpture*. Bielefeld: Kerber Verlag.

Rendell, Jane. (2011) 'Afterword: Working (through) the Field'. In Suzanne Ewing, Jeremie Michael McGowan, Chris Speed & Victoria Clare Bernie (eds.), *Architecture and Field/Work*. London & New York: Routledge.

Rosenthal, Rachel. (2010) *The DbD Experience*. London & New York: Routledge.

Said, Edward W. (1978) *Orientalism*. New York: Vintage.

Saville, Alice. (2016) 'Is Immersive Theatre Broken?'. 9 May. http://exeuntmagazine.com/features/is-immersive-theatre-broken/. Retrieved: 26 February 2017.

Schechner, Richard. (1978) *Makbeth: After Shakespeare*. Schulenburg: I. E. Clark Publications.

Schechner, Richard. (1994) *Environmental Theater*. New York & London: Applause.

Scopio. (2017) 'Interview with Willi Dorner: Bodies in Urban Space'. https://www.scopionetwork.com/node/330#1. Retrieved: 23 August 2017.

Serra, Richard. (1991) 'Quoted'. In Clara Weyergraf-Serra & Martha Buskirk (eds.), *The Destruction of Tilted Arc: Documents*. Cambridge: MIT Press.

Shaviro, Steven. (2014) *The Universe of Things*. Minneapolis: University of Minnesota Press.

Shepherd, Nan. (1977/2011) *The Living Mountain*. Edinburgh: Canongate Books.

Slater, Mel. (2009) 'Place Illusion and Plausibility Can Lead to Realistic Behaviour in Immersive Virtual Environments'. *Philosophical Transactions B. The Royal Society*, 364 (1535), pp. 3549–3557.

Smith, A.C.H. (1972) *Orghast at Persepolis*. London: Methuen.

Smith, Phil. (2001) 'Paper for DAISI on Acting'. (self-published).

Smith, Phil. (2002) 'Dread, Route and Time: An Autobiographical Walking of Everything Else'. *Reconstruction* (Summer 2002). Available at: https://www.academia.edu/167849/Dread_Route_and_Time_an-autobiographical_walking_of_everything_else. Retrieved: 18 August 2017.

Smith, Phil. (2009a) 'The Crab Walks'. In Roberta Mock (ed.), *Walking, Writing and Performance*. Bristol: Intellect, pp. 57–80.

Smith, Phil. (2009b) 'Actors as Signposts: A Model for Site-Based and Ambulatory Performances'. *New Theatre Quarterly*, 25, pp. 159–167.

Smith, Phil. (2010) *Mythogeography*. Axminster: Triarchy Press.

Smith, Phil. (2012) *Counter-Tourism: The Handbook*. Axminster: Triarchy Press.

Smith, Phil. (2013) 'Turning Tourists into Performers: Revaluing Agency, Action and Space in Sites of Heritage Tourism'. *Performance Research, On Value*, 18 (2), pp. 102–113.

Smith, Phil. (2014) *On Walking*. Axminster: Triarchy Press.

Smith, Phil. (2015a) *The Footbook of Zombie Walking*. Axminster: Triarchy Press.

Smith, Phil (2015b) *Walking's New Movement*. Axminster: Triarchy Press.

Smith, Phil. (2016) 'Pedagogy and the Zombie Mythos: Lessons from Apocalyptic Enactments'. In Victoria Carrington, Jennifer Rowsell, Esther Priyadharshini & Rebecca Westrup (eds.), *Generation Z: Zombies, Popular Culture and Educating Youth*. Singapore: Springer.

Smithson, Robert. (1972) 'The Spiral Jetty'. In Jack Flan (ed.), (1996), *Robert Smithson: The Collected Writings*. Berkeley, Los Angeles & London: University of California Press, pp. 143–153.

Solis, Julia. (2013) *Stages of Decay*. Munich: Prestel.

Sofer, Andrew. (2003). *The Stage Life of Props*. Ann Arbor: The University of Michigan Press.

Soule, Lesley Wade. (2000) *Actor as Anti-Character – Dionysus, the Devil and the Boy Rosalind*. Westport: Greenwood Press.

Spry, Tami. (2001) 'Performing Autoethnography: An Embodied Methodological Praxis'. *Qualitative Enquiry*, 7 (6), pp. 706–732 (London: Sage Publications).

Stanislavski, Konstantin. (1988) *An Actor Prepares*. London: Methuen Drama.

Steinitz, Kate Traumann. (1968) *Kurt Schwitters: A Portrait from Life*. Berkeley & Los Angeles: University of California Press.

Stephenson, Jenn. (2010) 'Portrait of the Artist as Artist: The Celebration of Autobiography'. *Canadian Theatre Review*, 144, pp. 49–53.

Szalwinska, Maxie. (2007) 'Site-specific Work Is Not Just About Location, Location, Location'. *Guardian*, 26 April.

Taylor, Heidi. (2004) 'Deep Dramaturgy: Excavating the Architecture of the Site-Specific Performance'. *Canadian Theatre Review*, 119 (Summer), pp. 16–19.

Taylor, Stephanie. (2002) *Ethnographic Research: A Reader*. London: Sage Publications.

Templeton, Fiona. (1990) *You – The City*. New York: Roof Books.

Thompson, Nato & Gregory Sholette. (2004) *The Interventionists*. Cambridge: MIT Press.

Tsing, Anna Lowenhaupt. (2015) *The Mushroom at the End of the World*. Princeton & Oxford: Princeton University Press.

Turner, Cathy. (2004) 'Palimpsest or Potential Space? Finding a Vocabulary for Site-Specific Performance'. *New Theatre Quarterly*, 20 (4), pp. 373–390.

Turner, Cathy & Synne K. Behrndt. (2008) *Dramaturgy and Performance*. Basingstoke: Palgrave Macmillan.

Turner, Cathy. (2014) 'Porous Dramaturgy and the Pedestrian'. In Katalin Trencsenyi & Bernadette Cochrane (eds.), *New Dramaturgy: International Perspectives on Theory and Practice*. London: Bloomsbury, pp. 199–213.

Turner, Cathy. (2015) *Dramaturgy and Architecture*. Basingstoke: Palgrave Macmillan.

Turner, J. S. (2002) *The Extended Organism: The Physiology of Animal-Built Structures*. Cambridge, MA: Harvard University Press.

Ulmer, Gregory L. (1994) *Heuretics: The Logic of Invention*. Baltimore: Johns Hopkins University Press.

Urry, John. (2000) *Sociology Beyond Societies: Mobilities for the Twenty-First Century*. London: Routledge.

Urry, John, (2007) *Mobilities*. London: Polity Press.

Van Eyck, Aldo. (1959) 'Het Verhaal van een Andere Gedachte' (The Story of Another Thought). *Forum* 7/1959. Hilversum & Amsterdam.

Wark, Mckenzie. (2013) *The Spectacle of Disintegration*. London & New York: Verso.

Warwick, Rhona (ed.). (2006) *Arcade: Artists and Place-Making*. London: Black Dog Publishing.

Wearing, Stephen, Deborah Stevenson & Tamara Young. (2009) *Tourist Cultures: Identity, Place and Traveller*. London: Sage Publications.

Welfare State International. (2017) 'The Trials of Lancelot Quail'. Unfinished Histories. http://unfinishedhistories.com/history/companies/welfare-state-international/the-trials-of-lancelot-quail/. Retrieved: 18 August 2017.

Whall, Miranda. (2017) 'Miranda Whall: Interdisciplinary Contemporary Artist: Crossed Paths'. http://www.mirandawahall.space/?page_id=2363. Retrieved: 16 October 2017.

White, Gareth. (2012) 'On Immersive Theatre'. *Theatre Research International*, 37 (3), pp. 221–235.

White, Graham. (1993) 'Direct Action, Dramatic Action: Theatre and Situationist Theory'. *New Theatre Quarterly*, 9, pp. 329–340.

White, Kenneth. (2003) *Geopoetics: Place, Culture, World*. Glasgow: Alba Editions.

Whitehead, Simon. (2006) *Walking to Work*. Abercych: Shoeless.

Whitehead, Simon. (2007) *Lost in Ladywood*. Abercych: Shoeless.

Whitely, Sheila & Shara Rambarran. (2016) *The Oxford Handbook of Music and Virtuality*. Oxford: Oxford University Press.

Wilding, Faith. (1971) 'Waiting. A Poem by Faith Wilding'. http://faithwilding. refugia.net/waitingpoem.pdf. Retrieved: 18 September 2017.

Williams, Mogg. (1996) *Selected Works: 1969–1996*. Pontypridd: Underground Press.

Williams, Raymond. (1997) *Marxism and Literature*. Oxford: Oxford University Press.

Wilkie, Fiona. (2002) 'Mapping the Terrain: A Survey of Site-Specific Performance in Britain', *New Theatre Quarterly*, vx (111) (Part 2, May 2002), pp. 140–160.

Wilkie, Fiona. (2004) 'Out of Place: The Negotiation of Space in Site-Specific Performance' PhD thesis, University of Surrey.

Wilkie, Fiona. (2015a) 'Sited Conversations'. In Victoria Hunter (ed.), *Moving Sites: Investigating Site-Specific Dance Performance*. Abingdon & New York: Routledge.

Wilkie, Fiona. (2015b) *Performance, Transport and Mobility: Making Passage*. Basingstoke: Palgrave Macmillan.

Wilson, Anna. (2016) 'Punchdrunk, Participation and the Political: Democratisation within Masque of the Red Death?'. *Studies in Theatre and Performance*, 36 (2), pp. 159–176. London & New York: Routledge.

Womanhouse. (undated) 'Performances: Faith Wilding/Waiting'. http://www. womanhouse.net/performances-1/. Retrieved: 17 September 2017.

Worth, Libby & Helen Poynor. (2004) *Anna Halprin*. London & New York: Routledge.

Wrights & Sites. (2003) *An Exeter Mis-Guide*. Exeter: Wrights & Sites.

Wrights & Sites. (2006) *A Mis-Guide to Anywhere*. Exeter: Wrights & Sites.

Wylie, John. (2007) *Landscape*. London & New York: Routledge.

Index

CPI Antony Rowe
Eastbourne, UK
February 25, 2019